ADVANCE PRAISE FOR *DEATH BY CHURCH*

It has been said that the best critique of the bad is the practice of the better. If this is true, then Mike Erre shows us "the better way" in this book. Rather than offering us a church-centered view of the kingdom, he provides us a kingdom-centered view of the church. And with this shift, everything changes—as it ought to. All I can say is amen and hallelujah!

ALAN HIRSCH
author of *The Forgotten Ways*
founding director of Forge Missional Training Network

Mike Erre reminds us that according to the Bible, there is no such thing as Lone Ranger Christianity. Unfortunately, while many love Jesus, they find the church irrelevant, and this should not be. *Death by Church* provides a no-nonsense, hard-hitting critique of the contemporary American evangelical church along with a clarion call for it to be a countercultural communal outpost of the kingdom of God. Not content with hand-wringing, Erre provides a way forward that is a theological feast, at once rich in biblical theology and practical effectiveness. I highly recommend it.

J.P. MORELAND
author of *Kingdom Triangle*
Distinguished Professor of Philosophy, Talbot School of Theology

Death by Church is one of the few books that actually don't leave you hungering for more. After you have finished the full course of this masterful meal, you will be full for days on end, feasting with leftover thoughts and enjoying tasty morsels of wisdom and insight. Rarely does a boxer in the ring stop throwing punches at his opponent and begin punching himself. This is a megachurch, culturally-savvy teaching pastor critiquing and challenging his own religious culture. That takes guts, and Mike pulls it off with amazing courage! This book will wonderfully aggravate some, confuse others, and challenge all! Mike is *dead on* with his scrutiny and patient in his application. The playing field of ministry has changed, and it is past time for all Christ-followers as well as leaders of local gatherings of disciples to passionately confess our consumeristic, self-absorbed, and self-aggrandizing ways in order to become the church God dreams we can be. If you have never been exposed to Mike before, trust me—he has a huge heart and is inviting people who love Jesus to travel a path that he is willing to travel himself. Mike is one of the few people I know whose spiritual curiosity and openness to the Spirit allows him to be led in places that surprise, delight, and inform. I wholeheartedly recommend this book.

DR. ROBIN J. DUGALL
pastor and adjunct professor in biblical studies at Azusa Pacific University

As Mike Erre demonstrates here, the Bible's sweep of kingdom theology lies at the heart of Jesus' message and ministry. This faith is radically evangelical, community building, and socially concerned, demanding transformed lives that transform culture and are committed to justice, the poor, and the environment. Mike speaks with passion, truth, and the breathtaking sweep of the kingdom into the black hole of "tolerance" and relativism that leaves everything up for grabs. This is a book for the whole church. It will ground new churches as they emerge and renew older churches with a proper theological grid for their life and ministry. This is a must read for our special moment in history, connecting us in a fresh way to Jesus, to each other, and to the world He loves and came to redeem.

DON WILLIAMS
author and former faculty member of
Fuller Theological Seminary and Claremont MacKenna College

Reading Mike Erre's *Death by Church* is best compared to experiencing the annual Death by Chocolate Festival in Napa Valley. The aftertaste of ashes from burned-out living is followed by the taste and training of true sweetness and the foretaste of heaven.

LEONARD SWEET
author and faculty member of
Drew University and George Fox University

Death by Church is a passionate and thought-provoking call to rediscover the meaning and purpose of the church. Mike Erre challenges current beliefs and inspires us all to capture the important mission of the bride of Christ. Because of its hope, clarity, and commonsense approach, *Death by Church* truly opens up the beautiful possibility of what could be.

MIKE FOSTER
president of Ethur.org
author of *Deadly Viper Character Assassins*

We are in the middle of an exciting and unsettling new reformation. New wine is bursting apart old wineskins, especially when it comes to our thinking about the church! In this bold and compelling work, Mike Erre helps Jesus' followers wake up to the many ways the conventional Western understanding of the institutional church has harmed people and hindered the advancement of God's kingdom. Erre calls on Jesus' followers to recapture His original vision of the kingdom as a humble community of exiles who reflect God's character in the way they worship God, care for one another, and humbly serve the world. I heartily recommend this book to all who have been understandably turned off to Christianity because of the ugliness of the church as well as to all who remain in the church but who sense that something profoundly important is missing.

GREGORY A. BOYD
author, pastor, and former professor of theology

Mike Erre

DEATH
by
Church

HARVEST HOUSE PUBLISHERS

EUGENE, OREGON

Cover by Abris, Veneta, Oregon

Michael Erre: Published in association with the literary agency of Mark Sweeney & Associates, 28540 Altessa Way, Ste. 201, Bonita Springs, FL 34135

Death by Church is published in association with the Conversant Media Group, P.O. Box 3006, Redmond, WA 98007.

ConversantLife.com is a registered trademark of Conversant Media Group. Harvest House Publishers, Inc., is a licensee of the federally registered trademark ConversantLife.com.

All emphasis in Scripture quotations is added by the author.

DEATH BY CHURCH
Copyright © 2009 by Mike Erre
Published by Harvest House Publishers
Eugene, Oregon 97402
www.harvesthousepublishers.com

Library of Congress Cataloging-in-Publication Data

Erre, Mike, 1971-
Death by church / Mike Erre.
p. cm.
Includes bibliographical references.
ISBN 978-0-7369-2496-2 (pbk.)
1. Church. 2. Incarnation. 3. Christian life. 4. Postmodernism—Religious aspects—Christianity. I. Title.
BV600.3.E77 2009
243—dc22

2008030536

Download a Deeper Experience

Mike Erre is part of a faith-based online community called ConversantLife.com. At this website, people engage their faith in entertainment, creative arts, science and technology, global concerns, and other culturally relevant topics. While you're reading this book, or after you have finished reading, go to www.conversantlife.com/mikeerre and use these icons to read and download additional material from Mike that is related to this book.

Resources: Download study guide materials for personal devotions or a small-group Bible study.

Videos: Click on this icon for interviews with Mike and video clips on various topics.

Blogs: Read through Mike's blogs and articles and comment on them.

Podcasts: Stream ConversantLife.com podcasts and audio clips from Mike.

conversant **life** .com

engage your faith

Acknowledgments

Thank you to...

Nathan and Hannah
    for your patience while Daddy was working

Justina
    for making this possible

Bruce, Stan, Mark, Peter
    for believing in me

Rock Harbor Church
    for the joy of learning together as a community

the elders and staff of Rock Harbor
    for allowing me to grow into this

Don, Todd, Ian, Gary
    for much wise council

my folks
    for lots of support and encouragement

Terry, Gene, and the good folks at Harvest House
    for your guidance, help, and expertise

Disclaimers

Before you dive in, I need to let you know a couple of things.

First, the views expressed in this book are mine and should not be understood as Rock Harbor's official position on these matters. Our community is made up of a lot of different folks from a lot of different backgrounds, and I doubt that all of us would all agree on every item discussed here. So in writing this, I am articulating my convictions on these issues; I am not speaking for our church.

Second, though I read many books as I prepared to write this book, several were highly influential. The works of N.T. Wright, Donald Kraybill's *The Upside-Down Kingdom,* Rodney Clapp's *A Peculiar People,* Barry Harvey's *Another City,* and Stanley Hauerwas and William H. Willimon's book *Resident Aliens* all deserve special mention.

The works of George Eldon Ladd and Derek Morphew's book *Breakthrough* were incredibly helpful in my understanding of the kingdom of God.

Finally, the work of Don Williams has been central to this whole project. Through long and personal conversations with him, listening to his lectures at our church, and reading his books and papers, I came to see the Bible and the church in an entirely new way. I cannot give him enough credit for some of the big ideas in this book. It is for this reason that I dedicate this book to him.

Don, thank you for introducing me to the ways of the King and His kingdom.

Contents

Introduction:
When Jesus Comes to Church

My impression has been that church is a place where Jesus is always found. This seems to be a fairly common idea around the Christian community. After all, Jesus Himself said, "Where two or three come together in my name, there I am with them" (Matthew 18:20). Which I always took to mean, of course, that Jesus was happy anytime His followers got together (for whatever reason), and so He would oblige our efforts by coming along. I had always heard this proof text used to verify that Jesus always shows up to church services simply because we've gathered.

And of course He must be pleased with us when we gather, right? We take time out of our demanding weekly schedules to worship Him; we sing, clap, and pay attention, and if we are really good, we give our money. So He must be glad we showed up, correct?

Obviously, none of us would say it this way, but I think this is the unconscious assumption that undergirds most of what we do at weekend church services across the country. Without a doubt, the passage in Matthew suggests that Jesus is present when several gather. The section from which the quote comes, however, deals with how to handle sin between two disciples. That passage as a whole addresses the issue of church discipline and conflict resolution. This is hardly the sure basis we think it is for our flippant assurance that Jesus is pleased simply because we show up and do church every week.

In fact, the only real interaction we get between Jesus and His church comes in the book of Revelation. There, Jesus speaks to seven flesh-and-blood first-century churches and has very interesting things to say. Our Lord seems to have an opinion on church polity and practice, and it isn't always positive.

Of course, we can demythologize the whole section (or book, for that matter) and end up with some nice sentiments about how the church has grown and developed over the years. But in so doing, we would lose the context (that the whole book was an epistle, written toward the end of the first century to encourage actual flesh-and-blood churches in the face of mounting persecution) and the power of Jesus' message to the church.

Contrary to popular opinion, Jesus doesn't always appear to go to church. The oft-quoted passage about Jesus standing at the door and knocking is written to a *church*.

> To the angel of the church in Laodicea write:
>
> These are the words of the Amen, the faithful and true witness, the ruler of God's creation. I know your deeds, that you are neither cold nor hot. I wish you were either one or the other! So, because you are lukewarm—neither hot nor cold—I am about to spit you out of my mouth. You say, "I am rich; I have acquired wealth and do not need a thing." But you do not realize that you are wretched, pitiful, poor, blind and naked. I counsel you to buy from me gold refined in the fire, so you can become rich; and white clothes to wear, so you can cover your shameful nakedness; and salve to put on your eyes, so you can see.
>
> Those whom I love I rebuke and discipline. So be earnest, and repent. Here I am! I stand at the door and knock. If anyone hears my voice and opens the door, I will come in and eat with him, and he with me (Revelation 3:14-20).

In other words, the image shows Jesus on the *outside* while the church is gathering, and He is inviting them to receive Him into their church.

Not only that, but Jesus is clearly aware of what is going on in each of the seven communities. Time and again throughout Revelation 2–3 He declares, "I know your deeds" (2:2,19; 3:1,8,15). He commends some for perseverance and faithfulness, and He denounces sexual immorality and false teaching in others. But in every case, He seems to have a strong opinion about what is going on.

This should strike fear into our liturgies, worship, and teaching. How much of what passes for "church" these days would Jesus Himself commend? And why do we rarely (if ever) even think to entertain this question? As long as people are coming and excited, most of us assume that God is moving. But NASCAR races and Mormon temples draw big crowds too.

The modern church is clearly in trouble. Declining attendance and participation are rampant. Sexual scandal and cover-up are commonplace. Books like this one are being published at breakneck speed, cataloging the failures of the church and offering solutions.

But behind the prescriptions and prognostications, behind the doubts and defeatism, beyond the debates about emerging churches and postmodern contexts is something that I think pleases Jesus: *hunger.* Hunger for deeper, wider, and higher community that genuinely and organically transforms the communities we belong to and the ones that surround us. I see a hunger for something beyond the individualized, self-absorbed, bloated faith that is the common fare of most churches.

Hunger for the power of the gospel—not only to forgive sin but also to transform what makes us sinful in the first place, bringing freedom, healing, and deliverance.

Hunger for grace—to see all those excluded and hurt by the church brought again into contact with Jesus and His bride and told of their pricelessness.

Hunger for joy—transcending our techno-isolation and consumer orientation, hunger to taste the joy, wonder, and awe of the world and people around us.

Hunger for justice—to see the gospel proclaimed and lived out in word and deed, corporately and individually, structurally and personally, globally and locally.

Hunger for worship—to see the offering of our whole selves as the only fitting response to God's mercy, holiness, love, and grace.

Hunger for truth—tired of talking heads proffering countless human opinions, always in conflict, we hunger for a definitive word, a voice with authority, a way of discerning what really matters and why.

Hunger for honesty—disgusted with the scandals of our churches and our hearts, we hunger to find places where we no longer have to hide our true selves from God or from each other.

This hunger, when combined with the sweeping cultural changes accelerating rapidly around us, has provoked many questions—both of orthodoxy and orthopraxis—that place us in the midst of a new reformation.

Like it or not, the generations to come will see this period in church history as a massive reevaluation of all things "church." This is cause for alarm to many, but it need not be so.

And yet, for all the press and pages spent on such a quest, nothing much has changed so far. We are in the midst of immense and unprecedented cultural change. That is well known and has been well documented elsewhere. A massive dialogue about what it means to be the people of God has arisen in evangelicalism between so-called emerging or emergent churches, traditional mainline Protestant churches, and more traditional evangelical churches (often of the megachurch variety). Much has been written from all three perspectives.

What often seems missing in this wider conversation are the anchors that should tether us to historical, apostolic, Christian faith and practice as we begin to experiment with methods and modes of being and doing church that are emerging with increasing momentum. The emerging church types and their missiologist friends are correct in this: Those churches that continue to do things the way they always have will suffer from the law of diminishing returns. We must prayerfully seek after new wineskins in order to engage and incarnate the gospel to our fragmented and increasingly fractured world. But the critics of the emerging church movement also have cause for concern: Nothing is wrong with the old wine, and it should not be cast out of churches that seek more authentic community and faithful witness.

Too much conversation in and about the emerging church is theologically imprecise and unhelpful at best and incorrect at worst. What we think and say *does* matter; no amount of epistemological gymnastics can demonstrate otherwise. The generations who have moved beyond the traditional understandings of what the church is and how it acts in the world give their critics fodder for critique when ambiguity reigns. I would like to propose that there are some nonnegotiables as we seek to know how God would have His people live in the world.

Regardless of whether one is in a mainline denomination or a leaderless house church, certain things must be true for this to be properly called *church*. Remember, our whims and reactions do not serve as the ultimate norm for the way we shape and do community; Scripture does. Much of the emerging theology and practice of church seems simply to be reaction to the abuses and failures of the modernistic church. Thus, I don't see too many *post*modern churches, but I see plenty of the *anti*modern variety. But the Protestant Reformation taught us that it is not enough to simply live in reaction to something—we must stand for something else, and that something else needs more justification than simply faulting the other way of doing things. We are people of the Book and of the Spirit. The Word of God and Spirit of God set the course, purpose, function, and practice of the community of saints. Therefore, revolt against the long-standing norms must be supplemented with biblical and pneumatological underpinnings for the emerging church movement to become a way station along the road to something truly and lastingly different.

I love the church universal and the church particular. As ugly and unfaithful as it may be at times, it is still the bride of Christ. We must not allow our disdain of some of modern praxis to turn into contempt for the body of Jesus Christ in this world.

This book attempts to outline some of the symptoms of what ails the Western church these days and to explore the root issues behind those obvious problems. From there, we'll offer anchors, postures, and pictures that should guide any spirit-led exploration of church. Finally, we'll move forward into what should be at the heart of our corporate witness to the world as salt and light: confession and repentance.

I write from an American evangelical perspective. I affirm the historic, orthodox creeds of the Christian faith. I pastor in a large, middle- to upper-class megachurch in Orange County, California. I acknowledge that the center of Christianity is no longer in the West and that we have much to learn from our brothers and sisters in developing nations. I am incomparably rich by the standards of poverty that most of the world lives by. I confess that it is easier to write this stuff than live it.

I write with some questions in mind. What constitutes a church as opposed to a religious organization? What is essential to its life and witness, and what is merely a reflection of the particular form of society in which it was embodied? What is the purpose of the church? Are some modes of belief and practice about church more pleasing to Jesus than others? Can someone be a part of a large church and not lose Jesus in the middle of it? Why are so many of us dissatisfied with the faith and practice that many in my generation have been handed? Why do the activities of the church matter to the church? How do they matter to our participation in God's redemptive work in the world?

I hesitate making specific applications for several reasons. I would not want to rob any of us of the hard work of prayer, discernment, and incarnation in whatever context we find ourselves. Modes and methods and models of church are part of what we must look past in order to free our imaginations from the confining assumption that what works one place will automatically work somewhere else. Also, my own church community, Rock Harbor, is still learning and growing. By no means do I, or we, have it much figured out. I'll include some of our story along the way to illustrate our attempts to live out the kingdom of God, but these are not suggestive. Were you to visit us, you would find us to be a pretty imperfect crew, united only by our love for Jesus and our desire to explore, experiment, and grow into what Jesus intends for His people.

My hope is that this book will provoke and inspire us to greater faithfulness to the way of Jesus together. And where we fall short, I hope that we'll have the courage to confess and repent of our mistakes along the journey.

Part 1

Symptoms:
Washing Feet in Dirty Water

Chapter 1

Descent into Irrelevance

We live in a time unlike any other time that any living person has known. It's not merely that things are changing. Change itself has changed, thereby changing the rules by which we live...

There is more to this change than simply a linear extrapolation of rapid change and complexity. Quantum leaps are happening that are nothing like evolution. They remove us almost totally from our previous context. Simply learning to do old chores faster or to be able to adapt old forms to more complex situations no longer produces the desired results...

Running harder and harder in ministry will not work in this new world...

Established churches are becoming increasingly ineffective because our past has not prepared us for ministry in the future. The discontinuity we have experienced because of these quantum leaps is comparable to the experience of the residents of East Berlin when the Berlin Wall came down. Nothing in their past prepared them for life without the Wall. Very little in our past has prepared us for ministry in today's world.

WILLIAM EASUM

America is simultaneously the most professedly Christian of the developed nations and the least Christian in its behavior.

BILL MCKIBBEN

G one now from the place of privilege as the center of Western culture, the church finds itself increasingly marginalized from the world around it. As a whole, God's people no longer answer the pressing questions of culture, or if we do, we do so in ways that alienate others or violate God's revelation of Himself. This chapter will highlight some of the ways the church is rushing towards obsolescence.

Many of us have already known that the Western church is in

serious trouble. We see this, at the very least, in the drastic rise of publications celebrating, explaining, or protesting its demise. The title of this book, *Death by Church,* is simply a shorthand way of saying that much of the church has ceased giving life, light, and hope to the world and has often dispensed exactly the opposite. This is not to say we don't have reason for great hope and optimism; we do. But such hope is no longer based on existing structures and methods. Those are becoming increasingly irrelevant (and in some cases harmful) to the world around us. No, we need new (or old, depending on how you look at it) ways of thinking and doing church.

This chapter seeks to lay out the case for why we need such change. Much of this is examined in greater detail elsewhere. By necessity, I will be oversimplifying and generalizing, but what I lay out here in broad strokes plays itself in particular instances all the time.

Our Witness to the World

For the vast majority of the last 2000 years, the church has been the sponsor and center of most of Western culture and civilization.[1] The catalytic cultural shifts around us, however, remind us that the world is no longer content with a single religious sponsor (what some call pluralism) or with the idea of religious sponsorship of culture in general (what some call secularization). Rodney Clapp identifies two of the most widespread responses from the church to this state of affairs. The first one he calls *sentimental capitulation.* Clapp argues that this response is, in essence, a capitulation to the post-Christian world's assertion that Christianity has nothing distinctive to offer or to embody to the culture around it. The church can still perform some perfunctory and sentimental roles (weddings, funerals, baptisms, hospital visits, and the like) but it exists only to be called upon when needed in a moment of personal or national crisis.

The second response that Clapp identifies is that of *retrenchment.*[2] This comes in several different varieties. One of the most popular forms of retrenchment comes from religious conservatives who insist that America was founded as a Christian nation and should be so again.

Another form is to ignore the political and public sphere altogether and focus on making people happy, wealthy, and content.

> Therapeutic and marketing techniques are key for these retrenchers—they preach a kind of religious Reaganomics: Ask yourself: are you spiritually better off, more comfortable and tranquil and satisfied, than you were four years ago? If not, then you need our church...They [both sentimental capitulation and retrenchment] are not stances that question the dominant culture; instead they embody it.[3]

The idea that the majority of the church no longer embodies an alternative counterculture but rather reflects the attitudes, practices, and beliefs of the world around it has been well documented.[4] Divorce and domestic abuse rates are roughly the same in the church as they are outside it.[5] Studies show the church to be just as racist and materialistic as the rest of American society. Theologian Michael Horton makes this assertion:

> Gallup and Barna hand us survey after survey demonstrating that evangelical Christians are as likely to embrace lifestyles every bit as hedonistic, materialistic, self-centered, and sexually immoral as the world in general.[6]

Only 6 percent of evangelicals give 10 percent or more of their income to their church. The average church attendees donate only 2.66 percent of their income, which is roughly the same percentage as those outside the church who give to charities. Those who are most likely to object to neighbors of another race are white evangelicals. The numbers of unmarried couples that are living together are higher in places where there are a greater percentage of evangelical Christians than in other places. The percentage of Christian men involved in pornography is the same as that in non-Christian culture. There are many more such surveys to be found, but this is just a sampling of what many of us know about ourselves and about our churches. Sider makes this conclusion:

Whether the issue is divorce, materialism, sexual promiscuity, racism, physical abuse in marriage, or neglect of a biblical world-view, the polling data point to widespread, blatant disobedience of clear biblical moral demands on the part of people who allegedly are evangelical, born-again Christians.[7]

We should not be surprised, then, that the world these days objects more to Christians than to Christ.[8] The hypocrisy of the church is what keeps most away from Jesus. "We have become famous for what we oppose, rather than who we are for."[9] According to one survey, the three most common perceptions of present-day Christianity are "antihomosexual (an image held by 91 percent of young outsiders), judgmental (87 percent) and hypocritical (85 percent)."[10] The authors rightly conclude, "Modern Christianity no longer seems Christian."

Again, the point isn't to debate the merits of this study or approach versus another one. I just find it interesting that most of those who were included in this study had a vast deposit of firsthand knowledge to draw from. These were kids who had been to church and knew Christians and Christianity.[11] This doesn't mean, of course, that we should tone down or soften the message of Jesus, or skip those parts of the Bible that aren't comfortable. It also doesn't mean that the non-Christian world around us is not paying attention. They are paying attention, but they are simply objecting to what they see. Because of this, young adults are abandoning the church in record numbers.[12]

The American church's descent into irrelevance hasn't come primarily from the influence of the "liberal media," "secular Hollywood," or any other external factor. It has come primarily from within. The enormous disparity between what we say we believe and how we live removes any moral or cultural authority to influence (or, in some cases, even to engage in) the cultural discussions around us.[13]

These are problems that will take more than vision statements, better leadership conferences, better sermon illustrations, and bigger auditoriums to address. More of "the way we've done it before" won't be enough. Alan Hirsch (quoting Sally Morgenthaler) makes this point: "According to 2003 actual attendance counts, adult church-going is at 18 percent nationally and dropping…Of 3,098 counties in the US, 2,303 declined in church attendance."[14] George Barna predicts that "by 2025 the local church as we know it now will lose roughly half of its current 'market share' and…alternative forms of faith experience and expression will pick up the slack."[15]

Pastors Gone Wild

The statistics regarding the health and longevity of clergy are staggering. If the clergy are doing so poorly, is it any wonder our churches suffer as well? Here is a sample from a recent study:

- Churchgoers expect their pastor to juggle an average of 16 major tasks.
- Pastors who work fewer than 50 hours a week are 35 percent more likely to be terminated.
- The typical pastor has his or her greatest ministry impact at a church in years five through fourteen of his or her pastorate; unfortunately, the average pastor lasts only five years at a church.
- Eighty percent of pastors believe that pastoral ministry affects their families negatively.
- Seventy-five percent report they've had a significant stress-related crisis at least once in their ministry.
- Fifty percent feel unable to meet the needs of the job.
- Forty percent report a serious conflict with a parishioner at least once a month.
- Forty percent of pastors say they have considered leaving their pastorates in the last three months.
- Thirty-three percent confess inappropriate sexual behavior with someone in the church.
- Twenty percent say they view pornography at least once a month.

- Twenty percent admit to having had an affair while in the ministry.

- Twelve percent of pastors say that since they've been in ministry, they've had sexual intercourse with someone other than their spouse.

- Fifty-one percent say that Internet pornography is a possible temptation for them; 37 percent admit that it's a current struggle.

- Thirteen percent have been divorced.

- Eighty percent say they have insufficient time with their spouse.

- Sixty-six percent of pastors and their families feel pressure to model the ideal family to their congregations and communities.

- Seventy percent do not have someone they consider a close friend.

- Ninety percent feel they're inadequately trained to cope with ministry demands.

- Forty-five percent of pastors say they've experienced depression or burnout to the extent that they needed to take a leave of absence from ministry.[16]

At the risk of presenting too many statistics, here is another set with similar findings:

- Fifteen hundred pastors leave the ministry each month due to moral failure, spiritual burnout, or contention in their churches.

- Fifty percent of pastors' marriages will end in divorce.

- Eighty percent of pastors and 84 percent of their spouses feel unqualified and discouraged in their role as pastors.

- Fifty percent of pastors are so discouraged that they would leave the ministry if they could but have no other way of making a living.

- Eighty percent of seminary and Bible school graduates who enter the ministry will leave the ministry within the first five years.

- Seventy percent of pastors constantly fight depression.

- Almost 40 percent polled said they have had an extramarital affair since beginning their ministry.

- Eighty percent of pastors' spouses wish their spouse would choose another profession.

- The majority of pastor's wives surveyed said that the most destructive event that has occurred in their marriage and family was the day they entered the ministry.[17]

Something has apparently gone very wrong in the preparation of, caring for, and role expectations of many clergy. They live the same disparity between belief and behavior that characterizes most Christian congregations. There are probably many reasons for this.

One of the foremost characteristics of modern American culture is reductionism. We love to reduce big things to little things, complicated things to simple things, worldviews to bumper stickers, theological diversity to uniformity. This comes to us as a gift of the Enlightenment worldview that sought to control the world through breaking wholes into their component parts in order to understand them better.

This has its costs. For instance, in my four systematic theology classes in seminary, I did not read the Bible. I read other books that systematized the Bible into various topics and categories so that each could be understood apart from the others. This isn't all bad, of course, but I wonder what violence this enterprise does to make sense of the Scriptures as a whole in the diversity of its entire witness. We have reduced salvation into four steps that allow me entrance into heaven when I die.

But in so doing, we have bypassed the gospel that Jesus preached—the gospel of the kingdom of God. This gospel deals much more with the "here and now" than the "then and there." In this case, our reduction has helped to create the disparity between belief and behavior that we see everywhere. If the gospel is only concerned with forgiveness and the life to come, the real discipleship to Jesus becomes optional.

We see this reductionism also applied to the church. Church has been reduced now to only a one-hour service on the weekends. Neil Cole makes this observation:

> It amazes me to consider how much effort and how many resources (time, money and people) are expended for a single hour once a week. We have made church nothing more than a religious show that takes place on Sunday, and after it's done we all go home, until church starts again next week, same time, same place. Is this what the bride of Christ is?[18]

Not only that, but the weekend services for many have become so complicated that the expertise of professional ministers is needed to sustain it. This creates a very unhealthy dynamic between pastors and churches. A reduced Jesus and a reduced salvation and a reduced church all put more pressure on clergy to meet the needs of their congregations.

Our preaching has lost its prophetic fire, so we settle for tips and techniques on how to be a better parent, spouse, husband, wife, or businessperson. The mystery of God's will can be solved in three easy steps, we learn prayer through acrostics, and worship becomes mindless repetition of sophomoric choruses. Often our church services (consciously or not) reinforce our materialistic and consumeristic assumptions and produce self-centered and self-absorbed "end-users who believe that God is a resource that helps an individual secure what amounts to an anemic and culturally bound understanding of the abundant life."[19]

Pastoral ministry has become so bankrupt that entire industries have been built up around helping pastors do their work for them. For instance, one large, popular evangelical magazine devoted over half its page count to advertisements for a bewildering array of pastoral or church help resources: 12 different seminary degrees were advertised, three different Bibles, 30 different Christian books, three conferences, five different church insurers or banks, two capital fundraisers, one sermon video clip resource, two church marketing firms, and two different resources to help churches be Web savvy. Nothing is wrong with any of this individually, but if this magazine is a resource that pastors turn to for help in ministry, might we wonder if all this helps or hurts us in the long run.

Same publication, different edition: Another ad (for a church sign company) promotes how one church grew from 200 people in attendance to 800 people in attendance in just 16 months. This is the endorsement from the pastor of that church, "To date, we're up 300 percent. The————sign by far is the number one reason." No mention of Jesus, prayer, or the Holy Spirit. I know this is an easy target, but I am amazed that this stuff just blithely becomes part of the evangelical pastoral culture. Which is easier—prayer or putting up a new sign?

Attendance, Buildings, and Cash

The dirty little secret behind all of this is that for many (and I include myself in this), pastoral ministry is a spiritualized form of getting our ego needs met. It is fundamentally narcissistic. Most of us talk a lot about the glory of God, but we prefer more tangible measures of success. Maybe this explains our fascination with numbers. What is the best-selling Christian book? Who are the best preachers or worship leaders, bloggers or conference speakers? How big is your campus? How many services do you have a weekend? How many people attend? How large is your congregation? How many podcast your services? Why do we find it necessary to identify the "10 Fastest Growing Churches" or "Top 100 Worship Songs" or "50 Most Influential Christians?" Why did numerical growth become the most significant indicator of success? Does Jesus evaluate churches the same way we do? The sin of pride takes our eyes off of Jesus and fosters competition and comparison in ways that damage our witness to the world.

Certainly the Scriptures record the numerical growth of the early church, but our obsession with counting, ranking, and succeeding is idolatrous. Like the disciples, we still argue about who is the greatest in the kingdom of God, but we use the ABCs to keep score: Attendance, Buildings, and Cash. I don't want to be misunderstood. There is no question that the ABCs matter as the resources that allow churches to minister. But these are tied to deeply spiritual issues in us and often are monuments to our own egos. We'd never say this, of course, but it's true. How could it not be? In a culture that measures performance from the day we are born (including developmental milestones, appropriate grades, and athletic success), how can we think that our motives in this stuff are totally pure?

In a different edition of the publication mentioned earlier, an advertisement for a fundraising company touted its partnership with a large church to raise more than $21 million in cash and more than $84 million in pledges. The ad "celebrates this extraordinary demonstration of generous giving" to share the gospel of Jesus Christ to the city of——and the world." Maybe that is true, but considering that pictures of the campus, the senior pastor, and the leader of the fundraising company are all prominently featured on the page, we must ask if this is also a celebration of something else.

I am convinced that one of the reasons so many people are turned off to the church (including pastors!) is that it all seems too explainable. How many pastors signed up to lead a revolution but are now caught in managing a spiritual business (complete with budgets, payroll, vision statements, and organizational charts)? So many churches seem to be growing because of the excellence, efficiency, and relevancy of their programming. Of course, none of this (by itself) changes anybody; only God can do that. But we certainly act as if our programs could.

We all feel as if we have to offer a church much like the Wal-Mart Supercenter down the street. People want a vast array of inexpensive products, convenient times and locations, and a smooth checkout, so we structure our churches the same way. The problem with this, obviously, is that nothing in Wal-Mart transcends the ordinary. The same is true for most of our churches. We have little to no awareness or expectation of the presence of God directly speaking and ministering to His people. The entire ministry is mediated by well-dressed and polite people with name tags and the professionals on stage. The way the room is arranged, the worship music timed down to the second, the sermon with three points and two illustrations, the closing hymn—all these can point to human beings doing their best to be substitutes for God's work in the lives of His people. No wonder clergy are blowing out in massive numbers. We've changed what church is and what pastors do—so much so that very few are able to keep this up for long. Our definitions of success are too often aimed at bigger, better, and more, and we work ourselves into exhaustion as mini-messiahs who are poor substitutes for the real thing. We may get glimpses of God's transforming or healing power, but those are the exception rather than the rule. The "church as vendor of religious goods and services" mind-set is antithetical to the Bible's insistence that the church is the bride of Christ (Ephesians 5:19-22), the temple of the Holy Spirit (1 Corinthians 3:16), and the household of God (1 Timothy 3:15). This mentality is harmful not only to the church's members but also to other churches as they compete with one another to deliver the best experience.

All of this adds up to the increasing irrelevance and isolation of the American evangelical church. Eddie Gibbs and Ryan Bolger comment, "The end result of this increasing isolation is that a spiritual culture now surrounds a secular church."[20]

Other capitulations are in our midst (more about those in the next chapter), but this quick survey reveals the terrain concerning our witness to the world and the health and well-being of our clergy. In both cases, the news is not good. But God's kindness leads us to repentance. I don't know about you, but I am still confident that God hasn't given up on us, His church. I think He is calling us to reexamine some things and reshuffle some priorities, but more importantly, He is calling us to wake up. To not just point to our shiny, happy megachurches and Christian bookstores and tell ourselves that all is well. Sometimes I wonder what would happen if we really started addressing the things that plague the church—things like pride, infatuation with power and influence, narcissism, idolatry, greed, envy, and hypocrisy. It is far too easy to point fingers at our culture and name these things in the world around us. It is a far more terrifying thing when us church folk start realizing that God's judgment starts with us.[21]

Chapter 2

Garage-Sale Jesus

How does the way of Jesus line up with the way of our consumer-oriented churches that try to make sure there's enough parking for everyone?

Hugh Halter and Matt Smay

Whether the evangelical subculture is conscious of it or not, the consumer spirit is deeply entrenched in its soul: that is, in many ways its soul is but a reflection of the larger culture's own narcissistic spirit. The consumer church mind-set [of getting the spiritual goods we want at the least cost to ourselves], which offers self-gratification and fulfillment to the individual, is not "redemptive." Rather, this mind-set is violent: It enslaves and violates those who have bought into it, causing them to spiral further inward and downward into the bottomless pit of their insatiable desires. The church must awaken and see itself as a peculiar people with a particular politics, a people whose mission includes shaping each other's lives through conversion and participation in the crucified body of the risen Christ.

Paul Louis Metzger

Alan Hirsch notes, "I have come to believe that the major threat to the viability of our faith is that of consumerism. This is a far more heinous and insidious challenge to the gospel, because in so many ways it infects each and every one of us."[1]

I am one among many who agree with his assessment. Consumerism has become the Caesar of our age. The mall is now a place of worship. Hirsch argues that "[if] the role of religion is to offer a sense of identity, purpose, meaning, and community then it can be said that consumerism fulfills these criteria."[2]

Consumerism is the new lord that demands our allegiance, and its tyranny reaches every one of us. I think of it this way. Does a fish know it's in water? Of course not—it knows of nothing else. Because it is immersed in water its whole life, it knows of no other option than being where it is. For a fish to have (in theory, anyway) a knowledge that it is in water, it would have to have a place outside of water from which to draw that conclusion. The point of this minor exercise is to understand that because we are immersed in consumerism, we struggle to leap outside of that mind-set to really see how much it controls all of us.

For many, the revolutionary Jesus has been replaced by the garage-sale Jesus. The term *Christian* was originally a noun; now it's also an adjective. We have Christian pocketknives, pens, purses, T-shirts, potpourri, board games, Halloween costumes, suckers, chocolates, bandages (with a picture of Jesus on them so "cuts heal faster"), wrapping paper, dog collars, energy drinks ("infused with the fruit of the spirit"), fans, key chains, calculators, watches, staplers, golf balls, jelly beans, MP3 players, bath salts, breath mints, bubble gum, lighters, guitar picks, tennis shoes, air fresheners, poker chips, yo-yos, socks, soap, moisturizing lotion, shea butter repair cream, tea, belt buckles, candles, sunglasses, nail clippers, water bottles, protein bars ("inspired by Scripture"), underwear, bottled water, packing tape, perfume, shot glasses, coffee filters, acne medication (effective because it contains "powerful faith Scriptures and a victory prayer"), tire rims, alarm clocks, tire gauges, and (one that I am particularly interested in) Christian hair-growth products![3]

Did I also mention that Jesus comes in all sorts of action figure varieties? There is Harley Jesus, Cowboy Jesus, Soccer Jesus, Football Jesus, Soldier Jesus (comes with dove *and* assault rifle), Surfing Jesus, Skater Jesus, Rock Climbing Jesus, and Homeless Jesus (complete with a sign that reads, "Will work 4 food").

This is big business. If it can have a Bible verse, be made in a cross shape, or have Jesus' picture on it, odds are that some enterprising retailer has stamped it as "Christian." In 2006, Christian retailing was a $4.6 billion business.[4] Beyond the shallow theology most of this represents, it raises questions about the way this business reflects the consumeristic tendencies of American religion.[5] We seem to have simply Christianized the secular American values of opportunity, success, ambition, and greed.

Advertising now promises to give us what religion used to deliver: meaning, purpose, significance, and identity. Ads no longer appeal to only the qualities of the product but now show us the kind of life the product leads to. Advertisers now intentionally play on the spiritual vacuum of American culture by enticing us with images of community, coolness, adventure, health, romance…things that most of us thirst for but never significantly achieve. Experiences of life are now commodified products. I don't just sit down for a cup of coffee; I have a Starbucks experience. And as Christianity has been pushed further and further from the center of American culture to the margins, these experiences and products take the place of what had earlier been considered sole purview of religion.

Now the church must compete with other institutions and experiences for a place in the hearts and priorities of people. It no longer holds sway over most of our culture. It no longer has privileged status among ideas, experiences, or even religions.

> The problem for the church in this situation is that it is now forced to compete with all the other ideologies and -isms in the marketplace of religions and products for the allegiance of people, and it must do this in a way that mirrors the dynamics of the marketplace—because that is precisely the basis of how people make the countless daily choices in their lives. In the modern and postmodern situation, the church is forced into the role of being little more than a *vendor of religious goods and services*.[6]

We end up playing by the rules of the marketplace (and therefore reinforcing them) in order to compete with everything else. We usually justify this in the name of winning people to Christ. Because we are no longer in the center of culture, we have to earn our way into the hearts of people. And certainly there is some truth to this. But at what cost?

Church growth experts have shown us the value of surveys and marketing techniques. We have learned to listen to our target demographic to see what barriers keep people from coming to church, and we adjust our churches accordingly. We cater to life stages and worship preferences and allow people their choice of time and venue. I hasten to add that not all of this is bad by itself, but these individual choices may add up to a capitulation to the consumerism we are trying to fight against in inviting people to be disciples of Jesus. We shop for churches because the church has been reduced to a once-a-week event that is aimed entirely at attracting people. We position people to be consumers, so they respond like consumers.[7]

Theologian John Drane calls this the "McDonaldization" of the church. McDonaldization is "the process by which the principles of the fast-food restaurant are coming to dominate more and more sectors of American society as well as of the rest of the world."[8]

Drane surveys George Ritzer's four characteristics of the McDonaldization process and applies them to Western expressions of church. The first characteristic is that of efficiency—finding the best means to achieve a particular end so that other consumers can be served. We see this in the prepackaged spirituality so common today. We have how-to manuals on every conceivable topic, all to be done in 30 minutes a day or less (in this way, much spiritual growth stuff sounds a lot like the infomercials we see for exercise products on TV). We have one-minute Bibles and curricula that we can work through in only fifteen minutes a day. Worship services are carefully planned out, and we dread going one or two minutes over lest the service immediately after start late. We allow others to do the thinking for us and serve it up to us in nice, tidy, efficient bundles. The obvious problem with this is that the spiritual life doesn't work this way—it is often anything *but* efficient. Our prepackaged church services and spiritual disciplines are not true to life or to Scripture. It is the difference between fast food and a home-cooked meal; one may be more efficient than the other, but when it comes to what is best for us, efficiency loses almost every time.

The second of Ritzer's characteristics is calculability. By this he means our obsession with counting and quantifying things. We love to turn invisible spiritual realities into things we can see and count.

We think that the more of something we have, the better it is. Certainly this appears to be true within the supersize culture we live in. This is McDonaldization at its worst. Our American fascination with numbers, ranking, and size borders on idolatry and a sell-out to the needs of our own ego. Besides, most of our church growth is simply taking people from other churches. The total percentage of Christians relative to the rest of the population is now declining steadily.[9] To value calculability, Drane argues, is to focus on filling the building rather than filling the people. We should not be focused on asking how many people attend. Instead the question should be, what kind of people are we becoming? Size is no longer a reliable predictor of faithfulness, as the growth of cults and country music indicate.[10]

Third, Ritzer points to predictability as another characteristic of the McDonaldization process.

> In a rational society people prefer to know what to expect in all settings and at all times. They neither want nor expect surprises… in order to ensure predictability over time and place, a rational society emphasizes such things as discipline, order, systemization, formulization, routine, consistency, and methodical operation…it is these familiar and comfortable rituals that make fast food restaurants attractive to legions of people.[11]

We see this in the American church culture's constant pressure to make things uniform and reproducible. We want to homogenize our processes of faith and discipleship into a set of steps that supposedly works for everyone. This is the danger in the church-conference mentality. We already know that just because God is doing something one place doesn't mean that He will do it again in another. But we just can't help ourselves. We run to the next new fix, program, idea, sermon series, or whatever. Because of our impatience with prayer and incarnation, we settle for what is merely predictable. Another word for predictable is *explainable*, meaning that we can structure and plan and manage outcomes. Again, there is a place for this, but it is often a substitute for reliance on the Holy Spirit and willingness to wait in dependence upon Him. We don't like to risk because we assume numbers are the most important measure for success, so predictability becomes key. I have yet to meet someone who really wants to be a part of something that is almost entirely explainable by human gifting, resourcefulness, and strategic planning, and yet we can't help but be enticed into thinking that the answers to our problems lie in imitating what some other community is up to. Maybe that is true or maybe not. But if we are not careful, God is robbed in the process.

Predictability is expressed in capital campaigns (if you do X and Y, you'll raise this much money), worship services (low lighting plus songs in minor chords equals reverence), and discipleship (here are the four stages of faith that everyone goes through so you can know where you are and what comes next, or take these four classes). The last word people would have used to describe Jesus if they really knew Him would be *predictable*. And He said the Holy Spirit is about as predictable as the wind. Jesus brings mystery, paradox, and tension—rarely did someone get a straight answer out of Him. This doesn't mean that we should be completely out of control, unpredictable, and spontaneous. Not at all. I just wish to point out how easily these things can become substitutes for the real work of Jesus and His Spirit in our lives.

Lastly, Ritzer mentions the issue of control, not as a characteristic unto itself but rather something that runs through the whole list. Churches seem to be intent on making disciples of churches, not disciples of Jesus. Very often our version of following Jesus gets held up as the only way to do it, and those who do it differently are rarely welcomed. Power and control undergird a lot of the ways we as pastors lead our churches. Vision statements can become a means of control; so can discipleship programs and spiritual gift tests. Of course, there is a difference between control and accountability. We need to exercise discernment and fight to maintain our unity. But we in church leadership often seem intent on getting everybody looking, acting, and talking the same way.[12]

I came across something recently that seems to embody the McDonaldization of the church dramatically.

Eddie Johnson, the lead pastor of Cumberland Church, espouses the franchising concept when it comes to the relationship between his church in Nashville, Tennessee, and North Point Community Church in metro Atlanta. On his blog, he states, "Just like a Chick-fil-A, my church is a 'franchise,' and I proudly serve as the local owner/operator."

According to Johnson, his job is to "establish a local, autonomous church that has the same beliefs, values, mission, and strategy as North Point." He completed a three-month internship at North Point and continues to receive training and support. He claims to rarely deviate from the "training manual."

"Just like that Chick-fil-A owner/operator," he says, "I'm here in Nashville to open up our franchise and run it right. I believe in my company and what they are trying to 'sell.'"

The pastor says people who are already familiar with the North Point "brand" will find a local congregation with the same fit. For those who have relocated from Atlanta, they'll get a taste of home and know what to expect in their new church.[13]

Meanwhile, on Eddie's personal blog, he reposted an entry entitled "Top 10 ways a North Point video church is a lot like Chick-fil-A," which leads with the following quote:

Just like Chick-fil-A, my church is a "franchise" and I proudly serve as the local owner/operator. Whether it sounds spiritual or not, North Point Community Church and their model of ministry is a brand. And that brand is now quickly becoming a franchise. The leadership of North Point made a strategic decision a few years back to "transport" their way of doing church by planting local Strategic Partnership churches all across the nation and eventually, the world...My job was and is to establish a local, autonomous church that has the same beliefs, values, mission and strategy as North Point...All that to say, I'm not trying to figure out how to "do church." Just like that Chick-fil-A owner/operator, I'm here in Nashville to open up OUR franchise and run it right. I believe in my company and what they are trying to "sell." I rarely, if ever, deviate from the training manual.[14]

By quoting from Eddie and pointing to his church, I don't intend to be unkind or unfair. He does make some good points. And I have no doubt that his (and North Point's) motives in this are nothing more than wanting to share the good news of Jesus with as many people as possible. I may have misunderstood him entirely (though this kind of language lends itself to misunderstanding).

The way he describes the franchise model, however, raises some questions. It seems to take the values of efficiency, calculability, predictability, and control to their logical conclusion. This is where McDonaldization leads us. When consumers can trust a church brand and pastors can simply import the franchise to a new location, the work of prayer and discernment about what *this* community needs and how *this* community should be reached with the gospel seems to be short-circuited entirely. It also lacks any resemblance to the counterkingdom of the first century that confounded the powers, principalities, and structures of this world. Where is the death to self required in discipleship in any of this?

A mall mentality can easily creep into the church. We design ministries with every need and age in mind and pursue greater and greater forms of excellence and relevance. We look at church "campuses" as our one-stop spiritual headquarters, and our church bulletins are filled with ministries to meet every conceivable need. Alan Hirsch makes this lament:

> In the end, the medium has *so* easily overwhelmed the message. Christendom, operating as it does in the attractional mode and run by professionals, was already susceptible to consumerism, but under the influence of contemporary church growth practice, consumerism has actually become the driving ideology of the church's ministry.[15]

The way we do church contributes to this misunderstanding. The vast majority of people in the church building are passively arranged (in comfortable chairs) to focus on a stage, upon which are gathered the most gifted (or sometimes hired) people in the church delivering what is hopefully an engaging spiritual experience. We leave church evaluating it by the same standards we use to evaluate movies: Did I like it? Was it good? Was it moving? All the while we are feeding the very beast of consumerism we are seeking to destroy. We've turned religion into just another consumer item that can be used to give us comfort, identity, and meaning—but which can just as easily be discarded when something else catches our eye. The church has become little more than a vendor of religious goods and services, and the consumers (us) slip into the role of the discerning customers who devour the religious goods offered by the latest and greatest vendor. Ninety percent of the people who attend a church service are passive consumers.

We consumers love the benefits of the competition between businesses in the marketplace. We don't mind their banal pandering because we've grown accustomed to being thought of as worthy of their attention. An entitlement mind-set ensues as we learn to give our time, money, and attention to those things that allow us to personally derive some benefit. This gets applied to the church as people *shop* for a church that meets the needs of their family or lifestyle.[16] One of the results of this is that many no longer see themselves as ministers who are gifted and empowered to join in the work of Christ on the earth. Instead, they see ministry as something that is done to them by somebody else. They become merely passive receivers of God's work instead of active participants in it. Our clergy often reinforce this assumption, and we end up with the mess we see in Western evangelicalism.

Bill McKibben sees a connection between this consumer mind-set and the disconnect between what Christians in the West say they believe and how they live. He is worth quoting at length:

> The more troubling explanation for this disconnect between belief and action, I think, is that most Americans—which means most believers—have replaced the Christianity of the Bible, with its call for deep sharing and personal sacrifice, with a competing creed...It is another (though sometimes overlapping) creed, this one straight from the sprawling megachurches of the new exurbs,

that frighten me most. Its deviation is less obvious precisely because it looks so much like the rest of the culture. In fact, most of what gets preached in these places isn't loony at all. It is disturbingly conventional. The pastors focus relentlessly on *you* and your individual needs. Their goal is to service consumers—not communities but individuals: "seekers" is the term of art, people who feel the need for some spirituality in their (or their children's) lives but who aren't tightly bound to any particular denomination or school of thought. The result is often a kind of soft-focus, comfortable, suburban faith...

Drive through latte-stands, Krispy Kreme doughnuts at every service, and sermons about "how to discipline your children, how to reach your professional goals, how to invest your money and reduce your debt." On Sundays children played with church-distributed Xboxes, and many congregants had signed up for a twice-weekly aerobics class called Firm Believers. *Your Best Life Now* by Joel Osteen—which even the normally tolerant *Publishers Weekly* dismissed as "a treatise on how to get God to serve the demands of self-centered individuals." It's just that these people, presenting their perfectly sensible advice, somehow manage to ignore Jesus' radical and demanding focus on *others*. You could eliminate the Scripture references in these bestsellers and they would still make or not make the same amount of sense.

The dominant theologies of the moment...undercut Jesus, muffle his hard words, deaden his call, and in the end, silence him. In fact the soft-focus consumer gospel of the suburban megachurches is a perfect match for emergent conservative economic notions about personal responsibility instead of collective action...for some reason the Christian Coalition of America—founded in 1989 in order to "preserve, protect and defend the Judeo-Christian values that made this the greatest country in history"—proclaimed [in 2004] that its top legislative priority would be "making permanent President Bush's 2001 federal tax cuts."[17]

The church growth movement taught church leaders that the key to a healthy church was that people have a positive experience in church. The program of the church needs to be excellent to attract a crowd. The speaker must be entertaining. The music must be excellent. The programs must be fast paced and offer relationship with nice people, and the parking must be sufficient. If we do this well, people will be attracted to the church, and this will expose the masses to the Word of God and the gospel. In this approach, we are really converting people to church attendance. The program takes most of the pastor's time. He is the director of an event. Christian fellowship is then reduced to individuals consuming church together.

All of this, I argue, is not the *cause* of the church's increasing irrelevance but is rather the consequence of a much larger and more foundational mistake. The church has forgotten that it is to be a witness to, a sign of, and a foretaste of the "now but not yet" kingdom of God. Central to the kingdom is God's desire to renew, restore, and reconcile all things. For the church to truly be the church, it must announce, embody, and participate in this work of God in the world. Philip Kenneson and James Street make this clear:

> If the convictions that animate the life of the church are at cross purposes with the convictions at the heart of this coming kingdom, then the church will fail to be what God has called it to be...To be this kind of community, the church must embody a different set of convictions from those that animate most of the wider society.[18]

We are now realizing that the monster of consumerism in the church is the monster we helped create. We built the church on a consumerist model, which focused on comfort and convenience and attracted a middle-class audience that demanded safety and security. In effect, people came to the services to be fed. The church became a feeding trough, and the members grew comfortable, fat, and lazy. This made embracing the need to focus outward and be missional a tough sell. Ironically, Jesus took just the opposite tack—following Him was dangerous and costly. He didn't always make His messages easy for everyone to grasp. He didn't make people comfortable, and He was often carving away followers rather than attracting new ones. Sadly, in today's church, the vast majority of the church's growth comes from "church hoppers"—people who move from one church to another based on comfort and preference. In other words, we're stealing sheep instead of going out and making new disciples.

This shapes our gospel. The gospel is grace—it is a gift—that has nothing to do with any sort of exchange or transaction between human beings and God.[19] God trains us to align our perceived needs to His agenda for the world because we simply can't determine for ourselves what it is we need.

So what should we do? Should we somehow use people's consumeristic tendencies against them and give them what they think they want in order to lead them to Christ? Or should we seek to embody countercultural community that prophetically challenges the consumer mind-set that holds us captive? We'll discuss this further in later chapters, but I think the way is clear on this one. We radically underestimate the power of consumerism if we think we can give people what they think they want *and* help them on their way to being disciples of Jesus.

The church has always been called to be a subversive counterculture that stands against the values, structures, and norms of this world as a witness to their emptiness and futility. Ultimately, the church is called to embody the upside-down way of the kingdom of God. We have lost sight of this truth, however. This is one of the reasons we find ourselves in the current mess we're in. Without a deep theology of what the church is (its essence), we can't adequately discuss and discern what the church does (its function). Most of us lack such a framework, so we turn to pragmatism (roughly, the view that something is good because it works) to justify our models and methods of church. Thankfully, we have much more to lean on.

Over the next several chapters we'll examine the idea of the kingdom of God and how it relates to the church. Jesus' message and ministry were centered on this idea. Though this will entail some heavy theological lifting, this background is necessary in order to adequately address some of the shortcomings we have highlighted. As we'll see, there are ways in which we can address the huge questions that face us.

Soil:
Back to Where
We Came From

Chapter 3

The King and His Kingdom

The kingdom of God? Time after time Jesus tries to drum into our heads what he means by it. He heaps parable upon parable like a madman. He tries shouting it. He tries whispering it...What he seems to be saying is that the kingdom of God is the time, or a time beyond time, when it will no longer be humans in their lunacy who are in charge of the world but God in his mercy who will be in charge of the world. It's the time above all else for wild rejoicing—like getting out of jail, like being cured of cancer, like finally, at long last, coming home. And it is at hand, Jesus says.

FREDERICK BUECHNER

I dentifying what ails the church is easy enough; offering practical corrections is another matter. In this chapter and those that follow, I want to lay a theological groundwork out of which we can address some of these issues. Not all of this is original with me, but I hope to dust off some ecclesiology (the study of the church) so it can both highlight and answer some of our present crises. We'll begin with the idea of the kingdom of God as it is presented throughout the Scriptures and then consider its relationship to the church. This will lead us to the call for the church to embody an alternative society that neither withdraws from the world nor uncritically engages it but rather witnesses to and serves as a foretaste of the redemption of God in Jesus Christ. This will then set the stage to come back and address the issues we have raised thus far.

The King and His Kingdom

I was raised in the church, attended youth and campus groups, and read a lot of Christian books, but not until I was in my thirties did

I hear much related to the kingdom of God. The gospel was always presented as going to heaven after you die, and praying the prayer of salvation. Certainly these are important things. But I now recognize that they represent only a narrow slice of what the Scriptures teach about salvation. This chapter is the longest and most complex in the book. The background we are about to cover is necessary, however, to the argument I am trying to make. If you'll stay with me, you'll find a significant payoff in a few chapters.[1]

The kingdom of God is the central theme of the Bible.[2] The foremost pronouncement of the Old Testament is that Yahweh is King.[3] The declaration of the New Testament is that Jesus is Lord. These statements are equivalent in nature and intent. At the heart of each is the worshipful proclamation of God's rightful rule, mediated by and through covenants (promises) of grace. This chapter is a short examination of pictures in the Scriptures that give us insight into the nature of the King and His kingdom.[4]

Whenever we get a glimpse into the heavenly realm, we see God exalted on a throne, surrounded by a sea of angels who are praising and worshipping His name. These images bind the whole of Scripture together.

> In the year that King Uzziah died, I saw the Lord seated on a *throne,* high and exalted, and the train of his robe filled the temple (Isaiah 6:1).
>
> Above the expanse over [the angelic beings'] heads was what looked like a *throne* of sapphire, and high above on the *throne* was a figure like that of a man (Ezekiel 1:26).
>
> As I looked, *thrones* were set in place, and the Ancient of Days took his seat...*Thousands upon thousands attended him; ten thousand times ten thousand stood before him.* The *court* was seated, and the books were opened (Daniel 7:9-10).
>
> At once I was in the Spirit, and there before me was a *throne* in heaven with someone sitting on it...Surrounding the *throne* were twenty-four other thrones, and seated on them were twenty-four elders (Revelation 4:2-4).

These images run throughout the Psalms as well. God is pictured time and again as a King reigning and ruling from a throne, and Israel is commanded to address and approach God in worship as King (see, for example, Psalm 93:1-2; 5:1-3; 9:11; 10:16). The whole Bible assumes this perspective. Israel regarded God as enthroned in their midst, dwelling between the cherubim (angels) in the innermost sanctuary of the tabernacle and later in the temple in Jerusalem (Numbers 7:89; Isaiah 37:16), where His throne was the mercy seat.

In Genesis we read of God speaking the world into existence from His throne. As King, He places humanity, made in His image, in the world to reflect and execute His sovereignty.[5] As king, He makes covenants (treaties) with Noah, Abraham, Israel, and David, and He promises a new covenant written on the heart.[6]

Creator and Redeemer

The Old Testament doesn't use the phrase *kingdom of God,* but as we'll see, it is present in various forms. The reign and rule of God in the Old Testament is presented as both universal in scope and particular in intention and manifestation.

Within the reality of God's universal and absolute reign, He creates the universe and makes all things good, including the gift of freedom given to both angels and human beings. They were free to love Him or to reject Him, to worship Him or to turn to something else. That is the purpose of the command for Adam and Eve to refrain from eating from the tree of the knowledge of good and evil—freedom only exists when there is freedom to do otherwise. God creates human beings in His image to be His vice regents, administering His kingdom over the world as His subjects.

Both angels and humans revolt, however. Satan, a rebellious great angel, leads a host of angels in a cosmic mutiny, seduces our first parents, usurps their domain, and establishes his counterkingdom. Their revolt and the counterkingdom, established against God's perfect reign, lead to judgment and the casting out of Satan to the earth and the expulsion of Adam and Eve from Eden. This Satanic counterkingdom becomes the backdrop for the rest of the Bible.

The good news for us is not only that God is creator but also that He is rescuer and redeemer. He doesn't stay far away from us in our sin and despair. His great purpose is to restore His fallen creation and renew it beyond the original. This begins with the calling of Abram to restore God's rule on the earth. God promises to bless not only his family but also all the families of the earth through him.[7] In doing this, He binds himself to Abraham in an unconditional, perpetual covenant (treaty). Thus God establishes his rule over a *people.* When Abraham's descendents find themselves in slavery in Egypt, God intervenes to deliver them.

Therefore, we must distinguish between the universal declaration of God's rule (over the heavens and earth, the angels and demons, space and time, life and death, and everything else) and the particular instances of that rule (such as whether or not a particular person or nation acknowledges this to be true). The coming of the kingdom of God involves God's intervention into human history. The universal reign becomes manifest in the particular. So the universal reign of God (He is King) is held in tension with the ongoing in-breaking of His kingdom in and through Israel into human history (He will be King).[8] Israel was to make the universal reign of God a reality in their time, and this serves as the focus for everything else.[9]

The dominant Old Testament picture of God is that He is King and reigns universally over all creation (2 Kings 19:15; Psalms 29:10; 99:1-4; Isaiah 6:5; Jeremiah 46:18;) and particularly over the ethnic tribe of Israel (Numbers 23:21; Deuteronomy 33:5; Isaiah 43:15).[10] This particularity was marked by several episodes in Israel's history that progressively shaped her understanding of the King and His kingdom.

The Exodus

God's deliverance of the nation of Israel took place on two levels. First, the nation was enslaved to Egypt and cried out to God from under the weight of their subjugation. But second, and more important, the tenth plague leveled against Pharaoh also included Israel in a unique way so that they too stood underneath the wrath of God. In the tenth plague, Israel was not immune as it had been during the previous nine plagues. This demonstrated that the nation (along with all of Egypt) was under God's righteous judgment and subject to His wrath. This was different from the nine previous judgments; in those, God made a clear distinction between the nation of Israel and the people of Egypt. But now, during the night of the tenth plague, God called His people to express their faith in Him through the shedding of the blood of a lamb. This was God's provision for the death of the firstborn in Israel. In this way, God passed over them when His wrath was revealed. The loss of the firstborn broke the stubborn will of Pharaoh and released the Israelites from their bondage.

The text makes clear that the ten plagues were not only the means by which God would deliver His people; they also formed an all-out assault on the false gods of Egypt.[11] The tenth plague—the killing of the firstborn—was directed at Pharaoh himself. Both Pharaoh and his firstborn son were thought to be divinely conceived, and this belief formed the basis of their authority. The death of Pharaoh's firstborn was an assault on Pharaoh's divinity.

Moses made it clear that each plague was the result of God's power (he predicted each beforehand), so the Egyptians clearly understood that these plagues were demonstrations of a powerful God. And the fact that the plagues (the first nine, at least, and the tenth, differently) were directed only at the Egyptians made it obvious that it was the God of *Israel* who was warring against them. The predictive nature of these events, as well as their focus and power, showed beyond doubt that God was King over nature and over all the gods of Egypt.

This twofold liberation was the subject of the song of freedom that Moses and Miriam sang in Exodus 15. And at the center of that song is Miriam's confession: "The LORD will reign for ever and ever." The Hebrew word *Melek* (king) comes from *Malak* (to be king, to reign). The concept here is *dynamic* because it refers to dominion, rule, and power. The kingdom of God, then, refers only in a secondary sense to the realm or area over which the king reigns. Its primary meaning is not the *realm,* but the *act* of God's reign. The reign of God is not a place but an event: God's intervention or breakthrough in and through the created order.[12]

The Mosaic Covenant

We also see God's kingship in His announcement to Moses: "You will be for me a kingdom of priests and a holy nation."[13] By defeating Pharaoh in battle, God, as the conquering king or *suzerain,* could enter into a treaty with a vassal nation (in this case it was Israel, not Egypt). The Mosaic covenant is a covenant between a conquering King and a people now under His rule. This agreement between Israel and the God of their forefathers now constituted a King forever reigning over a kingdom (*malkuth*) unlike that of any earthly king.[14] In other words, the idea of divine kingship presupposes the actual formation of a people that demonstrates God's exclusive claim upon the world.[15] That nation was delivered from bondage in order to be delivered into covenant with God. They were now constituted into a people under the kingship of God, governed by His law (the Torah).[16]

The Mosaic covenant clearly shows that God desired to bring the whole of human life under His rule. The law given to Israel includes rules and regulations governing all aspects of life (such as birth, death, marriage, clothing, lending, commerce, diet, agriculture, and justice). Not one aspect of life was exempt from God's rule, for it encompasses the events that take place in the midst of everyday life. Life was not divided into sacred or secular spheres; all of life was to be subject to God. This should warn us against reducing the rule of Jesus today to purely the so-called spiritual or religious parts of our lives.

The Kingdom of David

The blessings of the Mosaic covenant were most fully realized under the reign of King David. Despite the successes of God on behalf of His people, Israel was not successful in driving out the nations that had occupied Canaan before them. Although now dwelling in the land, the nation of Israel was continually and willingly led into idolatry and disobedience by the nations surrounding them. Their sin culminated in their desire to have a human king. From Abraham to Samuel, God was the only King of Israel. He raised up charismatic leaders to protect His people and do His bidding in times of great need. But the people were unhappy and wanted a king like the other nations. God assured Samuel (the last in a long sequence of judges) that the nation had not rejected him but God as King over them:

> But when they said, "Give us a king to lead us," this displeased Samuel; so he prayed to the LORD. And the LORD told him: "Listen to all that the people are saying to you; it is not you they have rejected, but they have rejected me as their king" (1 Samuel 8:6-7).

From this point on the question is this: When will God reassume His rightful, direct kingship over His people? Samuel had to come to a new understanding about the nature of the kingdom: God would be working through His representative kings. They were to be designated as servants of the Lord, though few actually honored that responsibility. God is King, Israel's only rightful sovereign, but He promises a king like David to rule over His people forever:

> The LORD declares to you [David] that the LORD himself will establish a house for you...Your house and your kingdom will endure forever before me; your throne will be established forever (2 Samuel 7:11,16).[17]

The essence of the house and the throne is the establishing of the kingdom. The dynasty or line of kings to follow David is the divine promise given to him.

The Exile

Shortly after this, the nation of Israel was divided into two kingdoms: the northern kingdom of Israel and the southern kingdom of Judah. Both nations were eventually sent into exile (though not simultaneously) after a long period of apostasy and rebellion. This was a devastating chapter in the history of God's people. Its significance is impossible to overstate. The temple in Jerusalem was destroyed, the people were scattered, and the walls of the holy city were torn down.

In this circumstance, the prophets began to deliver God's promise of a new redemption for His people. This redemption would eclipse previous revelations of God in both depth (the law would now be written on people's hearts) and breadth (the blessings God promised in Genesis 12 would now be for the nations, not just Israel).

Even though some eventually returned to the promised land, the Jews continued to languish under the oppressive rule of other nations. Yahweh had not yet come to Zion in triumph, redeeming Israel and setting her over the nations. Instead, the Jews saw themselves as slaves who were still in exile even though they were back in the promised land.[18]

As the exile continued, the language of the prophets became increasingly apocalyptic (focused on the *eschaton*—the final intervention of God's kingdom at the end of the world). To some extent their prophecies were about and were partially fulfilled in the return from exile and the restoration of the land and temple in the time of Ezra and Nehemiah, but their promises ranged far beyond this time frame. God would do a new thing (Isaiah 43:16-19) and come to the earth in a glorious new way (Habakkuk 3:1-15), similar to His coming and rescue in the original exodus.

This future orientation is so widespread that the prophets developed a shorthand way of referring to the promise of the kingdom. They used phrases like "the day of the Lord," "the latter days," and "in that day" to refer to the final revelation of God's power and glory at the end of human history. They saw a distinction between the present order of things and the one to come. The present age was characterized by the oppression of Israel and the flourishing of the wicked. The age to come would be marked by the vindication of Israel and the restoration of God's reign over all creation. The idea of a messianic figure who would usher in the transition from one age to the other soon gained prominence in Jewish writings.

The Old Testament ended with a great sense of anticipation and messianic hope and expectancy. The prophets announced the coming of the day of the Lord: the final and complete revelation of God and His kingdom to humanity. The Jewish hope was that God Himself would intervene—that just as He rescued His people from Egypt through Moses, so He would rescue His people from foreign oppression through the Messiah. A new king from the line of David, the heir to the throne of Israel, would establish His kingdom, slaughter the occupying army, tear down the pagan shrines, gather the Jews from their dispersion, cleanse the land, and rebuild Jerusalem. God himself would come to reign, glorifying his temple and welcoming any Gentiles who sought to live according to His law. The land would flourish with peace and prosperity.

But instead, 400 years of waiting and silence followed, and those Jews who had returned to the promised land found themselves under the rule of Rome, the dominant world power at the time.

The Life and Ministry of Jesus

All the Old Testament pictures and conceptions of God's kingship converged in the birth, ministry, death, and resurrection of Jesus of Nazareth. In this one person, the *eschatological* promises of God assumed human flesh and came bursting into human history. The Jews expected that the arrival of the age to come would signal the end of the present age of space and time.[19]

Instead, unexpectedly, the whole of the life of Jesus pointed to the inauguration of the world to come *in the midst of the present age*. People had all sorts of ideas about how to usher in the kingdom, but Jesus' claim was that it was already operative in Him.

This was significant. Jesus proclaimed and demonstrated the reality of the presence of the kingdom of God in His person. Moreover, Jesus did not merely retain His Jewish identity and heritage; He served as a "living capitulation of Israel's history. More precisely, Jesus did not merely copy the history of Israel, but realized it afresh in terms of His own life and obedience. By so doing, He re-presented not only Israel's past but also its future, as it would come to be through Yahweh's mighty consummating works."[20]

Jesus stood as the fulfillment of Israel's mission to proclaim and demonstrate the gracious and redemptive reign of God to the nations. This is seen in His teachings.

The central theme in the ministry and teaching of Jesus is the kingdom of God.[21] This is the essence of His teaching, the thread that ties His whole ministry together. His proclamation of the kingdom was the core of His message: "The time has come...the kingdom of God is near. Repent and believe the good news!" (Mark 1:15).[22] This good news is about God's closeness. The basic meaning of the phrase *has come* used here is not temporal (that is, Jesus is not saying that the kingdom of God is close like my vacation is close); rather, it is spatial (the kingdom is nearby, at hand, or within reach, much like this book is within reach). Jesus is saying that the Anointed One has come and if we reach out and touch Him, we touch the kingdom.

The phrase *kingdom of God* has been the subject of much scrutiny. To talk about the kingdom of God is to talk about God's rule or His act of reigning. George Ladd suggests, "The primary meaning of the Hebrew word *malkuth* in the Old Testament and the Greek word *basileia* in the New Testament is the rank, authority and sovereignty exercised by a king."[23] The primary emphasis of the phrase is on reigning and not on a realm or a group of people.[24] Or, as Allen Wakabayashi puts it, "The Kingdom of God is about the dynamic of God's kingship being applied."[25]

The kingdom of God is dynamic and all encompassing. It is always spreading, growing, and moving. It does not refer to a realm or place, but refers instead to God's will, power, and authority. It points us not to the place of God (in heaven) but to the act and nature of His ruling (from heaven). It is not a group of people, nor is it life in some future heaven. The kingdom advances now whenever people submit themselves to God's will (on earth as it is in heaven). Most importantly, the kingdom refers to the King: Jesus Himself. Jesus was the promised king, and His reign was the kingdom. The gospel was simply the good news of God's kingly rule, or of the one who inaugurates that rule—Jesus.[26]

An important key to understanding Jesus' use of *kingdom of God* is to note how some of His Jewish contemporaries used it.[27] Jewish rabbis used the phrase, *kingdom of God* originally to mean the rule of God over a person who keeps or begins to keep the written and oral commandments.[28] They felt that when a person confessed, "The LORD is our God, the LORD alone," indicating his or her intention to keep the Torah (the Jewish law, usually referring to the first five books of the Old Testament), that person came under God's rule and authority, and thus came into the kingdom of God. Having accepted God's authority over him or her, the person was able to begin keeping the commandments. This committing oneself to the kingdom of God is formalized by one's confession of the Shema (Deuteronomy 6:4), the declaration that there is but one God, but its practical expression is in the observance of the commandments.

Jesus spoke of the kingdom with the same understanding in Matthew 7:21: "Not everyone who says to me, 'Lord, Lord,' will enter the kingdom of heaven, but only he who does the will of my Father who is in heaven." Jesus spoke of God's kingdom being rooted in the confession of His authority and the doing of His will. He makes the same point in Matthew 6:10: "Your kingdom come, your will be done on earth as it is in heaven." The phrases are synonymous: People come into the kingdom when they accept God's authority and begin to do His will. In the story of the rich man in Matthew 19, Mark 10, and Luke 18, Jesus challenges the man to sell all he has, give it to the poor, and "come, follow me." The man turns away sad, and Jesus says, "How hard it is for the rich to enter the kingdom of God!" To join the movement Jesus is leading, one submits to His authority and thereby comes into the kingdom of God.

According to Jesus, this kingdom is limited. Only those who follow

Him are included. The kingdom should not be confused with God's providential (or universal) rule described in Isaiah 66:1: "Heaven is my throne, and the earth is my footstool." In this general sense, the Lord is king of the universe. Neither should it be viewed as an earthly political movement that rules by power and might or ordains Christian leaders to govern a largely unconverted world.

There *is* a final redemption or completion of the kingdom (more about that in a second), but both Jesus and other Jewish rabbis generally viewed the kingdom in a more practical, everyday way: doing the will of God. Jesus' demands for entering the kingdom of heaven were high. Among them was a readiness to leave family, property, and careers (see Luke 5:11,28; 14:25-33; 18:22). After a person joined Jesus' band of disciples, the demands for remaining at the center of God's kingdom remained high.

"Give us this day our daily bread" resonates with the values and priorities of this cultural context. Jesus expected His followers to make moving with God's redemptive activity their priority. Once committed to this program, they had no reason to worry about their basic necessities—food, clothing, and shelter. God would take care of these.

The Baptism of Jesus and Beyond

Jesus' baptism by John in the Jordan was significant in our understanding of the kingdom for a number of reasons. First, it signaled the beginning of Jesus' public ministry. Second, the Holy Spirit fell on Jesus and anointed Him for this messianic ministry. This anointing was reminiscent of the anointing of kings in the Old Testament (as in 1 Samuel 16:13). Third, Jesus receives the affirmation of the Father during His baptism as the Father speaks to the Son, "You are my Son, whom I love, with you I am well pleased" (Mark 1:11). The Father alludes to Psalm 2:7 and Isaiah 42:1, where Jesus' vocation as the messianic Warrior King and the Suffering Servant of the Lord are revealed. Jesus' disciples later wrestle with how these two themes fit together. They seem to be contradictory, but in fact, they seamlessly unite in Jesus' life and ministry.[29] The Father commissions Jesus not only to overturn Satan's kingdom but also to give His life as a ransom for many by taking away the sins of the world.[30]

Jesus not only proclaimed the message of the kingdom but also embodied its reality. He had authority over demons (Mark 5:1-20), sickness (5:21-43), and nature (4:35-41). He taught with uncommon authority and had the audacity to forgive sins. (Forgiveness has previously been tied to the functions and authority of the Temple.) The common thread through the accounts of Jesus' ministry is that He sought to free people from whatever held them captive (Matthew 11:1-5; Luke 4:16-19). In Jesus, the one true God confronts the ruler who holds God's people captive. But now the enemy is no longer a human ruler or a people, but the ruler (*archon*) of this world. Jesus has come to attack the strong man (Satan) and plunder his house (Mark 3:26-27). The reign and rule of God comes to the world through Jesus and is realized through healings, miracles, exorcisms, and the forgiveness of sins. These are signs and foretastes of the kingdom in a world that doesn't fully yet submit itself to the authority of God. God's kingdom breaks into this world whenever it is brought to bear and applied in our flesh-and-blood world.

The kingdom was breaking into the world through the ministry of Jesus, but there was much that was mysterious about it. Those closest to Jesus repeatedly found a great deal of His teaching and ministry puzzling. Particularly confusing was the way Jesus revealed who He really was. He forbade His disciples from announcing who He was (Mark 1:43-44), and He did not share the secrets of the kingdom openly (Mark 4:11) but rather explained that they were understandable to some but hidden from others (Matthew 13:11-13). When the disciples finally understand that Jesus is the Christ, Jesus immediately orders them to silence (Mark 8:30). Only Peter, James, and John got to see Jesus in His transfigured glory (Mark 9:2-13), and even then Jesus told them not to share this until He had risen from the dead. Demons were the only ones who seemed to consistently know the nature of Jesus' identity.[31]

But these weren't the only questions surrounding Jesus' life and ministry. Why did Jesus refuse to allow the crowds to crown Him king (John 6:15)? Why did He not speak out against Caesar and overthrow the Romans? Why did He condemn the religious leaders and their temple and eat with sinners? Why did some of the things promised in the Old Testament about the Messiah take place while others did not? Even John the Baptist doubted (Matthew 11:2-3). Had the kingdom really come, or was it yet to arrive? Jesus' disciples were confronted with irrefutable evidence that the kingdom had finally come, yet they were confused with the veiled way it was revealed, and they had to overcome their own Jewish assumptions about what the Messiah would be like.[32]

Now but Not Yet

The central mystery regarding the teachings of Jesus concerned the coming of the kingdom. Was it here and now? Or was it still to come? Some of the confusion about the nature of the kingdom stems from the bewildering array of statements that Jesus makes about its coming. In some cases, Jesus seems to teach that the fullness of the kingdom is still in the future (Matthew 6:10; 16:28; Mark 9:1; Luke 9:27; 21:31). Yet in other places, Jesus talks about the kingdom existing in the present time: "But if I drive out demons by the finger of God, then the kingdom of God has come to you" (Luke 11:20; see also Matthew 11:11-13; 12:28; 21:31; 23:13; Mark 1:14-15; Luke 10:9-11). In a number of other places, Jesus warns against speculating about the timing for the coming of the kingdom at all (see Luke 17:20-21). In fact, when the disciples asked Jesus directly about this, He didn't answer by pointing to *either* the current presence or the future coming of the kingdom. Instead, He told them (in essence) not to worry about it and to get to work sharing his message (Acts 1:6-8).

So we are left with a similar paradox regarding the kingdom as the one we examined in the Old Testament (that is, Yahweh is king, and Yahweh will become king). In this case, however, the mystery concerns the kingdom. In the words of one scholar, the kingdom is both *already* and *not yet*.[33] Jesus announced the arrival of the kingdom and yet talked about it still coming in all its fulfillment.[34] So in Jesus, we are in the presence of the future. Jesus reorients our view of time. Usually we take the present and project it into the future. Jesus' teaching, however, represents the opposite perspective. He speaks to the present from the prospective of the future. His teaching therefore contains both present and future elements held in tension.

A holistic understanding of the kingdom integrates both present and future elements. The kingdom must be understood as (1) the dynamic reign of God in the hearts of His people, (2) a reality now present on earth that people either enter into or reject, and (3) a future kingdom that will culminate with God dwelling with His people on a new earth.[35]

The Jews divided human history into two stages: this present age, where evil and injustice are prominent and Israel is oppressed, and the future age of salvation that is yet to come (Mark 10:30), inaugurated by the resurrection of the dead.[36] The Jews viewed the resurrection as belonging only to the age to come because this present age is still characterized by sin and death. The Jews had no conception of one man being resurrected in the middle of the present age. They thought that when God stepped into history to bring about the age to come, the righteous would be resurrected to share in the blessings of God's new world. Jesus' resurrection in the first century was puzzling to the disciples for precisely this reason. How could one man be raised from the dead in the middle of this present age? The only conclusion that they could draw was that because of the resurrection, the age to come had begun, right in the middle of this world.[37]

The best way to make full sense of Jesus' conflicting statements about the kingdom is to understand that in His ministry and person, the age to come broke into this present age. He was "the presence of the future." But evil still exists, Satan still rages, and we still long for the peace and justice of God. The kingdom of God is here but not fully here. Our world is fallen but in the process of being redeemed. We live at the intersection of the already and the not yet.[38]

The Parables of Jesus

The relationship between the present kingdom and the future kingdom is the central theme of the parables.[39] The present kingdom came near to people through the ministry and person of Jesus of Nazareth. The future kingdom confronted people with the realities of judgment and mercy. This tension left people with a choice (that is why He called them to repent and believe the good news). The way they responded to the kingdom in this life will determine their standing when it comes in all its fullness.

The danger was that men and women would misunderstand the hidden nature of the kingdom and miss its universal scope. So Jesus told parables that talked about how a little bit of leaven affects the whole meal (Matthew 13:33) or how a small seed grows into a giant tree. And the response demanded by the kingdom is deeper than words or intentions (Matthew 13:18-23; Luke 14:15-24). In the parable of the two sons, one son said yes to the request of the father but didn't follow through, and the other son said no but actually ended up doing what the father had asked. Jesus' point is that it is not our words, but our obedient response that counts in God's sight (Matthew 21:28-32).

But the Son of Man preaches the kingdom right now (Matthew 13:37-38). The kingdom is near in our present moment (Mark 1:14-15). The present is merely a shadow of the ultimate future that awaits us. The future kingdom is now suddenly present among us. Jesus was clear that His present kingdom was forcefully advancing, and this was most clearly seen in the response of the demonic realm to him (Matthew 12:28). Wherever Jesus was, demons understood and recognized His identity and authority. Isaiah had promised that the coming king would set captives free; Jesus came preaching the kingdom and attacking the house of the "strong man" (a reference to Satan) to plunder his possessions (Mark 3:22-27). Jesus pointed to the casting out of demons as a sure sign of the kingdom (Matthew 12:28), and they cried out in confusion because this event began "before the appointed time" (Matthew 8:29).[40]

And yet Jesus and the disciples believed in a dramatic future intervention of God and the Son of Man, which will bring this age to a close and consummate God's reign on the earth.[41] Jesus specifically taught about the delay of the kingdom in its future consummation in Matthew 25. In the parable of the virgins, some of them ran out of oil because the bridegroom was delayed (Matthew 25:1-13). So too in the parable of the talents, where the master reviews the work of his servants when he returns "after a long time" (Matthew 25:19). Jesus offers a similar parable in Luke 19:11-27 specifically to answer those who thought the kingdom would appear immediately.

Though our response is important, entrance into the kingdom is completely by grace. All we can do is respond to the invitation of Jesus (Matthew 22:14). We do not participate in the future kingdom because of our own merit. The parable of the workers in the vineyard shows no connection between how long the workers worked and how much they were paid (Matthew 20:1-16). Jesus seeks and saves the lost, not the other way around (Luke 15).

So in the person and ministry of Jesus, the kingdom is already present, but its presence isn't comprehensive or complete. The "already but not yet" dimension of the kingdom creates an unexpected interval of delay as this age continues while the next age is already present. We live, so to speak, at the intersection of this age and the one to come, of fallenness and redemption, of reality and anticipation. Aspects of the age to come can now be found right here in this present evil age. And yet the fullness of what God has in store for the world still remains in the future.

The words of Derek Morphew here provide a fitting close to this chapter:

> Even the highest point of Old Testament expectation was insufficient to express what really occurred in Jesus. The breakthrough of the future kingdom into the present world, before the present world had terminated, was beyond even Isaiah's anticipation. We find that the vision of the kingdom developed progressively through redemptive history with each new picture transcending the

previous one. The Exodus event moves to the Davidic monarchy, which then develops into the "day of the Lord" expectation in the prophets, reaching its highest point in Isaiah. But the coming of Jesus burst beyond everything that had preceded it, and what happened in Jesus is now the basis of what will happen when he comes again.[42]

Chapter 4

The Kingdom of the Church
or the Church of the Kingdom?

[The church] was designed with the particular mission of bearing witness to God's advancing kingdom of beloved community through participation in the crucified and risen Christ, and of being consumed by him on behalf of the world for which Christ died. As such, that beloved community should be breaking down divisions between male and female, Jew and Gentile, slave and free, and it should be confronting those demonic forces that distort and reduce people to races and classes, to rugged individuals in isolation, people whose value lies in how much they produce and consume. The church becomes a fallen power when it loses sight of its fundamental allegiance to God's kingdom, when it becomes proud and autonomous and thus distorted in its use of power, seeking political advantage in the secular sphere so as to win benefits for its members, benefits that will allow them to achieve and maintain a Laodicean standard of living and leisurely lifestyle, as they are—in the meantime—reduced to a function of the state, market, and consumer culture.

PAUL LOUIS METZGER

As I began to get my mind around the centrality of the kingdom of God, I immediately began to wonder how the kingdom relates to the church. Are they equivalent? Or is the kingdom bigger in some way? I had only heard the church and the kingdom discussed together by end-times doomsayers with fancy prophecy charts that had locust-looking things on them. They argued that that the church will be raptured from the earth when Jesus returns to set up shop as King over Israel.[1] I have been relieved to find answers to the questions I was asking. Clarifying the nature of the relationship between the kingdom and the church is absolutely critical if we are to recapture what God intended for His people.

My hope is that the previous chapter sufficiently established the following point: The kingdom is the focus of God's agenda. It is also the purpose of today's church. The church is not an end in itself, but rather a means to the end of extending the rule and reign of God throughout this planet.

This reign is not limited to human beings. God seeks to bring all things back into right relationship with Himself. Paul speaks of the reconciliation of all things, Peter talks of the restoration of all things and Jesus mentions the renewal of all things.[2] The salvation purchased by God and given to humanity is the total liberation and restoration of the universe. As Paul says, God is in the process of putting all things under Jesus' feet.[3]

In this new exodus, Jesus broke the power of Satan (the power behind all earthly "Pharaohs") and defeated his dark counterkingdom. Jesus carried away God's wrath as the Lamb of God, given as a sacrifice for our sins, and He rescued us from the power and principalities that hold this world captive. God has adopted us into His family and enlisted us to be agents of redemption in His ongoing work to reclaim all of creation for the gracious rule of the kingdom.

The salvation Jesus accomplished through His life, death, and resurrection was not for the Jews alone. The good news of the kingdom was to be proclaimed to all the nations by the followers of Jesus.[4] The Old Testament community of Yahweh the King becomes the New Testament body of Christ. The first-century church saw itself as the messianic Israel (formed because the rule of God drew near in the life and ministry of Jesus) in covenant with the resurrected Lord Jesus, thus continuing the story of Abraham and Sarah's descendants as those "on whom the fulfillment of the ages has come."[5]

As a result, the early church saw itself as the continuation and the culmination of the life and history of Israel. Thus, the activities and beliefs that set the church apart as a radical and subversive community in ancient Rome will make little sense if they are divorced from their connection to their Jewish antecedents.

As in the Old Testament, God formed a people for Himself who would both worship Him faithfully and witness about Him to the world.[6] After the exodus of Israel out of Egypt, God led Moses and the people to the foot of Mt. Sinai, where they received the sacrificial system (including the priesthood) and the designs for the tabernacle, which would allow God to dwell among His people (Exodus 20–27). When the tabernacle was completed, the glory of the Lord filled it (Exodus 40:34-35). The tabernacle, we now know, was the precursor to Solomon's temple, built hundreds of years later. At the dedication of the temple, the glory of God once again appeared and brought the work of the priests to an abrupt halt as they were overwhelmed with God's presence (1 Kings 8:10-11). The temple became the center of Israel's worship and festival calendar. The people believed that the presence of the temple was what separated Israel from the rest of the world: God's presence with them, His people.

So we see the significance of Jesus shifting the function of the temple from Jerusalem to Himself. He forgave sins without any reference to sacrifice, priesthood, or temple; He restored the cleanliness of lepers (usurping another temple function); He referred to Himself as the temple, and He taught that He had authority to cleanse the temple because one greater than the temple was here (John 2:19-22).

Even more strikingly, the New Testament writers taught that the church—the people of God formed as disciples of Jesus Christ—is now the temple of God (Ephesians 2:21-22), and the community of God is its priesthood (1 Peter 2:9). Paul teaches that even our bodies, indwelt by the Holy Spirit of God, are now temples as well (1 Corinthians 6:19).

Clearly, Paul understood Jesus to be the fulfillment of all the promises of the Old Testament. He is the seed of Abraham and the new Adam. Everything about the people of God in the Old Testament narrows down into and focuses on one person: Jesus of Nazareth. From Him comes the new people of God, the new humanity in Christ, made up of Jew and Gentile alike. This is the mystery revealed in Paul's ministry: The Gentiles and Jews were co-heirs of the promises of Israel. They together make up the community of God, for Gentile believers are now included in the tribal identity of Israel (Ephesians 2:12). This new humanity is being built into the temple of God (Ephesians 2:21-22), that is, the place where God dwells.

Peter writes to the church as if he were writing to the nation of Israel dispersed throughout the nations (calling them both the "elect" and the "Dispersion" in 1 Peter 1:1-2 NKJV)—language that would have been appropriate only to Israel. He reminds his audience that they once were not a people but are now a "chosen generation, a royal priesthood, a holy nation" (1 Peter 2:9-10). To quote Derek Morphew, this is not replacement theology, but *addition theology:* The people of God are now made up of Jews *and* Gentiles who have accepted Jesus as Savior and Lord. No longer does physical circumcision matter. Rather, circumcision of the heart is what counts (Romans 2:29; Galatians 5:6).[7] Barry Harvey makes this comment:

> Although the New Israel includes Gentiles, who at one time were "aliens from the commonwealth of Israel, strangers to the covenants of promise" (Eph. 2:12), Messianic Israel (that is, the church in Christ) does not exclude Jews. In other words, although the being and mission of the church are not identical to those of postbiblical Judaism, the overarching witness of the New Testament steadfastly maintains that the body of Christ exists in historical continuity with the being of the Jewish people (and then only by the grace of God). Christian faith, linked to the continuing existence of Israel by the divine economy of creation and redemption, articulated in Scripture, is finally nothing other than the particular, material, and historical life in community that the followers of Christ live with and before God, with and before the world.[8]

Jesus inaugurated the fulfillment of the kingdom of God in advance of its full and eschatological consummation. Of course, He was Jewish, and His ministry was focused almost exclusively on the Jewish people (Matthew 10:5-6; 15:24).[9] But it is also true that Israel, represented by its religious and political leadership, rejected Jesus as Israel's Messiah (Matthew 23:37-39; Luke 19:42-44). Still, large numbers of Israelites responded to Jesus in faith. Ladd summarizes the implications of this well:

It follows that if Jesus proclaimed the messianic salvation, if he offered to Israel the fulfillment of her true destiny, then this destiny was actually accomplished in those who received his message. The recipients of the messianic salvation became the true Israel, representatives of the nation as a whole. While it is true that the word "Israel" is never applied to Jesus' disciples, the idea is present, if not the term. Jesus' disciples are the recipients of the messianic salvation, the people of the Kingdom, the true Israel.[10]

Jesus' statement about building his church in Matthew 16:18 fits into this context.[11] Those who received His teaching Jesus saw as the inheritors of the kingdom, the renewed Israel, the people of God.

Heralds of the Ministry of Jesus

The New Testament writers use the word *keryx* (herald or announcer) to describe what occurred in the ministry of Jesus. He ushered in (or heralded) the age to come through both public proclamation and demonstration. Whenever Jesus spoke or acted, the *eschaton* (the future consummation of the world) was brought near, and eschatological events took place. When Jesus announced the closeness of the kingdom of God, its powers were unleashed. After Jesus began His ministry by announcing that the kingdom was at hand, the power and glory of the kingdom were immediately put on display through demonic exorcism (Mark 1:27) and two healings (1:41-42; 2:10-11). The announcement and the manifestation went hand in hand.

In Luke 4:18-19, Jesus unveils His agenda for ministry:

> The Spirit of the Lord is on me,
>> because he has anointed me
>> to preach good news to the poor.
> He has sent me to proclaim freedom for the prisoners
>> and recovery of sight for the blind,
> to release the oppressed,
>> to proclaim the year of the Lord's favor.

Jesus was quoting Isaiah 61, but He stopped midstream, leaving out Isaiah's reference to "the day of vengeance." Putting the judgments on hold, He emphasized God's deliverance. Later, when John the Baptist is put into prison and raises doubts about the ministry of Jesus, Jesus responds by pointing to His fulfillment of this passage. These verses are critical to understanding the nature of the mission of Jesus. In fact, some commentators believe the rest of Luke is a commentary on this passage. Only in this context do we get a picture of the implications for what the nearness of the kingdom meant.

This same ministry is now given to the church. This is critical to our understanding of the kingdom. The same ministry He did, we're to do, using the same power, message and methods.[12] Matthew 10:1-10 and Luke 9:1-6 record Jesus placing the same ministry on the 12. The two key terms used here are *power* (*dunamis*—the ability or empowering to make the announcement) and *authority* (*exousia*—delegated authority to act in the name of Jesus). This was completely in keeping with the nature of rabbinic discipleship in first-century Judaism. Disciples were trained to be like their rabbis, not only in character but also in ministry. Disciples were expected to continue and extend the teachings and ministry of their rabbi, and this is what we see in the commissions that Jesus gave His followers. What He taught (announcing the kingdom), they were to teach, and what He did (healing and casting out demons), they were to do as well (Matthew 10:24-25).

Luke 10:1-9 records the giving of the same commission to the 72. The fact that there is no difference between the two commissions is significant, for it shows that it was not meant to be restricted only to the 12 apostles. The 72, like the apostles, were to proclaim the message of the kingdom and demonstrate the ministry of the kingdom. Moreover, this commission was extended even beyond the 72 in several places after Jesus' crucifixion and resurrection.[13]

As part of this commission, Jesus told the disciples to wait for Pentecost—the coming and anointing of the Holy Spirit. In a sense, the disciples receive the same anointing for ministry that Jesus Himself received at his baptism.[14] If Jesus recapitulated the history of Israel in Himself and ministry (more about that later), then perhaps the disciples were to recapitulate the ministry of Jesus—and through them, the church also. The coming of the Holy Spirit was the last major event in the breakthrough of the age to come. Pentecost and Jesus' ascension to His place of authority at the Father's right hand provide the context out of which the kingdom was to expand. The King inaugurated His kingdom on earth, He is now reigning in heaven, and He is bringing that reign to fruition and fulfillment. The people of God, gathered and redeemed by the Son, are anointed with power by the Spirit to continue advancing the kingdom.

So the disciples (and by extension, the church) were to experience the triune God. Their destiny was to be incorporated into the inner life of the Trinity (2 Peter 1:4), and they were to receive Jesus' power to do His work. Like the disciples of a rabbi, Jesus' disciples were extensions of Himself, although more profoundly so. As people dealt with them, they dealt with Him. Through them in Jesus' name (His authority), those who believed were set free from Satan's kingdom, and they entered into the kingdom of God.

Jesus said in John 20:21, "As the Father has sent me, I am sending you." The disciples were being sent into the world to continue Jesus' mission in a way that was parallel to the way the Father sent Jesus into the world to redeem it. More than 40 times in the Gospel of John, Jesus teaches about His being sent from the Father. Being sent was central to Jesus' self-understanding, and so He would naturally commission the disciples similarly. In John's Gospel, immediately after sending the disciples, Jesus breathed into them the Holy Spirit. This episode is reminiscent of the climax of God's creation of human beings in Genesis 2:7, where God breathed the life of His Spirit into Adam and all human beings. So Jesus uses new-creation language here to convey His point. Jesus remade them in order to continue His mission of remaking all of creation.

The Relationship Between the Church and the Kingdom

With this background in mind, we are now in a better position to clarify the relationship between the church and the kingdom. Two extremes must immediately be eliminated. The first is to identify the church with the kingdom, and the second is to completely separate the church and kingdom so that they have no relationship whatsoever.[15] Neither of these positions does justice to the full scope of teaching about both the church *and* the kingdom. George Ladd famously clarified the relationship between church and kingdom through five points.

The Church Is Not the Kingdom

What was created out of Jesus' resurrection and ascension and the coming of the Spirit at Pentecost was a new, interim community (the church) that stood at the crossroads of this age and the one to come. Jesus never identified the kingdom with the church. When He used the term *kingdom* (*basileia*), He usually was referring to the rule, sovereignty, or kingship of God. Arthur Glasser makes this clear:

> In this he went beyond the rabbinic literature of his day that equated taking the yoke of the kingdom of God on oneself with acknowledging God as king and Lord. Whereas only 15% of Jesus' usages of the term *kingdom* have any reference to a domain or community over which the rule of God is exercised, we should not downplay this fact. He speaks of receiving the kingdom, entering it, belonging to it, shutting the kingdom against people, and even using keys to open it (Mt. 23:13; 16:19; Mk. 10:14-15; Lk. 11:52)... On the basis of Jesus' explicit teaching, there is not a great deal of evidence that he had the church in mind. But when we examine the things that he did, it appears clear that he was laying the groundwork for a mission-oriented community that would deliberately penetrate society after his pattern of seeking and saving the lost (Lk. 19:10).[16]

The church is the gathering of all those who call Jesus Lord and receive His message, while the kingdom is the dynamic reign of God over His people. The early church preached the message of the kingdom, not of the church (Acts 8:12; 19:8; 20:25; 28:23,31). Moreover, the many teachings about entering the kingdom are not equivalent statements about entering the church. As Ladd states, "The church is the people of the kingdom, never the kingdom itself."

The kingdom transcends the church in two ways. It existed before the church and will be God's kingly domain throughout eternity. The kingdom is also larger than the church—it represents the ultimate lordship of Christ over all people, principalities, and powers, so it is universal in scope. The church is the community of people who have embraced and submitted themselves to the rule of God, but the church itself is not the act of God ruling.

The Kingdom Creates the Church

Jesus' announcement of the kingdom demanded a response of faith. Those who responded to Jesus came under the gracious reign of God and entered into a new community. The disciples of Jesus, as we have suggested above, are formed into the new people of God. Matthew 16:18-20 ties the building of the church to the keys of the kingdom. The church is the human society and structured set of relationships that forms when the kingdom breaks into history and people respond.

The kingdom refers to the rule of God in our hearts *and* relationships— it is not primarily an individual thing. God was at hand in Jesus, living amid people and calling them to obedience. The church is the assembly of people who have welcomed God's reign in their hearts and relationships. The church consists of the citizens of the kingdom. It's the body of Christ composed of obedient disciples following in the way of Jesus. The church isn't a building, sanctuary, or program; it is the visible community of those who live by kingdom values.

The church is not the kingdom. The kingdom creates the church in the sense that Jesus formed the church out of His kingdom mission. The phrase *the church* refers to the people of the kingdom, but not the kingdom itself. God's people witness to the reality of God's kingdom through the proclamation of His redemptive work in Christ (both past and present) and their demonstration of the power of God through the ministry of the Holy Spirit.

The Church Witnesses to the Kingdom

The *telos* (or proper end) of the church is to witness to the reality of the kingdom. The church doesn't build the kingdom (Jesus does), nor does the church work to become the kingdom (the kingdom is received, not achieved). Instead, the church bears witness to the kingdom. This is illustrated by the commissions to the church in Acts 1:8 and Matthew 28:18. These commissions are extensions of those given to both the 12 (Luke 9) and the 72 (Luke 10). It witnesses to the reality of the kingdom in both word and deed. Through His followers, both the ministry and character of Jesus are extended into the world. As Israel witnessed to the kingdom in the Old Testament, the church witnesses to the kingdom in the New Testament.

Because of this, the church must demonstrate the presence of the kingdom. The church's witness is that the age to come has become real here and now. The world must look at the witness of the church and see what God has in mind for His followers; it is to provide an appetizer now for the full banquet of the reality of the kingdom in the future. The church must put on display the reality of the upside-down nature of the kingdom that will be most fully expressed in the future consummation of the kingdom. This witness also includes the way that those in the community now relate to each other in love.

The Church Is the Instrument of the Kingdom

The church has been entrusted with the proclamation of the message of the kingdom. This can happen many ways in many forms. The disciples proclaimed the same message Jesus did (announcing the kingdom), and they were commissioned as instruments of the kingdom to do the same works Jesus did (demonstrating the kingdom). They were empowered to heal the sick and cast out demons. Although their power and authority were derivative, they received the same anointing as did Jesus, and they performed the works of Jesus. The church presents itself as an instrument to be used by God for His purposes and to be anointed with His power.

The Church as Custodian of the Kingdom

In the Old Testament, the rule of God began with the call to

Abraham and was most fully expressed in the laws and covenants given to Israel at Mt. Sinai. The law was the clearest expression of life under God's rule, so Israel was to mediate the kingdom of God to the world.

In a similar way, those who received the message of Jesus came under God's gracious rule. They became the true sons and daughters of the kingdom. These disciples, those He gathered into a community, replaced ethnic Israel as custodians of the kingdom (Mark 12:9). Jesus makes this clear by giving the church the keys to the kingdom (Matthew 16:19) and referring to "binding and loosing," or including or excluding people from the participation in the benefits of the kingdom.[17] That is, the church has been entrusted with certain powers and responsibilities to be exercised as the instrument and custodian of the kingdom (including declaring God's judgment, forgiveness, and reconciliation).

We'll this end this section by quoting Ladd, which is fitting since so much of this chapter reflects his thought:

> In summary, while there is an inseparable relationship between the Kingdom and the church, they are not to be identified. The Kingdom takes its point of departure from God, the church from men. The Kingdom is God's reign and the realm in which the blessings of his reign are experienced; the church is the fellowship of those who have experienced God's reign and entered into the enjoyment of its blessings. The Kingdom creates the church, works through the church, and is proclaimed in the world by the church. There can be no Kingdom without a church—those who have acknowledged God's rule—and there can be no church without God's Kingdom; but they remain two distinguishable concepts: the rule of God and the fellowship of men.[18]

Chapter 5

Interlude: Why This Matters

The best criticism of the bad has always been the practice of the better. If much of the old church has to die (and I think it will, even without our pushing), then maybe it is because we have neither criticized the bad nor practiced the better with any social vigor. We have daintily gone to church while living like the rest of the world. Now I find people who are living the mystery of the church, and from that place going into the world. The church has always been a movement much more than this institution or that, a continual torrent of the Spirit flowing through the grist mill of human structures and human history.

RICHARD ROHR

Thanks for sticking with me. Here's where we've been:

1. The kingdom of God is the central focus of the Bible.

2. The kingdom is both universal (God is ruler over everything) and particular (He rules over a group of people and uses those people to actualize His rule on the earth).

3. The church of Jesus is not the kingdom but instead serves it, points toward it, seeks to embody it, and proclaims its message.

Gibbs and Bolger summarize this well:

The reign of God existed before the coming of the church and it will replace the church at the consummation of all things, when Christ will reign supreme and unchallenged. The church, for its part, is a servant and a sign of the coming kingdom, which was inaugurated with the coming of Christ and established, in its provisional form, with his ascension into heaven and the imparting of the Spirit. The

> church, as a servant of the kingdom, constantly points beyond
> itself to the Lord who is its head and who requires unreserved and
> comprehensive submission.[1]

Under the kingdom perspective, the church, in other words, ceases to be the focus of the work of God. I feel almost traitorous saying it this way. I have been raised to think of the church as God's work in the world. I have been taught (and have taught myself) that the goal is to get people involved in the church. They should attend more, give more, and serve more. I have not really been concerned about whether they are becoming disciples of Jesus or submitting more and more of their lives to Jesus' lordship. Instead, my focus has been getting people to get on board with the program of the church (assuming of course, that if they get more involved with the church, they'll get more involved with Jesus). But now we can see the catastrophic results of such an endeavor. When the church ceases being about the work of the kingdom and substitutes in its place the work of the church and its cultural assimilation (whether the Roman Empire or the consumer society), we elevate the church (its ministries, experiences, programs, and services) to a place where God never intended it to be. Church was to be the result of people working together in the kingdom, not the focus of the work itself.

This is not to say that the church is unimportant to God's plan. Not at all. The writings of Paul make that abundantly clear. I simply wish to point out that because we have lost sight of the kingdom, we have lost sight of the church also. We have made the church the point of God's work and not the kingdom. And in doing so, we have unintentionally substituted the gospel of the kingdom ("Repent, the kingdom is at hand") for the gospel of the church ("come to church to meet Jesus and grow spiritually"). We have substituted the work of the Spirit (transforming our inward character into the image of Jesus) for the work of the church (attending this class, this program, and this ministry). We have substituted the work of worship (which has always been the primary vocation of God's people) for passive consumption of church services (watching our paid professionals do their thing on stage).

I know I am being hyperbolic in some of this, but the good news of the kingdom is incredibly freeing and frustrating at the same time. It is freeing because when I see that the point of God's work is His kingdom, I realize it is not up to me as someone in the church to do God's work for Him any longer.[2] But it is also frustrating because I can better see how we have misunderstood this and found ourselves in the mess we're in.[3]

The Church as the Community of Disciples

Now we need to set up the next couple of chapters. We still have some theology to do as we draw out the implications of the kingdom of God and its relationship to the church. For my purposes here I want to make one point: The work of Jesus forms people into a *community*. But it is a community of a certain kind. N.T. Wright provides a definition of the church that represents what we have been discussing here:

> The church is the single, multiethnic family promised by the creator God to Abraham. It was brought into being through Israel's Messiah, Jesus; it was energized by God's Spirit; and it was called to bring the transformative news of God's rescuing justice to the whole creation.[4]

This definition captures what we'll be looking at through the remainder of this book. Through Jesus' announcement of the kingdom, people could enter the kingdom by responding in faith and repentance (Mark 1:14-15). The kingdom became available to any who responded to His message. Thus, the constituents of the kingdom came from "every tribe and language and people and nation" (Revelation 5:9). With a few profound exceptions, Jesus focused his earthly ministry almost exclusively on those whom he called "the lost sheep of the house of Israel."[5] But now that was no longer the case. This was a major point of contention for the Jews, who saw in Jesus the threat to their entire self-understanding and practice. Jesus and His church were to replace the temple as the center of the Jewish world (John 2:19-21). The law of Jesus fulfilled and then supplanted the law of

Moses. Animal sacrifice was no longer required for the forgiveness of sins, and the Lord's Day (Sunday) replaced the Sabbath (Saturday) as the day for worship.

The resurrection and ascension of Jesus assured the community He formed of His continued presence among them through the gift of the Holy Spirit. In other words, the community of disciples continued to exist as an extension of Jesus and His ministry. He entrusted His power and authority to them; they were to carry on the ministry of Jesus to the fulfillment of His mission. Their ministry and life were to look like His.

Jesus, then, formed and shaped His disciples into a certain kind of community. It wasn't the kind of community we think of—a group of individuals linked together through physical proximity and common interest. Rather, the community of Jesus was born through the regenerative work of the Holy Spirit. As people were joined to Christ in faith, so too were they brought into the community of disciples.

If the kingdom is the central message of the Bible and of the ministry of Jesus, if Jesus called His followers to continue His ministry of the kingdom through the power of the Holy Spirit, and if the community of disciples—later called the church—was not the kingdom but only stood in relation to the kingdom as a signpost or foretaste; then the ministry of the church should embody the ministry, values, purpose, mission, message, priorities, and methods of Jesus, or it is not truly the church. The church, in order to be true to its own nature and God's purposes for it, must never be an end in itself. It always should be pointing to something bigger. To be the body of Christ, it should be participating in the work of Christ in the world.

That is the point. If we witness to the kingdom, the community of the church should look like the kingdom. If the kingdom turns the world's values and priorities upside down, this should be reflected in the mission, ministries, and methods of the church. If the kingdom is inclusive, the church should be also. So in the next couple of chapters, we'll see how the earliest Christians understood themselves in this regard. In doing so, we'll try not to romanticize the early church (because we know from a clear reading of the New Testament that the early church was a mixture of success and failure, faithfulness and error, worship and idolatry). But that doesn't mean we don't have anything to learn from those who were closest to the life, death, and resurrection of Jesus and who were captured by His ministry and formed into the community that testified to the good news of Jesus and His kingdom from Jerusalem, Judea, and Samaria to the ends of the earth. We have much to learn from the earliest church communities and their Jewish and Roman contexts.

Some aspects of the self-understanding of the earliest Christians are instructive for us today. The current climate in the Western world more closely approximates the cultural setting of the early church than any in the last 1600 years.[6] We will look at the beliefs and practices that sustained the church in the midst of the Roman Empire, and in doing so, we'll be reminded of how the church today, which is at the margins of Western culture, can be a witness to the kingdom of God in our midst.

Chapter 6

More than a Ticket: Why the Four Spiritual Laws Need to Add a Few

The Gospels make it clear that Jesus was the embodiment—the incarnation—of the kingdom of God. When Jesus was present, so was the kingdom (see Matt. 12:28; and especially 3:2; 4:17). Though the world as a whole was and remains part of the domain in which Satan is king, in Jesus the domain in which God is king has been introduced into the world. The central goal of Jesus' life was to plant the seed of this new kingdom so that, like a mustard seed, it would gradually expand. Eventually that kingdom would end the rule of Satan and reestablish God, the Creator of the world, as its rightful ruler (Mat. 13:31-32). In other words, Jesus came to destroy the cosmic "power over" lord and establish the kingdom of God upon the earth (Heb. 2:14, 1 John 3:8).

GREG BOYD

We have seen that the kingdom of God was central to the ministry and message of Jesus. In Jesus, the kingdom broke into human history with astonishing power and love. This display of God's redemptive reign in Jesus provoked the greatest response from the demonic realm. Everywhere Jesus went, demons attested both to His identity and to His authority over them.[1] At the heart of biblical revelation is a cosmic battle. The battle between the kingdom of God and the kingdom of Satan serves as the backdrop to the ministry of Jesus and the rest of the New Testament. In this chapter, we'll examine the relationship between the kingdom of God and the kingdoms of this world and how this relates to the concept of salvation throughout the Scriptures.[2]

The Scriptures teach that the whole world is under the rule of a powerful, supernatural being who hates God, His creation, and His people (1 John 5:19). He is God's unequivocal enemy. Once a heavenly angel, Satan rebelled against God's rule in order to establish his own. He now hides behind the ways in which we see the world: assumptions, values, and the political and religious systems of this fallen world order. When Satan revolted in heaven, he led a hierarchy of angels who joined him. Through the serpent, he deceived Adam and Eve and usurped their God-given domain over the planet. Satan is now the "god of this world," ruling his counterfeit kingdom of darkness with a hierarchy of fallen angels. The worldview of the Bible is characterized by warfare.[3]

Humanity lives in this "present evil age" (Galatians 1:4). The kingdom of God wages war against the kingdom of Satan. This is the backdrop of God's redemptive intent. Beginning in Genesis 3, God reveals this to His people progressively, a little at a time. The whole Bible, therefore, is *eschatological*—working toward this end. Everything God does in redemption is determined, most importantly, by His plan to defeat Satan, overthrow his kingdom, and reestablish His own effective rule over all creation.[4]

The Jews thought that when the Messiah arrived, Rome would be expelled, idols would be destroyed, the land would be cleansed, and Israel would be restored and vindicated in all her glory. But Jesus' parables of the kingdom tell a different story. For instance, in the parable of the sower (Mark 4), Jesus sows seed, but Satan, persecution, and challenge spoil much of the crop. Jesus sees opposition everywhere. As it was with Him, so it is with us. Jesus was more realistic than most Christians today, for He saw Himself engaged in a great battle. Three times in the Gospel of John, Jesus refers to Satan as the ruler or prince of this world (John 12:31; 14:30; 16:11).

The Gospels record this battle for us. Jesus' disciples report of demons submitting to them in His name, He responds, "I saw Satan fall like lightning from heaven. I have given you authority to trample on snakes and scorpions and to overcome all the power of the enemy; nothing will harm you. However, do not rejoice that the spirits are submitted to you, but rejoice that your names are written in heaven" (Luke 10:18-20). Elsewhere in Luke Jesus defends His ministry by saying,

"But if I drive out demons by the finger of God, then the kingdom of God has come upon you."[5]

Immediately after His baptism by John, Jesus is led by the Spirit into the wilderness to be tempted by the devil. Once He begins His public ministry, He encounters demonic opposition almost everywhere He goes. At one point His enemies accuse him of being in league with Satan, so successful is His exorcism ministry. Jesus replies that He has come to bind the strong man (Satan) and to plunder his (Satan's) house, which is the world (see Mark 1:12-13; 1:21-28; 3:22-27).

The book of Revelation, which draws all the threads of Scripture together, opens heaven for us to see the battle between the church, a glorious pregnant woman, and Satan, "an enormous red dragon" (12:1-3). The dragon is ready to consume her child at birth, for He is the one who will rule the nations.

Behind this, in 12:7-11, is the heavenly battle between Michael and his angels and the dragon and his angels. The dragon and his angels are thrown down to earth. John writes, "The great dragon was hurled down —that ancient serpent called the devil, or Satan, who leads the whole world astray. He was hurled to the earth and his angels with him." Joy in heaven erupts because the "accuser of our brothers…has been hurled down." The war now rages on earth, and the church overcomes him by the blood of the Lamb and the word of their testimony in martyrdom, for "they did not love their lives so much as to shrink from death." The dragon, now on earth, goes after the woman's offspring (the church). "Then the dragon was enraged at the woman and went off to make war against the rest of her offspring—those who obey God's commandments and hold to the testimony of Jesus" (12:17).

Paul held this warfare worldview (see Romans 8:38-39; 2 Corinthians 2:11; Galatians 4:8-9) and warns us that the devil schemes against us. "For our struggle is not against flesh and blood, but against the rulers, against the authorities, against the powers of this dark world and against the spiritual forces of evil in the heavenly realms" (Ephesians 6:12). These powers are subject to the "ruler of the kingdom of the air, the spirit who is now at work in those who are disobedient" (Ephesians 2:2). As Paul preaches the gospel, the "god of this age" blinds the minds of unbelievers to keep them from seeing the glory of God in the face of Christ (2 Corinthians 4:4). Once people come to Christ, they are delivered from "the dominion of darkness" and transferred into the kingdom of God's beloved Son, in whom we have redemption and forgiveness (Colossians 1:13).

The New Testament is very clear that the life, death, and resurrection of Jesus signaled a decisive victory by God over the kingdom of darkness.

> When you were dead in your sins and in the uncircumcision of your sinful nature, God made you alive with Christ. He forgave us all our sins, having cancelled the written code, with its regulations, that was against us and that stood opposed to us; he took it away, nailing it to the cross. And having disarmed the powers and authorities, he made a public spectacle of them, triumphing over them by the cross (Colossians 2:13-15).

Paul also writes that Christ is now exalted in the position of authority in heavenly realms, "far above all rule and authority, power and dominion, and every title that can be given, not only in this present age but also in the one to come" (Ephesians 1:21-22).

But as we have seen from Ephesians 6, the war continues even though victory is assured. And as Adam and Eve were deceived by the serpent, so those in the Corinthian church were in danger of being deceived by false apostles, who were really Satan's servants in disguise. Satan himself, Paul writes, masquerades as an "angel of light" (2 Corinthians 11:14). Paul himself is not immune. He writes of a thorn in his flesh, a messenger from Satan, that torments him (2 Corinthians 12:7). When Paul wants to return to the Thessalonians, he comments that Satan kept him from returning (1 Thessalonians 2:18).

Where Is This in the Four Spiritual Laws?

The cosmic battle between God and Satan serves as background to our discussion of what salvation means in the kingdom of God. Many of us are recognizing the dangers inherent in the way the gospel has been proclaimed over the last century. From the Four Spiritual Laws to the Bridge Illustration or the Romans Road, God has used various presentations of the message of Jesus to reach countless people. These teach that the center of the gospel is Jesus' solution to our sin problem. God is holy and we are not. Our sin separates us from Him. Jesus died on the cross for our sins, and if we receive him, we receive forgiveness and are declared righteous so that we go to heaven when we die.

There is no question that the Scriptures teach this. But the real (and often overlooked) question is this: Is this the whole of the gospel of Jesus? The answer, biblically, is no. What is often shared is the truth, but not the whole truth. There is more to the gospel than this.[6]

This is not a trivial matter. What is left out of this truncated gospel is just as significant as what is left in. Jesus' ministry, resurrection, and ascension are often ignored, as is Pentecost. Moreover, this version of the gospel separates justification (being declared right with God) from sanctification (being formed progressively into the image of Jesus) in ways the Bible doesn't. We do this because we fear giving any appearance of being saved by our works. Righteousness is imputed, not earned or achieved. But the result of our misguided thinking is an inherent disconnect between what we believe and what we do.

Furthermore, this gospel is primarily about then (the future) and there (heaven) but leaves the here and now untouched. As a result, many people intellectually assent to the right information, but their lives don't reflect what they believe. This duplicity is implicit in the way the gospel has usually been presented.

One Message or Two?

Jesus preached the good news of the kingdom of God. Though God is King, the revolt in heaven has strayed to earth, so now we have a counterkingdom, the kingdom of darkness led by the rebellious angel Satan. Jesus comes to proclaim that God's kingdom is near (or "at hand") in Him in ways it had not been previously and that the rule of Satan has been overthrown.

How does this relate to the message of Paul in his Epistles? If Jesus proclaims the kingdom, Paul seems to proclaim the cross. How do these two gospels relate? The answer, of course, is that the gospel of the cross *is* the gospel of the kingdom. They are two sides of the same coin, or the same picture taken from two different angles. Paul, for instance, demands that we confess Jesus as Lord in order to be saved (Romans 10:9).

From Slavery to Freedom

N.T. Wright shows that the exodus is the defining picture of redemption in the Bible.[7] From that event (as we have seen previously), we learn that we need to be delivered from two things: the kingdom of darkness and sin that holds us in bondage (the "Pharaoh" of this world), and the wrath of God (Israel wasn't immune from the last plague—God provided a substitute). Like the Israelites of old, we need to be rescued from slavery and to have God's wrath lifted from us. The exodus points forward to the fulfillment in Jesus Christ. Matthew's Gospel shows that Jesus is the second, greater Moses. The same sense of powers in collision emerges in the ministry of Jesus. As He cast out demons, healed the sick, stilled the storm, and raised the dead, He was invading the prison house of the strong man and setting captives free.

Four separate but related themes emerge in the exodus from slavery in Egypt to the conquest of the promised land. They are given in the exodus, lost in the exile, and restored in the ministry of Jesus and His church, the New Israel (Galatians 6:16). Let's see how these four themes run throughout the Scriptures.

Deliverance

This includes rescue from slavery to Pharaoh through the Red Sea, the divine judgment expressed toward all of Egypt the tenth plague, and God's provision of safety for Israel by means of the Passover.

The first result of the exodus was deliverance from both the power of Egypt and the judgment of God. We must not miss either of these. Yahweh accomplished this salvation through the miraculous demonstration of His powers over the gods of Egypt and the power of Pharaoh himself (Exodus 11:5; 12:12). The tenth plague was to be against *all* the firstborn of Egypt: Hebrew and Egyptian alike. Animals were included also. This plague was a direct attack against Pharaoh himself, and all Egypt lay under his judgment. But because of His great mercy, God provides for His people. They were to slaughter a lamb at twilight and apply its blood to their doorposts. God would then be "pass over" them and spare them from His wrath.

Torah (the Law)

With the Red Sea and Pharaoh's chariots behind them, Israel follows Yahweh to Sinai, where He reveals Himself through fire, smoke, lightning, and thunder. The whole mountain quakes as God speaks to His people and gives them His law (Exodus 19:4; 20:1-17; 32:15-16). God presses social obligations on His redeemed people (at Sinai) that through them God's rule might extend to all aspects of their social order. Furthermore, God intends that they be a light for the Gentiles and that His salvation reaches "to the ends of the earth" (Isaiah 49:6). In the Old Testament, God intervened in human affairs by electing Israel and proclaiming Himself God and King over them. This meant that they would live under His direct rule and thus foreshadow the coming of the kingdom of God.

The Tabernacle

Many of God's commands centered on the building of the tabernacle, which would signify God's presence with His people. This was radical among the religious thought of the ancient Near East. In this, God demonstrates His desire to form a people for Himself that would declare to the world what He is like (Exodus 25:8–40:34).

The Promised Land

The destiny of God's people is to live under God's kingship, serve

Him in worship and obedience, and bring His revelation to the nations.

Once Israel was organized for travel and conquest, God moved them to dwell in the land He had promised Abraham and his descendents (Numbers 13:1-2; Joshua 1:1-3).

Exile and Restoration

Many years later, after an extended period of rebellion and apostasy, the nation of Israel was sent into exile as a result of the judgments of God. This exile included bondage to the nations as well as placement back under the wrath of God (Jeremiah 1:15-16; Ezekiel 7:5-9; Micah 1:16).

Israel's apostasy included a corruption of each of the blessings of the exodus. God had provided His people with the Torah (law), but they did not follow His decrees or keep his laws. As a result, God turned against Israel.[8] God had also provided the tabernacle and then the temple, but the people trampled His courts with meaningless offerings, and their incense became detestable to Him.[9] God had even brought Israel into the promised land, but the people defiled it and put themselves under a curse.[10]

But woven throughout the prophets are promises of something new, a coming restoration. God will not leave His people in exile forever. When it became increasingly apparent that the Israelites had repeatedly failed to sustain a kingdom characterized by righteousness and justice and had not fulfilled their proper role as a spiritual influence among the nations, the prophets began to speak of a kingdom not of a human king, but of God. Messianic expectations began to attach themselves to this kingdom. With the Babylonians' overthrow of the southern kingdom of Judah, these expectations increasingly pointed in the direction of a people of God assembled not as a political entity, but rather a community that would bless the nations. And in time there would be a new covenant and a new expression of the kingdom of God that would not fail (Jeremiah 31:31-34; 32:38-40; Ezekiel 36:26-27). Isaiah ties the end of the Babylonian captivity to the exodus (Isaiah 40–55) and states that Yahweh will do a new thing (43:16-21) that will be more glorious than anything that had gone before. He will restore all that had been lost to them. Let's look at some of the promises.

Return from Exile

The prophets likened Israel's deliverance from Babylon to the original exodus from Egypt. This would be a new Exodus.[11] Because the exile was twofold (bondage to the nations and being placed under divine judgment), God's promised restoration includes both *deliverance from the nations...*

> For though I sent them into exile among the nations, I will gather them to their own land, not leaving any behind. I will no longer hide my face from them, for I will pour out my Spirit on the house of Israel (Ezekiel 39:28).

...and *deliverance from judgment:*

> Remember these things, O Jacob, for you are my servant, O Israel. I have made you, you are my servant; O Israel, I will not forget you. I have swept away your offenses like a cloud, your sins like the morning mist. Return to me, for I have redeemed you (Isaiah 44:21-22).

A New Torah (Law)

> "This is the covenant I will make with the house of Israel after that time," declares the LORD. "I will put my law in their minds and write it on their hearts. I will be their God and they will be my people" (Jeremiah 31:33).

A New Temple

> "The glory of this present house will be greater than the glory of the former house," says the LORD Almighty. "And in this place I will grant peace," declares the Lord Almighty (Haggai 2:9).

A Renewed Land

> They will rebuild the ancient ruins and restore the places long devastated; they will renew the ruined cities that have been devastated for generations. Aliens will shepherd your flocks; foreigners will work your fields and vineyards. And you will be called priests of the LORD; you will be named ministers of our God. You will feed on the wealth of the nations, and in their riches you will boast (Isaiah 61:4-6).

A New King

> For to us a child is born, to us a son is given, and the government will be on his shoulders. And he will be called Wonderful Counselor, Mighty God, Everlasting Father, Prince of Peace. Of the increase of his government and peace there will be no end. He will reign on David's throne and over his kingdom, establishing and upholding it with justice and righteousness from that time on and forever. The zeal of the LORD Almighty will accomplish this (Isaiah 9:6-7).

The Coming of the King

As we shall see, the Messiah recapitulates Israel's history in Himself. All the promises to God's people are now focused in Him. He is the true Israel who brings Israel and the Gentiles back to God (see Isaiah 49:3-6). He comes fulfilling the promise given in Isaiah 40–66 of a new and final exodus for God's people. Mark's Gospel is most explicit in detailing the new exodus. Arthur Glasser makes this note:

> When the Psalmists sing of God as Redeemer, they make the Exodus their theme. And when the prophets speak of a new covenant beyond the covenant of Sinai, they expect God to act in an even greater way for the redemption of humanity and yet to be consistent with his actions at the Exodus (Jer. 31:31-34). It is for this reason that God's deliverance during the Exodus, Israel's wandering in the wilderness, and the conquest of the Promised Land are as significant for the New Testament as for the Old. It is in the New Testament that "One greater than Moses" makes possible a liberating and redemptive exodus, one that leads to a more lasting inheritance (Dt. 18:15-19).[12]

As Israel is baptized through the Red Sea and the Jordan, so Jesus is baptized through the Jordan. Like God in the first exodus, Jesus brings deliverance from the counterkingdom of demonic idols and lifts divine judgment upon all sin. The final exodus has begun.

As Jesus announced the inbreaking of God's kingdom in Himself, He turned Jewish messianic expectation on its head. Jesus trained His followers to extend His ministry (Mark 3:14-15). For the Jews, 12 is a magic number. Jacob's 12 sons formed Israel's 12 tribes in the first exodus from Pharaoh's kingdom. By selecting 12 apostles, Jesus reconstituted Israel for the final exodus. His mighty works and symbolic acts filled the air with wild hopes. Jesus recapitulated Israel's history in Himself but then twisted it in an entirely new direction and gave it an entirely new meaning.

As Israel wandered in the wilderness for 40 years, so Jesus is tempted in the wilderness for 40 days. As Israel left the wilderness to conquer the promised land, so Jesus leaves the wilderness in the power of the Spirit to conquer the kingdom of Satan, deliver His people, and cleanse and renew the land.

The exodus combines deliverance from idolatrous Egypt and deliverance from the wrath of God. So also, then, Jesus delivers God's people from the idolatrous kingdom of Satan (Mark 1–8) and then goes to Jerusalem to become the final Passover Lamb, delivering us from the wrath of God (Mark 9–16). N.T. Wright says that Jesus' ministry is a "counter temple movement." Jesus offers forgiveness Himself rather than through the temple (Mark 2:1-12). He cleanses the temple, symbolically stopping the sacrifices—a prophetic act of judgment on the old sacrificial system (Mark 11:15-17). He foretells the total destruction of the temple in a generation (Mark 13:1-2,30). This judgment results from Israel's rejection of Him.

Jesus now replaces the temple. He is God's forgiveness and our access into His presence. As the temple was the incarnational symbol of Judaism, Jesus is now the incarnational reality of the living God. He dwells, or *tabernacles,* in our midst. The glory of God, which dwelt in the temple, now dwells in Jesus: "We have seen his glory, the glory of the One and Only" (John 1:14). He, not the temple, is full of grace (the new Passover) and truth (the new Torah). In Jesus' culture, forgiveness was the prerogative of God alone. When Jesus started forgiving people on hillsides, in their own houses, and out in the streets, total anarchy seemed to have broken out. His actions amounted to nothing less than a massive threat to the entire religious, political, and social fabric of Israel. By offering forgiveness of sins, right here and now and for free, He was deliberatively bypassing the whole temple system.

The four blessings of the original exodus are found also in the new exodus, the ministry of Jesus.

Deliverance

As in the original exodus, deliverance comes in two forms. The first is a release from the bondage of Satan and his counterkingdom:

> Just then a man in their synagogue who was possessed by an evil spirit cried out, "What do you want with us, Jesus of Nazareth? Have you come to destroy us? I know who you are—the Holy One of God!" "Be quiet!" said Jesus sternly. "Come out of him!" The evil spirit shook the man violently and came out of him with a shriek (Mark 1:23-26).

> For he has rescued us from the dominion of darkness and brought us into the kingdom of the Son he loves, in whom we have redemption, the forgiveness of sins (Colossians 1:13-14).

The second aspect of the deliverance of the new exodus is rescue from the judgment of God:

> Look, the Lamb of God, who takes away the sin of the world (John 1:29).

> So they prepared the Passover...While they were eating, Jesus took bread, gave thanks and broke it, and gave it to his disciples, saying, "Take eat; this is my body."

> Then he took the cup, gave thanks and offered it to them, and they all drank from it.

"This is my blood of the covenant which is poured out for many" (Mark 14:16-24).

For Christ, our Passover lamb, has been sacrificed (1 Corinthians 5:7).

A New Torah

In the beginning was the Word, and the Word was with God, and the Word was God...The Word became flesh and made his dwelling among us (John 1:1,14).

To the Jews who had believed him, Jesus said, "If you hold to my teaching, you are really my disciples. Then you will know the truth, and the truth will set you free" (John 8:31-32).

Do not think that I have come to abolish the Law or the Prophets; I have not come to abolish them but to fulfill them (Matthew 5:17).

A New Temple

Jesus answered them, "Destroy this temple and I will raise it again in three days"...But the temple he had spoke of was his body (John 2:19,21).

Don't you know that you yourselves are God's temple and that God's Spirit lives in you? If anyone destroys God's temple, God will destroy him; for God's temple is sacred, and you are that temple (1 Corinthians 3:16).

A New Promised Land

But our citizenship is in heaven. And we eagerly await a Savior from there, the Lord Jesus Christ, who, by the power that enables him to bring everything under his control, will transform our lowly bodies so that they will be like his glorious body (Philippians 3:20-21).

But in keeping with his promise we are looking forward to a new heaven and a new earth, the home of righteousness (2 Peter 3:13).

The creation itself will be liberated from its bondage to decay and brought into the glorious freedom of the children of God (Romans 8:21).

The New Exodus

Jesus comes to fulfill the controlling narrative of the Bible and to inaugurate God's kingdom crashing in upon us. He comes to liberate us, not from Pharaoh's Egypt, but from Satan's kingdom—the kingdom that stands behind all earthly kingdoms. Jesus comes as the second Moses to lead His people out and release them from the kingdom of darkness that manifests itself in the kingdoms of oppression that rule this world. The Jews wanted a Davidic warrior-king to liberate them from Rome; Jesus saw beyond Rome to the darkness that stood behind her.

So it is the kingdom of God that is preached over against the rule of the kingdoms of the world, but that is only half of what we need. We can get out of Egypt and still have the wrath of God against us because of our sin. To fulfill the full promise of the kingdom (or the promise of the exodus), Jesus does two things. First, He comes as the warrior-king to break the back of the enemy and to set the captives free. Then, as the Servant to the Lord, He suffers and dies as the Passover Lamb who takes away the sin of the world.

At the last meal with His disciples, Jesus reveals the full meaning of the Passover. They didn't understand it completely then, but His words and acts on that final night together were not easily forgotten. When He was crucified outside the walls of Jerusalem, He died as the Passover Lamb, the end and consummation of the sacrificial system. The wrath of God that should have fallen on us fell on Jesus.

We don't have two messages, but two problems: Satan's influence and God's wrath. The first half of Mark's gospel deals with the first problem. Then, after Peter's confession, Mark devotes the rest of his narrative to the second problem. When Paul proclaims Jesus Christ crucified, he is proclaiming the sacrifice for our sin, but he is also proclaiming the risen, reigning Lord, the great king who is ruling and bringing down the powers of darkness. That brings our message together—the message of the cross is the message of the kingdom, but there is more to the message of the kingdom than only the message of the cross. The cross is central, but Jesus has come to do more than die for our sins. Jesus brings the presence and power of the kingdom against the counterkingdom of Satan and seeks to establish His just, righteous, and gracious rule over people and creation.[13]

We are the new and renewed Israel, grafted into the Old Testament people of God (Romans 11:17-24). To be a Christian is to experience the new exodus: deliverance from Satan's kingdom and the wrath of God through the cross. But we must not think that the good news is simply to accept Jesus and go to heaven one day. When we leave Egypt we go to Sinai. We receive Jesus, the new Torah, who speaks the very words of God (John 3:34). Through his Word and Spirit we become human again, like Him. Little by little He reverses the effects of the fall. But we also receive from Jesus the new temple worship. Jesus' message and ministry lead us into the presence of God, the King. There we grow in praise, surrender, sacrifice, intercession, and intimacy with the living God. Finally, our journey to Sinai takes us to the promised land. The new order is already breaking in with Jesus' resurrection from the dead and the gift of the Spirit poured out upon us, and one day we will receive our new bodies and worship the King forevermore.

Chapter 7

Hammer and Tongs

> The power of the Gospel lies not in the offer of a new spirituality or religious experience, not in the threat of hellfire...which can be removed if only the hearer checks this box, says this prayer, raises a hand, or whatever, but in the powerful announcement that God is God, that Jesus is Lord, that the powers of evil have been defeated, that God's new world has begun.
>
> N.T. WRIGHT

If this analysis of the breadth and depth of the exodus as a picture of salvation is correct, then the implications are significant. The church is already grasping many of these, but I want to put them now in their proper kingdom context so that they may rest on a better theological foundation. This was huge stuff for me to learn. As I have said, I was born and raised on the gospel message that started with this question: "If you died tonight, would you go to heaven?" And certainly if that were the entire gospel message, that would be more than we deserve. But there is more. And the fact that we don't talk much about it leads to the disconnect between belief and behavior that we discussed in chapter 1. Here are five helpful truths about the gospel that can help us bridge this gap.

1. The gospel is not only about *then* and *there* but also about *here* and *now*.

My friend Don Williams writes this:

> We have a thin understanding of the gospel and Christian life—salvation becomes either a past event (I got saved) or a future hope (one day I will go to heaven). But, salvation at its core is our transfer

from the kingdom of Satan into the kingdom of God. There, we live a grace-based life together in the power of the Spirit. Jesus' bold and unflinching call, "Follow me," releases us from our old lives as He unequivocally attaches us to Himself.[1]

The reason the resurrection and ascension of Jesus and the coming of the Holy Spirit at Pentecost are so important to the church calendar is that they make possible our understanding of God's work in us and through us into the world. The reigning and ruling Jesus forms and sends His new community, the church, into the world to be partners with Him in ministering the cosmic nature of the gospel.

This means that the question of what happens to me after I die is not the fundamental question of the Scriptures. The New Testament, true to its Jewish roots, regularly insists that the major, central, framing question is that of God's purpose of rescue and re-creation for human beings *and the whole world*. N.T. Wright puts it this way:

> When God saves people in this life, by working through his Spirit to bring them to faith and by leading them to follow Jesus in discipleship, prayer, holiness, hope and love, such people are designed—it isn't too strong a word—to be a sign and foretaste of what God wants to do for the entire cosmos. What's more, such people are not just to be a sign and foretaste of that ultimate salvation; they are to be *part of the means by which* God makes this happen in both the present and the future. This is what Paul insists on when he says that the whole creation is waiting with eager longing not just for its own redemption, its liberation from corruption and decay, but *for God's children to be revealed:* in other words, for the unveiling of those redeemed humans through whose stewardship creation will at last be brought back into that wise order for which it was made. And since Paul makes it quite clear that those who believe in Jesus Christ, who are incorporated into him through baptism, are already God's children, are already themselves saved, this stewardship cannot be something to be postponed for the ultimate future. It must begin here and now.[2]

Salvation is not just something you gain when you die. Even Matthew, who uses the term *kingdom of heaven* (or better, *kingdom of the heavens*) instead of the phrase *kingdom of God,* isn't thinking of some otherworldly existence. That would have run against the grain of everything he believed as a faithful Jew. For the Jews, heaven isn't somewhere up in the sky but is instead God's dimension of the universe. In using the phrase *kingdom of the heavens,* Matthew is referring to the rule of heaven—that is, God's kingship, being brought near in the present world. "Let your kingdom come" was a prayer for an immediate and concrete "here and now" reality, not some future heavenly place. This is more than seeing sin as the breaking of God's commands and seeing salvation as the deliverance of human beings from the wrath of God toward those who disobey. This is only part of the whole biblical picture.

Our worn-out theology of escaping from this world does not do justice to the here-and-now work of Jesus through His Spirit. Nor does it adequately convey the mission of the church in the interim between Jesus' first and second coming. Jesus does more in this present life than simply forgive sins or offer assurance of a better life after we die (though, as I mentioned earlier, if that were all He did for us, that would be far more than we deserve). Jesus delivers people from the pain of sin, brokenness, and addiction. He renews people's identities so they no longer see themselves simply as victims, addicts, failures, or sinners. He heals hearts, minds, and bodies. He delivers captives out of the domain of darkness and into the kingdom of light. The then-and-there gospel of Jesus, who forgives our sins only so that we can go to heaven when we die, shortchanges the power of the present announcement of the kingdom's nearness and availability. Far too often and for far too many, the response to the gospel is a simple, private transaction instead of the life-altering and communal entrance into the kingdom that Jesus describes.

In Revelation 11:15, John talks about the kingdom of this world becoming the kingdom of our Lord Jesus. In a sense, the message of Jesus is that transformation has already begun, and we, the redeemed of Jesus, get to play a part. By following Him, we become like Him and take on His mission, authority, priorities, and power. We extend kingdom life by and through the community of those who have responded to the kingdom.

2. **The gospel is holistic and comprehensive; it is not concerned with souls and sins alone. God wants to redeem the whole person and all of creation.**

Redemption in the kingdom concerns the whole person, not just a list of wrongdoings. As we have seen, the work of Jesus is to bring us out of exile in whatever way we are enslaved. The good news is the presence and coming of the kingdom of God. It is about the rule of God being applied to all of creation—every part of human beings and the world. The work of salvation in its full sense is about whole human beings, not merely souls; about the present, not simply the future; and about what God does through us, not merely what God does in and for us.

Our traditional conceptions of salvation are blatantly more individualistic, focusing on one's individual reconciliation with God through a personal relationship with Jesus. The emphasis seems to be only on giving Jesus our sins and not on every area and aspect of our human life. It is more concerted with getting souls to heaven than with bringing heaven to earth. This narrow gospel focuses only on the salvation of the human soul, but the gospel of the kingdom includes the salvation of human beings within the context of the larger story of God restoring all of creation.

The entrance of sin and death into the world afflicted all of creation, so the consummation of the kingdom includes an entirely new creation (Romans 8:20-22). This new and cosmic salvation is spoken of as the renewal, restoration, or reconciliation of *all things*. Paul talks of God's purpose: "to bring all things in heaven and on earth together under one head, even Christ."[3] The goal of all unfolding history is salvation and blessing: the defeat of Satan and his kingdom and the redemption and restoration of this fallen creation with a greater glory than it has ever known.

In 1 Corinthians 15:28, Paul speaks of a future time when God is "all in all." Romans 8 furthers this picture. There, Paul applies the imagery of the exodus to the creation as a whole. Like the children of Israel in Egypt, creation is in bondage at the moment. And creation, like the enslaved Israelites, yearns and expectantly waits "for the day when God's children are revealed, when their resurrection will herald its own new life." [4]

This was seen and foreshadowed by the Old Testament prophets, who understood that the rule of Messiah will bring justice and peace to the whole world (see Isaiah 11:1-9; 55:1-13). They knew that the great future of God with His people lies in the renewal of the entire universe, heaven and earth together. Isaiah writes, "I will create new heavens and a new earth; the former things will not be remembered, nor will they come to mind" (65:17).

This means the concerns for social justice, the environment, and the salvation of individuals all are intertwined and cannot be so neatly separated as many modern commentators would have us believe (more about this later). The gospel is as broad in scope as the whole universe; it's as all-encompassing as the whole of human life. Anything less is not the gospel of the kingdom of God and of His Christ.

3. The gospel is, at its core, an exchange of sovereignties.

Many stress acceptance of Jesus for the forgiveness of sins, assurance of salvation, and eternal life, and then they leave it at that. But even more fundamental to the gospel is the *exchange of sovereignties*.[5] Either we live in Satan's counterfeit kingdom of darkness or we live in the kingdom of God. Of course this language seems hopelessly outdated, as does the language of spiritual warfare. One cannot take the Scriptures seriously, however, and not draw similar conclusions. The sacrifice and resurrection of Jesus have defeated the powers of evil. Conversion to Christ, therefore, is a turning away (repentance) from loyalty and allegiance to what is evil and choosing instead to be loyal to Christ and stand under His reign and rule.

When we call Jesus *Lord,* we use the very name given to God in the Greek Old Testament. This declaration is a surrender of our own sovereignty and autonomy and leads to our submission to Him. Paul makes this confession central to kingdom life (as in Romans 10:8-9). When we declare Jesus is Lord, we are renouncing all other claimants for the title. Nothing else—no person, thing, idea, habit, and so on—can have a higher claim on our lives. All idols (including the worship of oneself so prevalent today) must be pulled down, repented of, and crushed at Jesus' feet. Anything that takes the place of Jesus in our hearts, our devotion, or our passion must go. As Elijah the prophet said to the nation of Israel, "How long will you waver between two opinions? If the LORD is God, follow Him" (1 Kings 18:21).

To say that Jesus is Lord is to worship Him and nothing else.[6] Psalm 115:8 and 135:18 teach that we become like what (or whom) we worship. If we worship sex, we become filled with lust; if we worship money, we become greedy; if we worship people, we then constantly seek their approval. If we worship power, we become controlling and demanding. When we enter into the kingdom of God, we are transferred from death to life, from slavery to freedom, from self-centeredness to God-centeredness. But these are all reflections of one fundamental exchange: We are transferred from the kingdom of death and darkness into the kingdom of God and His Son, Jesus. This is all entailed in declaring that Jesus is King.

This saves us from the unbiblical idea that intellectual assent to the message of Jesus is considered saving faith.[7] It is far too easy to "pray the prayer" and then go on living by one's own rules and desires. Under the small gospel, where Jesus deals with only my sin problem, this is common. But the gospel of the kingdom removes such confusion. To step into the kingdom is to submit to Jesus' authority as king. There is no middle ground.

This doesn't have anything to do with being saved by works. We evangelicals are rightly suspicious of anything that smacks of earning our way into God's favor. But the gospel that pictures my relationship as a spiritual transaction (where I get Jesus' righteousness credited to me and He has my sin credited to Him) leaves out both discipleship (how do I grow) and mission (what do I do now). This results in the disconnect between belief and behavior that we briefly looked at in chapter 1.

4. The gospel is both *now* and *not yet*.

As George Ladd notes, the words *to save* and *salvation* refer to both a future eschatological blessing and a present one. Both the "now" and the "not yet" need to be held in tension to understand Scripture's insistence that, at the same time, we are saved, we are being saved, and we will be saved.[8] *The kingdom of God* is a comprehensive term for all that messianic salvation included.[9] In other words, salvation isn't only a gift belonging to life after death or life after Jesus returns. It is also a gift to be received and enjoyed in this present age. So our presentations of salvation must address *both* aspects of the work of Jesus: He comes to give us fullness of life under God's gracious rule (and that life will come into all its fullness in the age to come), but we can receive that life *now*.

Furthermore, understanding the "now but not yet" nature of the gospel of the kingdom of God helps to explain some of the duality and paradox of the Christian life. The Scriptures declare, for instance, that we are entirely new creations (2 Corinthians 5:17). And yet at the same time, we are told that we also have an old nature that must be put to death (because, paradoxically enough, it died with Jesus on the cross—Colossians 3:5). So we live in the midst of tension between the old nature and the new, between the now and the not yet (2 Corinthians 4:8-9; 6:8-10; also compare 1 John 3:6 with 1 John 1:8). The duality we experience is eschatological—two ages coexist within us. The spirit/flesh language of Paul expresses the "already but not yet" nature of the kingdom. The flesh reveals the continuity that one still has with one's old life. The Spirit fuels the continuity one has with one's new life. Understanding this tension keeps us from despair (believing we are not strong enough to stand up under the temptations of this world) or perfection (believing we will reach a point in this life where we'll no longer struggle with sin). We are not simply waiting for the end to come; we are already living in the end, which began with the death and resurrection of Jesus.

5. The gospel embraces the reality of spiritual warfare.

Most of the church today suffers from one of two extremes regarding the reality of the demonic. On one hand, many so obsess on this issue that they see demonic oppression behind every traffic ticket, past-due bill, or piece of burnt toast. But, usually in reaction to these folks, others simply pretend that spiritual warfare is part of a nice fairy-tale world that the Scriptures describe but that has no place among our modern scientific sensibilities.

As we have noted, understanding Jesus' teaching about the kingdom of God forces us to confront the reality of other kingdoms in the world. And looming beyond the earthly kingdoms is the spiritual kingdom of Satan. Rather than dismissing the battle between kingdoms as a relic of a pre-scientific worldview, we should see it as a backdrop for much of the New Testament teaching regarding the church.

Jesus doesn't just simply save souls. He creates a new order—a new community, a new Israel—where mercy and justice reign, and He extends it into every area of society. He liberates us from Satan's kingdom and the idolatrous political, religious, and legal structures that hold us in bondage. The salvation that Jesus brings releases us from the authority of the powers and principalities of this age, and it allows us to reclaim our standing in God's world as agents and ambassadors.

If the church is to take on the ministry of Jesus, this needs to become part of how the gospel sets people free. Rather than making spiritual warfare the domain of specialists (or just plain weird people), the New Testament assumes that normal, ordinary people live with regard to the spiritual battle around them. Presenting spiritual warfare in a gentle, non-freakish way in our churches would go a long way toward explaining why things in this world are so wicked.

We set new Christians up for failure when we omit those parts of the New Testament that deal with the warfare that rages around us. As life moves along and hard and difficult things happen, this omission usually causes them to think that God has let them down or that something is wrong with them. But in reality, one of the primary solutions that the Scriptures give to the problem of why bad things happen to good people is that we live in a war zone, and no one should be surprised that there are casualties. We handicap disciples of Jesus by not showing them how standing for Jesus and His kingdom brings us into conflict with the counterkingdom established by the enemy. Through the Scriptures and the Holy Spirit, believers are equipped to engage in warfare in the power of the name of Jesus. This isn't always Hollywood-style "exorcist" stuff (though sometimes it is); often the battle rages through our thoughts and judgments about ourselves and others.

When Jesus proclaimed and demonstrated the reality of the kingdom, demonic confrontations were commonplace. Though not as common in the Western world (for reasons that we don't have time to get into here), these confrontations still take place. I have come to see the reality of the "warfare worldview" in my own life and in the ministry of our church community. I hesitate talking about spectacular occasions of demonic confrontation because spiritual warfare is most often much less visible as it takes place in our hearts and minds. But I do so because I have seen with my own eyes the reality of what we have been talking about in the last couple of chapters.

We are constantly choosing between two kingdoms: life and death, light and darkness, truth and lies, freedom and slavery. At times, we may, consciously or not, allow our adversary to have authority or position in our lives.[10] The Scriptures call these "strongholds" or "footholds." Often demons attach themselves to us through these places and need to be confronted. Sometimes this can result in some obvious physical manifestations.

I remember one young man who came into my office complaining of an addiction to pornography. We talked, and as I began to pray for him, I sensed (kind of a "gut feeling") the presence of the enemy in his life. I simply said, "Jesus, I sense the presence of the enemy," and he began to convulse, bent over, and began to drool. This is a normal, Christian college kind of guy. There was no reason to think he was acting or having a psychotic break. I recruited some help from some other pastors, and we prayed that Jesus would deliver this guy from whatever was plaguing him. After a few moments, he returned to normal and has said that the battle with porn has been different ever since.

I had the opportunity to pray for another person in our church community who had confessed to sexual sin. I wish I could adequately describe what happened. A group of us gathered first to pray and confess our sins. Then he walked in. I am telling the truth—his *face* looked shrouded, dark, and slightly contorted. I know it sounds crazy, but I can remember it exactly. We began to pray, and I felt the Lord leading me to place my hand over his heart. I simply declared that Jesus was Lord and started to ask Jesus to war against anything unholy in his life. He started to cough in the strangest way. He seemed to be trying to vomit, though nothing was happening. He bent over, his face twisted into a sneer, and he continued to make the weirdest noises. This went on for ten minutes, after which he sat back up, panting, and said, "They're gone, they're gone."

The group of us praying for him just sat back, amazed and thankful.

We have seen this happen several other times. I share this because I am the *least likely* person to have ever been involved with this sort of thing. But I have seen the truth of Paul's statement: "The kingdom of God is not a matter of talk but of power" (1 Corinthians 4:20). When we take the kingdom seriously in our practice and preaching, the enemy opposes its progress. I have seen the salvation and power that the name of Jesus brings to real people with real issues. This is more than a ticket to heaven; this is salvation here and now.

Part 3

Roots:
Followers of the Way

Chapter 8

The Big Story of God's People

I look into the subculture of many versions of the Christian faith that
are operative in America today and see Christians wringing their
hands in fear, hoping that Jesus will come back and get them out of
this "mess." On the other hand, I look at the world around me and
see a cultural context that is closer to the world of the early church
than any other culture in the last two thousand years. The irony is that
these same Christians are open about their desire for a return to a
version of faith that was modeled by the early church and described
in the pages of the New Testament book of Acts. In other words,
we want the fruit of the early church but not the context of suffering
and demand that produced such fruit. How American. How selfish.
How consumptive. How anemic. Let us listen anew to the teachings
of Jesus while we walk through the pages of Scripture to the cross.
As we do, our personal and corporate imaginations will bring us into
a new (and ancient) identity: sojourners and aliens testifying to an
alternative life rooted in the revelation of God in Jesus Christ.

TIM KEEL

A summary: The God who creates everything (Genesis 1–2)
allows His creatures the freedom to rebel against His rule
(Genesis 3). Sin, violence, and alienation fill the world as a result
(Genesis 4–11). God moves to reclaim the world by calling one man,
Abram, and promising to bless all the world through the nation that
will be made up of his offspring (Genesis 12:1-3). This nation, Israel, is
redeemed through the exodus and brought into covenant relationship
with God. The rest of the Old Testament is the story of God's faithfulness in the midst of Israel's faithlessness. As Israel is sent into exile, God
promises to snatch a remnant from the lion's mouth (Amos 3:12) and
make it the new focus of His redemptive design and the beginnings of
national restoration. Israel begins to look forward to a king who will

109

reign like David (Isaiah 11:1-9; Jeremiah 30:8-9; Amos 9:11-15) and lead the nation to be vindicated above other nations (Psalm 137; Isaiah 51:4-5). It anticipates a new covenant (Jeremiah 31:31-32; Ezekiel 34) and a new Jerusalem (Isaiah 2:2-3; 28:16-17).

Jesus of Nazareth reconstituted a true Israel by choosing 12 disciples (one for each of the 12 tribes of Israel). Jesus began to call Israel back to her true nature and identity, and He promised that His followers would see the kingdom of God in all its fullness (Matthew 19:28; Luke 12:32). As His life and ministry progressed, Jesus took onto Himself the past and the future of Israel. He was called out of Egypt (Matthew 2:15), baptized by John, and tempted in the wilderness. He proclaimed Himself the temple, forgave sins, and declared lepers to be clean. As we have seen, Jesus was a living recapitulation of Israel's history through His own life and obedience. Where Israel failed, He succeeded. In doing so, He revealed to the world what God's rule looked like and foreshadowed the redemption that awaits the whole world.

Jesus' earthly ministry culminated in His crucifixion, resurrection, and ascension. Under the Mosaic covenant, the nation of Israel was blessed when it was faithful to God and cursed when it wasn't. Even though the Jews of Jesus' day lived in the promised land, they considered themselves still in exile (because pagan Rome ruled over them) and therefore still under the curses of the covenant. Because Jesus recapitulates Israel, He takes Israel's curse upon Himself on the cross and exhausts it in a stunning climax.

Only within this story—the story of God's redemptive intent for the world through a particular nation—can we appreciate the resurrection of Jesus for what it represents. To the Jews, resurrection meant more than simply life after death. It became associated with and symbolic of the renewal of Israel, returned from exile, and reconstituted in the promised land under a new covenant (Ezekiel 37:1-14).[1] Because Jesus, as the living summation of Israel's life and destiny, was the one resurrected, His followers saw Him as the person through whom all the promises given to Israel would be given to the world.

God restores Israel through Jesus and then begins to directly fulfill the promises given to Abraham in the Old Testament.[2] His invitation was for people to "abandon their agendas, including those agendas which appeared to be sanctioned in, or even demanded by, the Torah and the Prophets. He summoned them to follow him in a way of being the people of Yahweh which was, according to him, the true though surprising fulfillment of the whole scriptural story."[3] Jesus was inviting the nation of Israel to reclaim its identity as a city set on a hill and its mission to be salt and light to the earth. In the midst of competing ideas about how Israel was to be Israel, Jesus announced He was renewing Israel and suggested any attempt to create a new Israel apart from Him and His words was doomed to fail.

Jesus' announcement of the kingdom was coded with imagery to indicate that the centuries-old exile of Israel among the nations was finally ending and that He intended to reconstitute a new community of God, formed around Himself. This means, among other things, that "what Jesus was to Israel, the church must now be for the world. Everything we discover about what Jesus did and said within the Judaism of his day must be thought through in terms of what it would look like for the church to do and be this for the world."[4]

The Nature of the Kingdom Community

Central to understanding this call of Jesus is the idea that it concerned itself less with the salvation of individual souls and more with the formation of a renewed Israel, a community of disciples that would collectively embody the kingdom once Jesus ascended to the Father. The kingdom of God and the community it creates are primarily public and therefore social entities. To be brought into the kingdom involves membership, citizenship, adoption into a new family, new loyalties and allegiances, and a fundamentally new identity. This is no mere "personal relationship with Jesus." To be a citizen of the kingdom is to be given privileges and obligations that entail relationships with other people. These dimensions of kingdom life supersede individual faith, experience, and practice. Kingdom citizenship reorients our relationships to the King, to the other citizens of the kingdom of God, and to other kingdoms. That is why so much of the New Testament contains ethical teaching regarding relationships with other members of the kingdom and with those who stand outside it.

This wars against our Western notions of individualism. One of the hallmarks of modernity is the fragmentation of life into different spheres: public and private, economic, social, political, religious, rich and poor. We rarely see ourselves as part of a movement far greater than ourselves and part of a universal history that gives meaning to our lives because it shows us our place in the cosmic story. So instead of true community, we are offered (and settle for) cultural counterfeits of pseudo-community: loose associations based on self-interest or mutual benefit. This community usually costs somebody very little—no risk, no discomfort, no inconvenience, no hanging around with others who aren't like us. This further caters to our individual consumer preferences. We love to be around people who are like us. In fact, the subtle and not-so-subtle reality of consumer preference leads us to fail to grasp just how individualizing and damaging such a mind-set can be.

Jesus' announcement about the kingdom of God refers to the rule of God in our hearts *and* relationships. God was at hand in Jesus, living amid people and calling them to obedience. The church is the assembly of people who have welcomed God's reign in their hearts and relationships. The church consists of the citizens of the kingdom. It's the body of Christ composed of obedient disciples following in the way of Jesus. The church isn't a building, sanctuary, or program. It is the visible community of those who live under the authority of the King.

And this King has decreed that independence has no place in His kingdom. Instead, collective interdependence is demanded. Privacy and individual rights are supplanted by mutual submission and relational accountability. Those who yield their hearts to the King find they must yield their relationships also. The reign of God creates, orders, and sustains a collection of relationships that bind the King and His subjects together.

Just Me and Jesus?

One of the most damaging aspects of modern life has been the replacement of community, belonging, and responsibility with individual identity and rights. The primary entity of marketplace democracy is the individual. Western civilization is now based on the assumption that society exists…

> to supply our needs, no matter the content of those needs. Rather than helping us judge our needs, to have right needs which we exercise in right ways, our society becomes a vast supermarket of desire under the assumption that if we are free enough to assert and to choose whatever we want we can defer eternally the question of what needs are worth having and on what basis right choices are made. What we call freedom becomes the tyranny of own desires. We are kept detached, strangers to one another as we go about fulfilling our needs and asserting our rights. The individual is given a status that makes incomprehensible the Christian notion of salvation as a political, social phenomenon in the family of God. Our economics correlates to our politics. Capitalism thrives in a climate where "rights" are the main political agenda. The church becomes one more consumer-oriented organization, existing to encourage individual fulfillment rather than being a crucible to engender individual conversion into the Body.[5]

This individualization also pervades the American understanding of religious life. Faith is thought to be exclusively an individual concern, something that shapes our private lives but does not (or should not) bleed into the public sphere.

> What I think or feel about God is between me and my conscience. "Spirituality" is an amorphous, ever mutable engagement between two isolated selves—the human individual and "God," both apart from the world, change, time, place and community.[6]

The predominant structures of the American church today center around and favor the locus of individual choice. Often our gospel appeals are little more than spiritualized pop psychology focused only on self-fulfillment. For example, Joel Osteen's *Your Best Life Now* seems to be a far cry from Jesus' message: "If anyone would come after me, he must deny himself and take up his cross and follow me."[7]

Indeed, given such blatantly communal and social language in the Bible as exodus, kingdom, church, family, and household, it can be difficult to comprehend how we have managed to so thoroughly privatize New Testament faith. Pastoral ministry has now been reduced to marketing and psychotherapy—disciplines that both concentrate exclusively on the individual. The message of the gospel is treated the same way. The American gospel concerns itself solely with the inner, private world of people as they exist only in relation to God. There is usually no talk of community, tradition, or public accountability. (After all, who are *you* to stand between me and God?) Faith exists as a private exercise, a personal option, an individual choice.

But this is not New Testament faith. It is not of Jesus or His apostles, nor is it the understanding of the earliest Christians. Reception of the kingdom, far from being a matter solely between the individual and God, amounts to being grafted into a new people.[8] People believe the gospel and through it become God's covenant people. The early church never saw itself as a collection of individuals gathering to pursue their own individual spiritual programs for growth. To view the church in these terms is to deny the very purpose for which it was called into existence: to testify to the reality of the kingdom-inaugurating agenda of Jesus Christ. By His Spirit and through His people, He is working to put everything back the way He wants it.

The earliest Christians used various Greek terms to describe their Jesus-shaped community, including *oikos* (a family or household*), polis* (a city or group of citizens), and *ekklesia* (the assembly of citizens in a city). But what is important is the way the early community of Christians saw themselves in relationship to Jesus, to each other, and to the world. They existed as a subversive counterculture in the midst of the global military superpower of Rome. They embodied a *koinonia* (a term referring to the ways a *polis* organizes and its citizens relate to it and to each other) that was remarkable in the ancient world. All of these are communal pictures.

From the standpoint of the rest of the New Testament, the life, death, resurrection, and ascension of Jesus resulted in the formation of a new community, created by the Holy Spirit, that existed alongside the cities, nations, and empires of this world. Georges Florovsky describes it this way:

> Christianity entered history as a new social order, or rather a new social dimension. From the very beginning Christianity was not primarily a "doctrine," but exactly a "community." There was not only a "Message" to be proclaimed and delivered, and "Good News" to be declared. There was precisely a New Community, distinct and peculiar, in the process of growth and formation, to which members were called and recruited. Indeed, "fellowship" (*koinonia*) was the basic category of Christian existence. Primitive Christians felt themselves to be closely knit and bound together in a unity that radically transcended all human boundaries—of race, of culture, of social rank, and indeed the whole dimension of "this world."[9]

To put it another way, the church understood itself to be a parallel culture, a distinct community that existed within the social, economic, religious, and cultural structures of the Roman Empire.[10] This community was comprised of people from every tongue, tribe, and nation. The redemption wrought by Jesus Christ superseded the barriers of hostility that existed between Jews and Gentiles and reconciled them together into what Paul calls a new humanity. This mystery, that the Gentiles are now joined together with Jews in the new people of God, is essential to Paul's understanding of the church.[11] To be in Christ is not to be alone but to be with others who are in Him, to constitute with them an organic unity, and to transcend the division and hostility that had separated Jew and Gentile, male and female, and slave and free (Galatians 3:27-28). Evangelism in the early church involved attracting and inviting people into a new society—a "new humanity," to use Paul's words. The great Commission is not simply a conveyance of information, not a mere inward acknowledgment, but a making of disciples from all nations in community. In our terms, this is a call for people into a different way of life together—a departure from the old ways of life that formerly defined them and made them what they were.

The early Christians saw themselves as continuing Israel's story under different circumstances. The church understood itself as messianic Israel covenanted with her risen Lord (Acts 2:38; 5:30-32). It saw itself, under Jesus as the new temple and the firstfruits of a new humanity, reborn in Jesus.

The Church as a Parallel but Subversive Community

The distinctive character of this community as a witness to the reality and future coming of the kingdom was based on Jesus and His embodiment of the kingdom. Instead of resorting to violence and coercion, the community of Jesus embodied the practices of forgiveness, reconciliation, and the bearing of one another's burdens. Whatever segregation a person experienced in the world was wiped away and replaced by one's identification with Christ and His community (as we saw in Galatians 3:27). He or she was called a "new creation" and was given gifts of the Spirit to use in service to Jesus and His church (1 Corinthians 12:7). The celebration of the Lord's Supper sought to reverse the social stratifications of the day and extended unity and solidarity to all regardless of race, gender, class, background, or economic status.[12] Church discipline, public confession and reconciliation, and high moral standards set the early Christian community apart from other religious societies in the first century who held that faith had little or nothing to do with how one lived. Jesus needed to teach His growing band of disciples how to conduct themselves in their world. It would be just the opposite of the conventionally accepted values, norms and relationships of ancient Near Eastern society and of modern culture today.[13] These activities were signs that God was at work in the world. Barry Harvey's words are suggestive:

The first-century church understood itself to be a definitive sign that the process of gathering together the commonwealth over which the God of Israel would rule at the end of the ages had already begun in the midst of the present age. The very existence of the Christian community made this destiny known to a fallen world that did not know either what it was—the cherished creation of God—or its ultimate destination—that *polis* which will descend from heaven like a bride adorned for her husband (Rev. 21:2). The early Christians thus referred to themselves as the *ek-klesia*, a people "called out" of the world so that they might be sent back into it as the provisional assembly (*ekklesia*) of this other city.[14]

The revolutionary practices of the early Christian community provided the surest proof to skeptics that the fledgling church was unlike any other religious society in the Roman Empire. Michael Green, in his fantastic work *Evangelism in the Early Church*, identifies several factors that allowed the ancient New Testament communities to have such a powerful witness to the world.[15]

1. Their fellowship showed qualities unparalleled in the ancient world. Nowhere else would slaves and masters, Jews and Gentiles, rich and poor engage in table fellowship and show real love for each other. In times of plague and disaster, the Christians shone by means of their service to their communities. This was not a dull uniformity—the issues addressed in Romans 14 show us that. Instead, the community transcended barriers of race, class, sex, and education unlike anything else in the Roman Empire.

2. The character of their adherents was transformed. They shared with those in need and refused to have anything to do with idolatry and its by-products. They renounced magical practices. They stood out for their chastity, their hatred of cruelty, their civil obedience, and their good citizenship and payment of taxes.

3. Particularly in the second and third centuries, the

community faced criticism, hatred, persecution, and death with joy. They commended Christ regardless of circumstance (Acts 5:41; 8:8; 13:52; Romans 5:2-5,11; 1 Thessalonians 1:6). The early church father Tertullian boasted, "The oftener we are mowed down by you, the more in number we grow. The blood of Christians is seed." The manner in which they went to their deaths caused much admiration.

4. Believers were filled with power. Healings, exorcisms, and other miracles seemed to accompany the proclamation of the Christian message.[16]

This, then, was what God was doing in Jesus. He was creating a *people* through whom the promises given to Israel were to be given to the world. This work was fundamentally *communal*. The church was not to be a collection of individuals who each found spiritual nourishment and fulfillment in Jesus. Instead, the church—as a community of the redeemed—was to witness to, point toward, and seek to embody the kingdom of Jesus to the world.

Chapter 9

One Is the Loneliest Number

I confess that I have come to feel the primary reality of which we have to take account in seeking for a Christian impact on public life is the Christian congregation. How is it possible that the gospel should be credible, that people should come to believe that the power which has the last word in human affairs is represented by a man hanging on a cross? I am suggesting that the only answer, the only hermeneutic of the gospel, is a congregation of men and women who believe it and live by it...Evangelistic campaigns, distribution of Bibles and Christian literature, conferences, and even books such as this one... are all secondary, and...they have power to accomplish their purpose only as they are rooted in and lead back to a believing community. Jesus...did not write a book but formed a community.

LESSLIE NEWBIGIN

*C*ommunity is one of the most used and abused words in the modern Christian vocabulary. Though the idea is utterly central to God's work of redemption, it remains beyond most of us. Rather than focusing on ways that church can better foster community among its people (through small groups, for instance), I want to look at our salvation and witness (and indeed the church itself) in more communal terms.

Much in modern life works against biblical notions of community, as does the rugged American-style individualism that is culturally heroic. For us to overcome this, we need to till much soil in our hearts and in our churches. Consider the practice of evangelism, for instance. Conversion in the first century was not just a private matter between the individual and God, but a social act with profound public and social consequences. Biblical evangelism in our current setting would not be simply declaring a message to someone but rather initiating

them into the world-changing kingdom of God. To think of evangelism as proclamation is not enough—it is all the activities related to the
community of God as they draw and admit persons into a society, a
set of principles, a body of knowledge, a way of living. Converts must
understand that they are becoming members of a new race, humanity,
or family. Ours is not primarily a private or hidden faith. Christians
are to understand witness as corporate and not only or even primarily
individual. When we understand evangelistic witness as corporate,
organic, ongoing, and flowing naturally from a Christian way of life,
then we are prepared to participate in and recognize conversion in its
thousands of forms.

Modern evangelism should call people to become a part of a new
people, a holy nation, a contrasting and alternative community. The
big revivals and crusades that were popular in the nineteenth and
twentieth centuries were aimed primarily at awakening latent faith of
people reared in Christian homes and communities. In this form of
evangelism, people did not need to learn and participate in a new way
of life embodied in a particular visible community. They only needed
to be individually convinced and convicted. These evangelistic forms
tended to isolate and appeal directly the individual. We began to so
focus on the inwardness of faith and so concentrate on the moment of
decision that we really didn't have much to say after someone decided
to accept Christ. In the early church, evangelism was primarily a matter
of inviting people to become part of a new way of being human—
literally a new creation, reborn in Jesus Christ, which was itself the
firstfruits of what God was going to do with the whole world. This
represents a radical break from the dominant individualistic mind-set
that separates us from each other.

The early Christians lived and worked within the confines of normal
first-century life in the Roman Empire. In other words, they did not
restrict their activities or associations to a private religious sphere of
individual life. Rather, they were formed in connection to the real
goings-on of public life: buying and selling, celebrating and mourning,
marrying and parenting, working and resting, planting and harvesting.

They contributed to the general welfare of whatever town or village they happened to live in. The first-century church never withdrew from society to focus on spiritual matters, leaving the secular concerns of regular life to others. No, such distinctions were unknown in the ancient world. But their communal beliefs and practices nourished their discernment and faith so that they were able to live in the world while they lived and proclaimed the lordship of Jesus.

I am not advocating community merely for the sake of community. The Christian claim is not that life is better when we live together rather than alone. That is simply a veiled appeal to self-interest. Rather, life is better lived in the community of faith because the church is the only community formed around the truth.[1] The community formed by Jesus recognizes that kingdom life is so at odds with the life of this world that only a community can sustain faithful witness to it. This, in turn, reshapes our ways of thinking about the mission of the church. It may not cause us to do anything differently, but it reorients our vision about what we currently do and why.

Christianity is more than a matter of new beliefs. Following Jesus is an invitation to be part of an alternate society that is formed around Him. Right living within this community is more of the challenge than having the right beliefs. The creation of the church is the creation of new people who have aligned themselves with the seismic shift that has occurred in the world since Christ. Due to the cultural situation in the West, we have an unprecedented opportunity to discover what has always been true—that the called-out ones of the church embody an alternative social reality that the world can never know by itself.

The reality of this community was called a "mystery" by the apostle Paul (Ephesians 3:6). The Old Testament taught that Jews and Gentiles would be united into one body, but this far exceeded the imagination of the Jewish people. Moreover, this community would testify to the powers and principalities of the world about the wisdom of God. The church visibly testifies to God's wisdom by its very existence. The existence of the church provides a testimony to the powers. The hostile powers seek to frustrate the work of God, and they believed they had succeeded when they conspired against Christ in the crucifixion. But they were merely instruments in God's hands. The death of Christ had been the very means He had devised for the accomplishment of His plan. So because of the church, the hostile powers, after an apparent triumph, have become aware of a divine wisdom they never suspected. As the church arose out of Christ's death and testified to the hidden purpose of God, the forces of darkness saw that they had played into their own defeat.

This requires more than simply a small-group ministry. We must reorient our methods and message so that this becomes central to the ways we conceive of, practice, and talk about the kingdom. This is the subject of the next several chapters.

Chapter 10

The Church at the End of the World

> There exists in every church something that sooner or later works against the very purpose for which it came into existence. So we must strive very hard, by the grace of God, to keep the church focused on the mission that Christ originally gave to it.
>
> C.S. LEWIS

> The healthy Church understands itself as the presence of Christ in the world with a mission to embody, proclaim and enact the salvation of the world through the *Mission Dei* accomplished and inaugurated by the life and ministry of Jesus and completed at the *eschaton*. Such a church acts as a communal witness to the overthrow of the powers of evil and to the reign of God over all creation.
>
> ROBERT E. WEBBER

The early Christian community didn't exist for its own benefit. It existed within the world *for the sake of* the world. It was to proclaim the good news of the gospel, which is the power of God. It saw itself playing a critical role in the inauguration of God's messianic kingdom. Made up of members from every tongue, tribe, and nation, the church was a people that had no physical space to build or defend and no distinct place of gathering. Spread across the empire, disciples of Jesus were bound together, not by geography or economy, but instead by the distinct nature of fellowship they shared in and through Jesus Christ.

They saw themselves as living within the structures of the world, but also as people who continued the mission of Jesus within those structures. As emissaries and ambassadors of another King and another kingdom, they were constantly reminded that they had no lasting home in the empire. Instead they were…

> looking forward to the city with foundations, whose architect and builder is God…They admitted that they were aliens and strangers on earth. People who say such things show that they are looking for a country of their own…they were longing for a better country, a heavenly one. Therefore God is not ashamed to be called their God, for he has prepared a city for them (Hebrews 11:10,13-14,16).

The early church believed that God was not limited within or contained by their assembly. They knew that "the earth is the LORD's, and everything in it" (Psalm 24:1). Yet they believed that their *ekklesia* somehow participated in the life of the triune God and participated in the mission of God to redeem all of creation. The reconciled community called the church did not merely house the missions program of God or send missionaries into the world; it *was* the missions program of God. The existence of the church is the embodiment of Christ's mission.[1]

The church's mission was to be an outpost of heaven, a colony of aliens living in a land that was not their own, calling the powers and principalities of the world and over the world to account in the name of the risen Lord Jesus, who sat in the position of greatest authority at the right hand of the Father. This community was gathered together by the Holy Spirit as a new humanity, who through repentance and faith was being re-created according to the image of Jesus. They were to represent the reign and rule of God and to invite people to live under the present reign of God and to witness to the future reign of God at the end of this age. The church is an eschatological people who proclaim the hope that is and the hope that is to come. In this we proclaim the ultimate destiny of the world. The early church existed in the world but embodied a kingdom that was not of this world. They lived for the sake of the world as a parallel community that neither separated itself from it nor capitulated to it.

The Mission of the Kingdom

Our line of thinking thus far has been as follows. The church today in America and the West is in trouble. Whatever measure is used—attendance, life change, health of clergy—the results are the same. We face an era of cultural change unprecedented for hundreds of years. Part of this cultural change involved the removal of the Christian church and message from the center of Western culture to the margins. This is not necessarily an altogether bad thing.

From the opposite direction, we have been looking at the message of the kingdom of God and all that it entails. Already we have begun to see the ways in which modern Christianity has truncated, domesticated, ignored, or forgotten altogether elements of Jesus' radical message about the kingdom. For instance, the full biblical concept of salvation in the kingdom has been replaced with the (true but incomplete) idea that salvation concerns (mostly) individual human souls and sin so that one can be guaranteed of heaven after death. This is also compounded by the lack of real kingdom ecclesiology (the study or theology of the church) that takes seriously the call of the church to witness to the reality of the kingdom of God in its midst.

As we have seen, the church is a witness to and servant of the kingdom. The church participates in and anticipates the kingdom, but the kingdom is larger than the church and is not yet fully present in the church or the world.[2] One of the ways that the kingdom is larger than the church is that the focus of the kingdom is the redemption of all creation. The message of the kingdom of God is cosmic in its proportions. God's work in Christ is not only for the salvation of individual people; it is ultimately aimed at redeeming and restoring all that God has made. When the Scriptures depict the end of this age, they give us the following picture. The veil preventing us from seeing Jesus clearly will be removed. Every knee will bow and every tongue will confess that Jesus Christ is Lord. The dead will be raised and judged, and creation will be restored. God will dwell with His people in a world in which evil has been wiped away entirely. And at that time, God's new world will be exactly as He wants it—we will see His will done on earth as in heaven.

The kingdom is also larger than the church in the sense that church can only bear witness to the *present reality of the kingdom*. Along with creation, the church waits in anticipation for the consummation of the kingdom that is still in the future. Thus, while the church bears witness to the kingdom, it cannot be identified with it because it falls short of the fullness of the kingdom.

Clarifying the relationship between the kingdom and church is essential to understanding precisely the nature of the mission given to the church. If the church witnesses to the kingdom (and does not see itself as the kingdom), the church should reflect the values, priorities, methods, and messages proclaimed and demonstrated by Jesus as He embodied the kingdom and brought it near. In other words, the church is most true to God's mission for it when it reflects the kingdom. The further away it gets from kingdom values and priorities, the less it should be properly called church. As N.T. Wright suggests, as Jesus was to the Jews, the church is to be to the world.[3] In other words, all that Jesus was as the embodiment of the *missio dei* to Israel, the church, through the work of the Holy Spirit, seeks to be and do in implementing the kingdom of God in the world. Jesus empowers the church to continue His mission and ministry in the ways He Himself brought it about.

These days, a church can be defined as almost anything. A result of this lack of clarity has been a distorted view of how the church relates to the kingdom. For some (though they may never say it this way), the church *is* the kingdom. They think that by building the church, they are building the kingdom. And certainly that sometimes might be true, but most often a church centered on building the church builds nothing more than adherents to itself, and not citizens of the kingdom and disciples of Jesus.

For others, the church and the kingdom don't have much to do with each other. Some believe the kingdom that was offered by Jesus to first-century Israel (and rejected by them) will be manifest during the (future) millennial reign of Christ, when Jesus returns and reigns on earth over Israel and the nations. Until then, the church exists to do the work of God in the world, drawing as many to Christ as possible.

Both views result in something very damaging: *They make the church an end in itself.* If the goal is simply to get more people into church, it is no wonder that we'll employ whatever methods possible to do so, whatever their underlying theology. If the goal is for the church to grow, it is not surprising that conferences, seminars, tips, and techniques multiply by the thousands to help churches grow numerically. If the function of the church is to simply build the church, we can do almost anything to justify doing so. If we need a $200 million church campus to reach more people, we build it without a thought given to what we are saying to the world around us when we do so.

If the church, however, is to reflect the message, methods, values, and priorities of the kingdom of God in Jesus, then the church no longer exists for itself. It is only an instrument, a servant, and a witness to the kingdom. This is not merely an issue of semantics, nor is it a matter of abstract or esoteric theology. This matters. I believe that the mess we are in is the direct result of this confusion. We have lost sight of the kingdom and why it matters and how it informs the ways in which we live as the church. The church is a witness to God's reconciling and redemptive activity in the world. It is a sent community (called out by God) to be a sending community (raising up disciples that participate with God in His mission in the world).

The rest of this chapter will be spent in examining the nature of the *mission of the church* in light of its call to witness to the kingdom.

The Big Picture

"The whole Bible, both Old and New Testaments, is a missionary book, the revelation of God's purpose and action in mission in human history."[4] The truth of this statement has radical implications for the church. The mission of God—*missio dei*—is His work to rescue and redeem the world from the power of Satan (1 John 3:8). Christopher Wright defines *mission* as "our committed participation as God's people, at God's invitation and command, in God's own mission within the history of God's world for the redemption of God's creation."[5]

The church's mission, properly understood, finds its identity in its formation by the Holy Spirit to be sent into the world to join God in His work. God has a mission within all creation to restore it to its original design and bring everything back under the gracious reign of God. This redemptive work is best understood as the announcement and inauguration of the kingdom of God in the world in and through the presence of Jesus of Nazareth. The big picture of the relationship between church and mission would look something like this.

First, God exists within Himself as the community of Father, Son, and Spirit.

Second, God creates all things and declares them to be good. Human beings, created in God's image, are created for fellowship (it was not good that the man was alone) and dominion (caring for the world God made). They originally existed in right relationship to Him, to the world around them, and to each other (Genesis 1–2).

Third, sin and death entered the world due to human disobedience and brought corruption and decay to God's good creation (Genesis 3–11).

Fourth, God determines to rescue and redeem humanity through the calling of Abram and the ultimate formation of the nation of Israel (Genesis 12:3). In the story of Israel, we see the foreshadowing of what will be the reality in Jesus Christ.

Fifth, God sent Jesus Christ to redeem the world. The one who made the world now seeks to redeem it.[6] Through His death and resurrection, Jesus defeated the powers of Satan, sin, and death, thereby allowing for the possibility of reconciliation between God and all things. Jesus announced that the redemptive work of God is present in the kingdom of God. As the second Adam, Jesus reverses what resulted through the first Adam's rebellion. Though the focus of this reconciliation is human beings, God seeks to bring redemption beyond humanity to all areas of life in creation. The existence of the church stands as testimony that the powers and principalities that govern this world have already been defeated.

Sixth, God is working out His redemption in the world through the work of the Holy Spirit and the called-out community formed by Him—the church. The church is reconciled into relationship with both the triune God and with others. The church does not exist for itself, but is sent by God back into the world to participate in God's mission to redeem all things. The church is therefore a witness to the reality of God's reign in the world, but it is also a sign or foretaste of the fullness and consummation of the kingdom.

Seventh, the church witnesses to and hopes for the future coming of Jesus again to earth, at which time Satan, sin, and death will be destroyed and a renewed humanity will dwell forever with God in a new heaven and a new earth.

Eighth, at the end of history, the powers of evil will be destroyed, and Jesus Christ will reign forever in the new heavens and new earth. This culminates in Revelation 21–22 with, as N.T. Wright suggests, the "marriage of heaven and earth."

This is the ultimate rejection of all types of Gnosticism, of every worldview that sees the final goal as the separation of the world. It is the final answer to the Lord's Prayer that God's kingdom will come and his will be done on earth as in heaven. It is what Paul is talking about in Ephesians 1:10, that God's design, and promise, was to sum up all things in Christ, things both in heaven and on earth. It is the final fulfillment, in richly symbolic imagery, of the promise of Genesis 1, that the creation of male and female would together reflect God's image in the world. And it is the final accomplishment of God's great design, to defeat and abolish death forever—which can only mean the rescue of creation from its present plight of decay...What is promised in this passage, then, is what Isaiah foresaw: a new heaven and a new earth replacing the old heaven and the old earth, which were bound to decay...But unlike in Ezekiel's vision, where the rebuilt Temple takes eventual center stage, there is no Temple in this city (21:22). The Temple in Jerusalem was always designed, it seems, as a pointer to, and an advance symbol for, the presence of God himself. When the reality is there, the signpost is no longer necessary.[7]

The church must orient itself around this epic story in order to fully capture and express God's mission for it. Salvation is not just offered to individual souls, but is worked for and witnessed to in all aspects of creation. Mission is not just the bringing of people to Jesus; it is also the labor of the church to allow all aspects of human life to flourish, just as God intended.

Mission, Missional, and Missionary Positions

There is much discussion these days about the dimensions of the church's activity in the world. Is the church merely responsible for the saving of souls? Or is it to engage in issues (political or otherwise) that pertain to the bringing about of a just society? Can we share Jesus by doing good in the world? Or must we do good only to share Jesus?

These are questions that many have wrestled with. I do not propose to solve them. My goal here is to address the issue of mission from a kingdom perspective. While receiving a lot of attention of late, the ideas carried in the words *mission, missional,* and *missionary* are central to a church's understanding of itself, and not always obviously so.

For the church to witness to the kingdom, it must understand itself as being central to the ultimate intention of God to redeem all of creation. This means that the church is concerned with the salvation of human souls, but not exclusively so. Many see here the tension between evangelism and social action (or justice). Evangelism is typically thought to be the spiritual work of the church in proclaiming the gospel and persuading and inviting people to believe in Jesus Christ. Social justice has been construed as the more practical work of making the world better through addressing the individual and systemic issues that cause human misery and suffering.

The church has bounced back and forth between different understandings of the relationship between evangelism and social action. Some argue that one or the other has priority, or that one should lead to the other, or that they should be held together in partnership. All these positions overlook the call of the church to bear witness to the kingdom, and as a result, each assumes a false dichotomy between bringing people to a saving knowledge of Jesus versus making their lives better.

If God is restoring *all of creation,* and He has invited the redeemed community to be participants in that renewal, then the distinction between evangelism (saving souls) and social justice (doing good) no longer holds. Think of the ministry of Jesus. He proclaimed (in word) and demonstrated (in deed) the reality of the kingdom and the promise of its future coming. Both His teachings and His miracles bore witness to the reality and coming of the kingdom. Paul uses exodus language in Romans 8 to describe creation: It is "groaning" and "in bondage" (descriptions of the Israelites under Pharaoh). He argues that Jesus' resurrection has also to do with the liberation of creation and its rescue from bondage and decay. (Interestingly, Revelation records for us that "all of creation" will be worshipping God. I wonder what that means.)

The separation of social justice (usually built on Jesus' public ministry and miracles) and evangelism (usually focused on Jesus' death and resurrection) forces onto the teaching and ministry of Jesus what simply was not there. Both Jesus' words and works called people to the kingdom, and so should ours. Jesus' teaching on the kingdom admits no division between the spiritual and the physical or practical.[8] We may make a distinction between them, but to separate them does violence to their original intent. As we witness to the reality of the kingdom in Jesus, both words and deeds are necessary. In Jesus' own ministry the interconnection between healing one's body and forgiving sins makes this point powerfully (Mark 2:1-12).

To construe the debate in terms of evangelism versus social action turns our vision away from the proper end of the church's mission. If the mission of the church is to bear witness to the kingdom in and through its own life, then these no longer may be separated. We must not mistake either side of this debate as expressing the fullness of the kingdom.

So we must reintegrate what should never have been separated: the ministry of Jesus that focused on the kingdom, and the events surrounding Jesus' death and resurrection. This leads us to see the gospel not as a story of Jesus' dying for the private sins of individuals and not as some political and social work that got Jesus killed. It is something much bigger than the sum of those two diminished perspectives. It is the story of God's kingdom being launched, on earth as in heaven, generating a new state of affairs in which the power of evil has been decisively defeated, the new creation has been decisively launched, and Jesus' followers have been commissioned and equipped to put that victory and that inaugurated view into practice. Atonement, redemption, and salvation are what happen on the way because engaging in this work demands that people themselves be rescued from the powers that enslave the world in order that they can in turn be rescuers.

Missional Church

Because of this, the church no longer exists to serve its own ends; it exists for something far larger. Craig Van Gelder has identified three different ways the church has understood itself (as it relates to its mission) throughout church history.[9]

Van Gelder begins with the Established Church, "which is the institutional expression of the primary location of God's presence on the earth, through which the world can encounter God." In other words, the Established Church understands itself to be God's presence in the world. The church was the physical place where one could encounter God and receive salvation. The focus of the Established Church was on its purity and membership. Distinctions were made between the visible and invisible church in order to explain the sin and failure of the church on earth. Debates were held about what constituted membership in the true church, which was equivalent to salvation. Was it participation in the sacraments or the hearing of the Word? Or both, as Calvin suggested?

Certainly there is some truth to this view. Both Paul and Peter speak of the church as the new temple of God and do not shy away from all that imagery denotes.[10] They speak not of sacred space or clergy, but of sacred people. While it contains some truth, the Established Church's self-understanding was lacking in some important ways that are captured by the other two views listed below.

Next, Van Gelder discusses what he calls the Corporate Church, "an organization with purposive intent to accomplish something on behalf of God in the world." This way of understanding the church puts the emphasis on seeing the church in primarily (though not exclusively) functional terms where the church is responsible to accomplish the task God has given to it (such as being obedient to live out the Great Commission, for example). Here mission is understood as something that the church must do. People in the church are recruited, trained, and sent to do God's work in the world. Again, there is truth to this, and many of our churches today operate from this perspective, but something is still missing.

Finally, Van Gelder examines what he calls the Missional Church.[11] The Missional Church "exists as a community created by the spirit that is missionary by nature in being called and sent to participate in God's mission in the world." Instead of doing God's work in the world (as the Corporate Church suggests), God's people join God in *His work* in the world. This distinction may seem trivial at first, but it is of great significance in how the church understands itself and its mission. Only this last view makes sense of the great, epic story described above.

The missional church reorients our thinking about the church in regard to its mission. Here, God becomes the primary agent of redemption in the world, not the church. The church isn't to become an end in itself; it merely participates in and witnesses to the work of God *already going on* in the world. It neither initiates nor sustains such work. It only seeks to pay attention and prayerfully discern where the Spirit is moving so that it can join in. Seeing God as the primary acting agent changes the way we think about both the church and the world. The whole of creation is now included in the scope of redemption. This shows the failures of the Established Church's view of itself—the church is not the primary location of God in the world; the world is.

Moreover, the church is no longer responsible (by itself) to carry

out activities in the world on behalf of God. A more balanced kingdom perspective sees the Spirit-led missional church as participating in
God's mission. All we do is try and catch up with what God is doing.
In doing so, the church becomes a sign that God's redemption is now
present in the world, a foretaste of what that redemption is like, and
an instrument to carry that message into every local context and to the
ends of the earth. In living out this identity, the focus of the church
shifts primarily to one of discerning and responding to the leading of
the Spirit.

In the ministry of Jesus, the future has already begun. The Holy
Spirit is moving all things toward the final consummation. The church,
under the leading work of the Spirit, now lives between the times—
the now and the not yet—and is called to participate in God's work
beyond the church. Discerning this work is essential for the church's
ministry.

The kingdom of God gives birth to the missional church through
the work of the Holy Spirit. Its nature, ministry, and organization are
formed by the reality, power, and intent of the kingdom. Understanding the redemptive purposes of God that are embedded within the
kingdom of God provide an understanding of the church as missionary in nature.[12] Ecclesiology, our understanding of and participation
in the church, comes to expression and identity in relationship to
God's mission in the world. Congregations created by the Spirit exist
for the purpose of engaging the world in bringing God's redemptive
work in Christ to bear on every dimension of life. In being true to
their missional identity they can never function primarily as ends in
themselves.

Chapter 11

Missional Church 101

We must start with those who are our mission field. We start with *their* assumptions, *their* experiences, *their* worldviews, *their* emotions. When we start there, everything changes: our posture with people, our livelihood, what we do with our spare time, who we spend our time with, how we structure the fabric of our lives. Yes, church is what we're concerned about because we're deeply entrenched in its minutia, but we can't make transformative adjustments if we start there and work outward. We must go out and then let church reemerge as a reflection and the natural outgrowth of our missional way of life.

HUGH HALTER AND MATT SMAY

I f the church is no longer its own but rather exists as a witness to the kingdom of God through participating in God's work beyond its walls, then much about ministry and mission in the American church needs to be rethought. A very obvious example is the way in which we talk about missions. If the church itself is missionary in nature, then to have a missions program separate from other programs or missionaries set apart from other people is mistaken. Relationship to Jesus always has meant involvement in His mission (Matthew 4:19; 10:1,40; Mark 6:7; Luke 10:1-2). In other words, the community of the church was born out of the mission of God and His kingdom and not vice versa. The church is first the product of mission (it is called out of the world and called together as the church) before it is the agent of mission (it is called out and called together to be sent into the world to witness to the kingdom).[1]

The church, by nature, is a missional community—a community that exists by, in, and for mission. But community is not merely utilitarian, a tool for mission. No, the mission itself leads to the creation of an authentic community, in the spirit of Jesus Christ.[2]

The church was birthed out of the mission of God, and not the other way around. This means that we don't take Christ to a region or people group, but we instead show up and pay attention to the work that Jesus is already doing. We have to move away from the current mind-set about church, ministry, and mission and think again about our participation in *the ministry of Jesus* in the world.[3] This change is difficult for us because it means we are no longer the initiators or sustainers of mission and ministry. Instead, we are focused on discerning the movement of God's Spirit as we seek to join Him in what He is already doing. This involves waiting, asking, seeking, knocking—disciplines and activities that cannot be mass-produced or consumed.

This is all stuff that is relatively new to me. I have lived in each of Van Gelder's churches and am currently in a church that is attempting to make the shift from being a corporate church to being a more missional (or, as I prefer, a more kingdom-minded) one. This has been a process that has been going on for several years. We first tried to balance out our emphasis on weekend services through the creation and sustaining of a ministry of smaller communities called Life Groups. This was coupled with weaning our church off of a video venue model toward a team approach to teaching and worship leading. In each of these moves we were attempting to make our church less personality dependent and more adaptable to what we sensed God was doing around us.

We then introduced a series of initiatives that were lumped around a vision called Giving Ourselves Away. We began a ministry-equipping center to help inspire and train people toward whatever ministry was going on in their everyday lives. We created a special staff position called Outbound for those who would join our staff with the intention of soaking in all they could from us and then moving on to positions of greater influence within the kingdom. Lastly, we embarked on something we called the GO Campaign, which was our attempt to mobilize our community toward missional immersion adventures centered around four places of local ministry and to raise $1 million for 12 different causes at home and around the world. We are trying it again this year and look forward to seeing how God changes our community as a result. Again, I share all this for the sake of illustration, not suggestion, because we are still very much in process on all these things. I just want to highlight our attempts to embrace what we are discussing together in this book. All theology should be practical. What's the point in all this theological work if, in the end, nothing changes?

Rethinking Church

Mission means *sending,* and it is the central biblical theme describing the purpose of God's action in human history. God's mission began with the call of Israel to receive God's blessing in order to be a blessing to the nations. God didn't remain distant; He took on human flesh and dwelt among us in the form of Jesus Christ. Upon Jesus' ascension, He sent the Holy Spirit to tabernacle within each of us, and He entrusted to us the role of ambassadors (2 Corinthians 5:16-21). In other words, the church is a sent people: "As the Father has sent me, I am sending you" (John 20:21; see also 17:18). A genuine missional impulse is a *sending* one rather than an *attractional* one.

Getting people to church can no longer be the end game of ministry. Within a kingdom perspective, the church witnesses to the work of God in the world, pointing it out, celebrating it, nurturing faith, and reminding each other of God's grace and truth. The goal isn't to get people to church and think that once that is done, everything else will take care of itself. Church gatherings are instead the inevitable (and joyful) result of people joining with others who are living under God's reign, pursuing Him and His purposes for them in the world. Instead of getting people more involved in the church and her programs, we should instead teach and equip disciples to prayerfully discern where God is moving in the rest of their lives and empower them to cooperate in *that* work.

Our talk of churched and unchurched people reflects a fundamental mistake. It assumes that church (meaning, for the most part, the building or the services) is where the majority of the action is. We invite people to come to church in order to receive and learn about Jesus. This can no longer be the case if the church is to be true to its nature and mission.

Church keeps the past, present, and future work of God in view. Looking back, the church reconnects itself to the long line and larger story of God's people, maintaining its memory of God's work in history. Looking forward, the church lives now in light of what is coming: consummation, judgment, and the renewal of all things. And living in the present, the church seeks through participation and incarnation to join God in His redeeming work, serving as a testimony of the gracious nature of God's rule. In doing this, the church tells the truth about itself. It cannot do this through the means and methods of the world (such as violence, politics, or marketing techniques) nor though subservience to the world. Instead, it lives as a countercommunity, witnessing to the reality of God's kingdom in the world and in anticipation of its future fulfillment.

If the kingdom gives birth to the church (and not the other way around), then what matters isn't church location, style, or structure but rather whether or not the kingdom of God is embodied in the life of the community. As we move to embrace the mission of the kingdom, traditional understandings of the importance of church services and ministries decrease dramatically in importance.

The church is an anti-institutional institution. It is not true to its own cultural identity unless it constantly examines itself and its shortcomings in light of the kingdom and the Scriptures. Our fervent desire is to see the church surpassed by the reality of the kingdom so that all nations and all of creation will recognize the lordship of Jesus until finally and truly "the kingdom of the world has become the kingdom of our Lord and of His Christ" (Revelation 11:15). So the church regularly celebrates the hope of its demise, the hope that it will not endure forever.

We will now turn our attention to aspects of the early church community that will help us to see ours in an entirely new light. Once we abandon our fascination with the church as an end in itself, we are free to move the focus of the church from an hour-a-week corporate gathering to the ordinary avenues and mundane stuff of life.

> The church gets in trouble whenever it thinks it is in the church business rather than the Kingdom business. In the church business, people are concerned with church activities, religious behavior and spiritual things. In the Kingdom business, people are concerned with Kingdom activities, all human behavior and everything God has made, visible and invisible. Kingdom people see human affairs as saturated with spiritual meaning and Kingdom significance. Kingdom people seek first the Kingdom of God and its justice; church people often put church work above the concerns of justice, mercy and truth. Church people think about how to get people into the church; kingdom people think about how to get the church into the world. Church people worry that the world might change the church; Kingdom people work to see the church change the world...If the church has one great need, it is this: to be set free for the Kingdom of God, to be liberated from itself as it has become in order to be itself as God intends. The church must be freed to participate fully in the economy of God.[1]

Part 4

Branches: Growing into Who We Already Are

Chapter 12

The Confessional Church and the Subversive Jesus

Perhaps we must stretch our imaginations to comprehend the radical quality of the threat posed by the resurrected Jesus to the political and religious authorities of the day. As North American Protestants we are quite comfortable with Jesus. How much do we allow him to threaten anything or anyone anymore? Certainly we have our moral issues where we challenge our culture's assumptions and behaviors in the name of Jesus. But I suspect for a broad swath of Christians, Jesus is a Lord at home in our celebrity-oriented culture. Jesus Christ, super-star. No tables get overturned; rarely are demons denounced. No brood of vipers get condemned and no authorities get provoked.

ANDREW PURVES

The ministry of Jesus is a vivid demonstration of the dynamic character of the kingdom of God. We will examine His ministry, which sets the parameters and possibilities of the mission of today's church among the nations. Jesus' kingdom ministry is to be continued and extended as the church moves out in mission to the nations. In this chapter, we will see that for the church to properly witness to the kingdom it must be *confessional,* that is, oriented around the confession of Jesus as Lord.

To say that the church is to be confessional is to say that in order to be faithful in its witness to the kingdom, the church must consistently proclaim (or confess) the kingship of Jesus. The title *Christ,* when affixed to Jesus, was a kingly term that meant "anointed one." It referred to the prophets' practice of anointing the kings of Israel to signify God's choice and blessing. As we have seen, though, God

Himself anointed Jesus through the Holy Spirit. This was no ordinary king; He was far greater any of them. In Jewish terms, then, to say "Jesus Christ" was to say that Jesus was the Christ, a reference to the kingship of Jesus.

Jewish concepts of the messiah and the kingdom of God would be lost on a Hellenistic Gentile audience, so the confession applied to Jesus quickly morphed into "Jesus is Lord" (*Kyrios*—a title used of Yahweh in the Old Testament and used of Caesar throughout the first century), as the message of the kingdom of God spread into non-Jewish territory. Saying that Jesus is Lord is roughly equivalent to saying that Jesus is the Christ. Both confess the sovereignty of Jesus as King of kings and Lord of lords.

The announcement of the good news of the kingdom moved through various iterations. At first, Jesus' message was simply the announcement that the kingdom was at hand. Then, as the disciples preached to the Jews, they preached the good news about Jesus, that He was the promised Messiah, crucified and risen again. But when the message of Jesus reached a Gentile audience, the announcement became more focused: that Jesus was Lord (*Kyrios*). Jesus went from preaching the kingdom to being the content of kingdom preaching after His death and resurrection. But in all cases, the lordship and kingship of Jesus is upheld and heralded. This confession became the core of the Christian message: Jesus Christ is Lord.[1]

Lord of All of Life

For the earliest Christians, accepting Jesus was primarily a very this-worldly exercise in renouncing one lord and proclaiming allegiance to another. It was, fundamentally, an exchange of sovereignties. When we call Jesus Lord, we surrender to Him exclusively and completely. We submit ourselves to Him and renounce all other lords. No ideology, political philosophy, drug, or person can have a higher claim on our lives. All our idols must be pulled down, repented of, and crushed at Jesus' feet. Anything that takes the place of Jesus in our hearts, our passion, and our devotion must go.

Because of the connection between the confessions that Yahweh is King and Jesus is Lord, certain parallels may be drawn. For instance, even a cursory reading of the Old Testament is enough to show that *every* area of life was to be given over to God. Everything was spiritual in the sense that God was concerned with the whole of human life. Nothing was seemingly too mundane for God's purposes and glory. The same is true when one follows Jesus. There is no distinction between what is spiritual and what is not, between what is sacred and what is secular. All of life belongs to Jesus and comes under his lordship.

It's also not enough simply to say Jesus is Lord. We need to show people that we mean this by actually living as if we believe it to be true. As Paul said, we are living letters whose message is constantly being read by others (2 Corinthians 3:1-3). The only way to truly announce the message of the kingdom is to live it (1 Corinthians 11:1; Philippians 3:17; 1 Thessalonians 1:6-9; 2 Thessalonians 3:9; Titus 2:7-8). A consistency between message and messenger is imperative if people are going to be receptive to the message. There is often little integration between our relationship with Jesus and life as we live it. Yet the kingdom demands the opposite. It is not identified by sacred spaces, places, times, or even people. The kingdom is on the move because God is making His enemies His friends, reclaiming His good creation, and bringing this occupied planet under His lordship.[2]

The Lord of All Other Lords

The confessional nature of the early church community got it into trouble with Rome. From the Empire's point of view, Christians were atheists (they denied the divinity of the emperor and did not worship the other pagan gods), cannibals (they consumed the body and blood of Christ), and enemies of human progress and Roman order.

Though their lives were exemplary and winsome, their confession was not.[3] As the kingship of Rome became more and more focused on one man, worship of the emperor as the divine *kyrios* (lord) became common.[4] The imperial cult (as the worship of the emperor was called) was designed to unify the various peoples and deities around the central image of the emperor. Images of Roman emperors began to crop up in temples and other public places so those under Roman rule could worship them.

For the Greeks, this was not a matter for debate or concern. They were not exclusive in their worship, so the emperor could be added easily to their pantheon. In the Roman Empire, religion existed to serve the demands of the state. The Romans believed that for the gods to continue to bless the empire with peace and prosperity, they had to continue to be pleased with the worship of its subjects. So all those living in Roman lands were required to worship the emperor as the representation of all the gods who made Rome great.

For Christians, however, Jesus was Lord. There were no other gods besides Him. To say that Jesus was Lord was to say that Caesar was not. For their refusal to bow down to Caesar's images and confess their allegiance to him, Christians came to be seen as a subversive presence in the Empire. The Christians insisted that their allegiance to Jesus was exclusive. Anyone who would be identified as a Christian had to draw the line here: Jesus is Lord, and there is no other.

Thus the proclamation that Jesus is Lord subverts all other narratives (Roman or otherwise). Luke records for us the accusation leveled against the early church by some men in Ephesus: "They are all defying Caesar's decrees, saying that there is another king, one called Jesus" (Acts 17:7). Rome tried to gain power by subjugating all other gods under the lordship of the Caesar, so the Christian assertion that Jesus is Lord became a deeply subversive claim that undermined the rule of the Caesars.[5] The Roman authorities viewed them with suspicion and ultimately considered them a subversive sect. N.T. Wright makes this comment:

> They were therefore classified as a *political* society, and as such came under a ban on corporate ritual meals. That is, they were seen not just as a religious grouping, but one whose religion made them a subversive presence within the wider Roman society.[6]

The early Christians did little to assure the Romans of their benevolence in this. They regarded themselves as a *polis* (city), *ekklesia* (assembly), *oikos* (family), and *politeias* (commonwealth). All of these were political and social terms used widely in the empire, and in using these, the ancient church set itself up alongside the structures and institutions of Roman culture as a parallel but distinct society. The message of Jesus and His kingdom paralleled and subverted the worship of the emperor in other ways also.

The Christian use of the term *gospel* (or *evangel*) was also very subversive. In the Greco-Roman world from which the early church adopted it, a gospel was a public proclamation of, for example, a military victory announced by a herald who ran back to the city and, with this welcome political news, occasioned public celebration. Also, within the Roman cult of emperor worship, announcements of the birth of an heir to the throne, of the heir's coming of age, of his accession to the throne, and so forth were called *gospels*.

The Gospel writers were announcing the coming of a different king leading a different kingdom. The peace of Rome—*Pax Romana*—came through the torture and humiliation of Rome's enemies. The peace of Christ—*Pax Christi*—came through the suffering and death of the one true King Himself. The peace and community of Christ did not come through conquest and ambition; rather, it came through suffering and reconciliation. Rome was pictured as the *body politic* with Caesar as the head of the body. Paul instead uses this image to picture the body of Christ.[7] Rodney Clapp makes this point well:

> The clincher is that if the early church had wanted itself and its purpose to be construed in privatistic and individualistic terms, there were abundant cultural and legal resources at hand for them to do just that. The early church could have easily escaped Roman persecution by suing for status as a *cultus privatus,* or "private cult" dedicated to "the pursuit of a purely personal and otherworldly salvation for its members" like many other religious groups in that world. Yet instead of adopting the language of the privatized mystery religions, the church confronted Caesar, not exactly *on* his own terms but *with* his own terms.[8]

By selecting and adapting Roman language and structure, the church challenged both the assumptions and practices of Roman society on their turf using their terms. In doing so they proclaimed their allegiance to Jesus, their Lord and King, in a manner that required its members to renounce loyalty to Caesar as God. Thus they intentionally confronted Roman society with a social and this-worldly alternative that incorporated elements of its host culture while remaining a distinct people.[9]

A Colony of Heaven

This parallel community existed within and alongside Roman society but included people from all over the world and had no geographic or political boundaries. From Philippians 3:20 ("our citizenship [*politeuma*] is in heaven"), William Willimon and Stanley Hauerwas demonstrate that the church should be thought of as a "a colony of heaven." They suggest this term because a colony is a "beachhead, an outpost, an island of one culture in the middle of another, a place where the values of home are reiterated and passed on to the young, a place where the distinctive language and lifestyle of the resident aliens are lovingly nurtured and reinforced."[10]

This designation is helpful because it places the church as a confessional community within the real world of other kings and other kingdoms. It allows us to picture what it means to witness to the kingdom in the midst of the culture of this age. The early church understood that its existence not only embodied God's future redemption but also witnessed to the overthrow of evil and the present (and future) coming of the kingdom of God.

Willimon and Hauerwas distinguish between the activist church (a church more concerned with building a better society than with building a better church), the conversionist church (which concerns itself exclusively with the salvation of individual souls because no amount of good works within society can counter the effects of human sin), and the confessional church, which they see as a radical alternative.

> Rejecting both the individualism of the conversionists and the
> secularism of the activists and their common equation of what
> works with what is faithful, the confessing Church finds its main
> political task to lie, not in the personal transformation of individual
> hearts or the modification of society, but rather in the congrega-
> tion's determination to worship Christ in all things.[11]

This is at the heart of what it means to proclaim Jesus as Lord—to worship him in all things. Worship is both the central practice of the church and the eternal purpose of the church.[12] It is what most clearly sets the church apart and what the church is most clearly called to be and do. In worship we are set again in the midst of what is real and reoriented to the true state of things. We are brought back into the cosmic story of creation, fall, redemption, and re-creation, and we both remember and anticipate the work of Jesus. To grow in the kingdom is to have one's whole life increasingly conformed to the pattern of worship. To grow morally means to turn one's life into worship.[13]

We often hear that God is the audience for our worship, and that is certainly the case. But we don't always understand that there is another audience as well, a watching world.

> As we engage in the practice of worship and display the *telos* of
> creation in the redemption of Jesus Christ, we are bearing witness
> to the good news. For worship to be witness, we simply have to
> do the work of the people of God [the liturgy]. We do not have to
> twist or skew worship away from its real purpose in order to bend
> it toward witness.[14]

Subversive Worship

In every way, the message of Jesus and the kingdom subverted the message of the emperor and Rome. To the first-century world, Rome was invulnerable, and the emperor was the lord of heaven and earth. In the book of Revelation, two of the seven churches addressed were centers of emperor worship in Asia Minor (Smyrna and Pergamum). To them and the other communities living under the lordship of

Caesar, John reveals that what lies behind the seemingly invincible juggernaut of Rome is a puppet king. John saw that the emperor is not lord of the earth; Jesus is. And the worship of the emperor was just a faint parody of the praise and service of Israel's God in heaven (Revelation 17–18). The lion turns out to be a lamb (Revelation 5:5-6), martyrs turn out to be conquerors (Revelation 12:10-11) and there is one throne at the center of the universe, and Caesar is not on it (Revelation 4).

The *Pax Romana* was made possible by the cross. People so feared crucifixion that they would think long and hard before rising up against the emperor. It's stunning in this light that the church chose the cross as one of its primary symbols. What could the choice of such an instrument of torture, domination, fear, intimidation, and death possibly mean? For the early church, it apparently meant that the kingdom of God would triumph not by inflicting violence but by enduring it—not by making others suffer but by willingly enduring suffering for the sake of justice—not by coercing or humiliating others but by enduring their humiliation with gentle dignity.[15]

To say it another way, in worship the church confesses the lordship of Jesus over against the rival lords of this world. In worship the church makes visible the good news about the kingdom of God. But to do this faithfully today we must reexamine our worship in the West. The debates between hymns and choruses, choirs and drums, contemporary or traditional completely miss the point. It reveals a sickness in the American church that must be cured. We have divorced worship from justice and obedience, and we often substitute slick, planned-to-the-minute song lists that are poor alternatives to the presence and power of the Holy Spirit. The Scriptures talk more about the kind of worship that God hates than the kind of worship He finds acceptable.[16] Our songs rarely call into question the assumptions, biases, or prejudices of our world and are often more about us than God. Does our worship call us to confront the reality of sin and death in our world with the hope and grace of Jesus? Does our worship expose our blind spots, our unbiblical assumptions, or our unconsidered lifestyles? Does our worship remake our mundane lives, giving them the power and perspective needed to both lament evil and celebrate goodness?

The church, as an alternative community defined by Jesus' way of life, must continually be reminded of who, how, and what it is. But for the most part, our worship has lost its confessional, confrontive, and subversive nature. We see faith in Jesus as a private preference, so worship becomes that also. Worship is only what happens when we are singing in church. Our likes and dislikes take the place of radical engagement with God, His community, and His world. Because of this, people are now more concerned with being fed in worship (and teaching) than in encountering the living God and honoring Him in any way they can.

To witness to the kingdom, the church must confess its king, and it does this most clearly in the practice of worship. In worship we see things as they are and bathe our minds in the alternate reality of the kingdom of God. As the Caesars and Herods of this world come and go, the church reminds itself again and again of the invisible but more important reality: Jesus is Lord, and He is in the process of bringing everything together under His reign. We, the church, exist as a sign of that ingathering, and we, in our worship, testify to its reality.

What is important for our purposes is to notice that the worship of a confessing church is primarily *subversive*. It strikes against the empires and lords of our age who proclaim themselves arbiters of justice, beauty, goodness, or truth. It wars against our individualistic and consumerist preferences by demanding we bow our knee to Jesus regardless of circumstance or mood.

How lacking is this understanding of worship today! In its place, we have settled for church understandings and practices that reinforce the prevailing assumptions of the world instead of challenging them. But the church must proclaim and embody the upside-down nature of the community given over to God's rule.

To a culture that says accumulation is the path to joy, we must say in and through our worship that simplicity and generosity are where joy is. Greed isn't redemptive, and the gospels of Donald Trump and Joel Osteen don't offer a worldview that is ultimately rewarding or worthwhile. The church is and has always been intended to create a new kind of society that sits right next to the world as we know it. In that very regular flesh-and-blood world, the church stands and confesses the lordship of Jesus and the reality of His kingdom. To a culture that is obsessed with looks and beauty, the church stands and declares that external appearance is fleeting and that all the plastic surgery in the world can't make people beautiful if they are not beautiful inside already.

The rule and reign of the resurrected Christ isn't intended to be lofty theological talk; it is meant to change how we relate to each other and to the world, here and now. It is meant to be put on display, to subvert the other things that beckon for our attention and call for our worship. The church is to be a dynamic colony of heaven, a countercultural community whose purpose is to reshape individuals, institutions, and societies with the message and power of the Lord Jesus.

The confession that Jesus is Lord and the message of His kingdom is a gospel that is big enough to embrace earth and heaven, this life and the next. It expresses itself in a life lived to the glory of another, and in a community that worships faithfully and subversively.

To those who think stepping on others is the best way to get ahead, we witness to the reality that we gain our lives by losing them and sacrificing for others. To those who seek revenge, we acclaim that forgiveness and reconciliation are intoxicating and liberating. To those who are lost in the wilderness of sexual confusion, we proclaim the simple purity and fidelity that exists between a bride and groom. Among everything else the church ought to be, in its confessional worship, it is a place that simply tells the truth about the world and its destiny. This is a group of people who resist the values of greed, consumerism, materialism, revenge, power, manipulation, lust, and self-indulgence. It proclaims and embodies a new and better way. Willimon and Hauerwas summarize this well:

The confessing Church, like the conversionist church, also calls people to conversion, but it depicts that conversion as a long process of being baptismally engrafted into a new people, an alternative *polis,* a countercultural social structure called Church. It seeks to influence the world by being the Church, that is, by being something the world is not and can never be, lacking the gift of faith in vision, which is ours in Christ. The confessing Church seeks the visible Church, a place, clearly visible to the world, in which people are faithful to their promises, love their enemies, tell the truth, honor the poor, suffer for righteousness, and thereby testify to the amazing community-creating power of God. The confessing Church has no interest in withdrawing from the world, but it is not surprised when its witness evokes hostility from the world. Witness without compromise leads to worldly hostility. The cross is not a sign of the Church's quiet, suffering submission to the powers that be, but rather the Church's revolutionary participation in the victory of Christ over those powers. The cross is not a symbol for general human suffering and oppression. Rather, the cross is a sign of what happens when one takes God's account of reality more seriously than Caesar's. The cross stands as God's eternal no to the powers of death, as well as God's eternal yes to humanity, God's remarkable determination not to leave us to our own devices.[17]

Chapter 13

Worship in the
Upside-Down Church

> Jesus planted the seed of the kingdom of God with his ministry, death, and resurrection and then gave to the church, the body of all who submit to his lordship, the task of embodying and living out this distinct kingdom. We are to be nothing less than "the body of Christ," which means, among other things, that we are to do exactly what Jesus did…John teaches us that "whoever says, 'I abide in him,' ought to walk *just as he walked*."
>
> GREG BOYD

The worship and the confession of Jesus form and shape the church into an alternative social reality—a colony of heaven. This colony lives alongside the kingdoms of the world while reflecting and seeking to embody the reality of the kingdom of God in both its presence and anticipation. Our witness to the kingdom is communal—we live primarily as a community of worshippers. And this witness is confessional—in word and deed we declare that Jesus is Lord. This already sets us at odds with the world around us. This is as it should be.

The values and norms of our society become so deeply ingrained in our minds that we find it difficult to imagine alternatives. Throughout the Gospels, Jesus presents the kingdom as a new order breaking in upon, and overturning, old ways, old values, old assumptions. If it does anything, the kingdom of God shatters the assumptions that govern our lives. Everything—including our expectations, assumptions, and demands—are reversed in the kingdom of God. Those whom we declare good are not seen that way from God's perspective and vice versa. Tension, paradox, irony, surprise, and mystery all infect the teachings of Jesus. Everything is flipped upside down: the first are the last, to lose our life is to save it, adults must become like little children, sinners receive forgiveness and blessing while the religious miss the great feast, the "poor in spirit" are blessed while the religious leaders are cursed. Nothing is what it seems in the kingdom.

So we must gather on a regular basis for worship. The pressures and images of the present world system dominate our lives so thoroughly that we must regularly reorient ourselves around Jesus and His kingdom. We must regularly gather around a common table in order to confront a world that seeks to divide us from each other. We must pray together to remind ourselves that life in the kingdom is lived through asking, seeking, and knocking, not through our own efforts. In a world like ours, what we do together when we gather is a matter of life and death. We gather to submit our dreams, hopes, desires, and ambitions to Christ, His Spirit, and His church. We gather to recognize His work in our lives and to carry our crosses together as we follow Him. We are unified in our humanness, sinfulness, and confession. Ours is the true story, the story that all the others stories are echoes of. As Karl Barth says, the church exists "to set up in the world a new sign which is radically dissimilar to [the world's] own manner and which contradicts it in a way which is full of promise."[1]

My understanding of this has been altered dramatically over the past few years. As a disciple of Jesus I have woken up to the radical and revolutionary nature of Jesus Christ.[2] That in turn has led me to better see the revolutionary and subversive nature of the church. But *subversive* is exactly the last word that many would use to describe the modern church in America. Instead of countering culture and embodying a new alternative reality, we often reinforce cultural ideals and assumptions instead. How else can we understand the existence of a health-and-wealth gospel or of a therapeutic Jesus who doesn't want to confront sin and conform me to His image, but instead wants to help me through my issues?

Worship often reflects this cultural conformity. Why do we always need happy, shiny songs when so much of life isn't that way? Why don't worship leaders realize they are teaching theology when they choose the songs they do? Why is it that worship is supposed to make us feel better but rarely does? Why doesn't worship confront us more often with the holiness, grandeur, and majesty of God? Why does so much of it seem shallow and hollow and trite and simply about *me?* Where are the prophets, the mourners, and the theologians who will write our laments and anthems?

I am primarily a teacher of the Scriptures, so I have always approached church services thinking the teaching was the focal point, or "end zone" of the service.[3] Worship (by that I meant only the singing and responding part of the service) was merely a prelude, an appetizer to the main course, or the introduction to the message. But the Scriptures have convinced me otherwise. Worship is the "end zone" and the point of our gathering. My job as a teacher is to call people to worship and obedient response. Worship is the point; information isn't. I love how Paul puts it in Romans 12:1: "Therefore, I urge you, brothers, in view of God's mercy, to offer your bodies as living sacrifices, holy and pleasing to God—this is your spiritual act of worship."

This is also all over the Psalms. Worship is our response to God's initiative. It is responding with our whole lives to everything God is and everything He has done. It is reminding ourselves of His past faithfulness, celebrating or lamenting our present circumstances, and anticipating the day when Jesus returns and all is made right. Confessional worship, I have come to realize, is a response to the revelation of God. We don't confess that Jesus is Lord until we have seen Jesus. So my job as a teacher is to reveal the God within and beyond the Scriptures so that people may worship in response to Him. This has changed the way I teach and the way we, as a community structure our services. Instead of leading with worship, we put the teaching part of the service toward the front so that the back half of the service is spent worshipping: lamenting, celebrating, praising, thanking, responding, reconciling, repenting, confessing, listening, singing, and so on. We call that time of worship our response time, and we ask

God to do the work we cannot as we respond to what we have just heard.

I have learned to love this time of response—not only for myself but also for our church. In it we get a chance to reflect and engage instead of immediately running off to pick up our kids or rushing to lunch. We sit in it, so to speak. And by sitting in it, we are confronted by the reality of the King and His kingdom.[4]

Kingdom worship also dismantles the sacred/secular distinctions so prevalent in modern church and cultural understanding. Designations of sacred space, time, or activity are resisted when the confession of the kingdom (Jesus is Lord over everything) is taken seriously. The secularization of the modern world (believing that some realms exist apart from God's presence) is confronted when the church worships Jesus as risen Lord over all. Confessional worship means that all things are given over to God—including those things formerly thought to be secular or unspiritual.

One prominent value of the modern approach to life is the desire to dissect and categorize something in order to understand it. Thus, modernism introduced distinctions and categories that would have been rarely understood or practiced in the ancient world: natural versus the supernatural, public practice versus private belief, physical versus spiritual, faith versus reason, and sacred versus secular.[5] Confessional worship confronts the legitimacy of these categories and seeks to see everything as having been made to reflect the glory of God. So we bring all that we are, and all that is our world, to God in worship. Nothing is marked off or separated out. In doing so, we reawaken to the possibilities of redemption in all areas of life.

Chapter 14

Flesh and Blood: The Incarnational Nature of the Church

Jesus Christ is the supreme act of divine intrusion into the world's settled arrangements. In the Christ, God refuses to stay in his place. The message that sustains the colony is not for itself but for the whole world—the colony having significance only as God's means for saving the whole world.

STANLEY HAUERWAS AND WILLIAM WILLIMON

There is nothing so secular that it cannot be sacred, and that is one of the deepest messages of the Incarnation.

MADELEINE L'ENGLE

The Incarnation is one of the central paradoxes and mysteries of the Christian faith. That the eternal Word of God became flesh and was born into a Jewish family in the first century is so mind-blowing that we can hardly conceive of its reality. Jesus confined Himself to that time, that place, even that *culture,* and He worked from within it to advance the kingdom. Jesus used Jewish forms and methods of teaching, often using cultural examples or physical settings to make a point. He adapted His message to His audience so that it became good news to them regardless of their station in life. In Jesus' life and ministry, He contextualized His message and methods in order to be heard in a particular historical situation.

The Incarnation fits squarely within the scriptural emphasis that God is dwelling more and more fully with His people. In Genesis 1–2 He creates human beings to live in full and intimate relationship with Him and with each other. In Genesis 3 Adam and Eve choose to live outside the way God made them to live. The first thing that happened after sin entered the world was that Adam and Eve's relationship with God and with each other was interrupted. God begins to restore humanity by calling Abram in Genesis 12 and promising to form the nation of Israel through him.

Fast-forward hundreds of years as the children of Israel are encamped at the foot of Mt. Sinai. As part of the covenant with Israel, God instructs the community to make a tabernacle so He can live and dwell among them. After they're settled in the promised land, the tabernacle becomes a temple, where God resides permanently with His people in the land He had promised to them.

The prologue of John's Gospel reveals God's desire to live among us most dramatically. There the eternal Word of God became flesh and tabernacled (made His dwelling) among us. John intentionally uses Genesis and Exodus language to evoke the significance of the Incarnation. It wasn't enough for God to dwell among humanity; He was so intent about being close to us that He put on a human body. Jesus was, of course, fully divine, just like the Father. At the same time, He was fully human, just like us. He was tempted just as we are, and these temptations were real. They proved that Jesus was not a cheap human imitation, but was in actuality the real thing. When Jesus walked the earth, God was taking up residence in the most intimate way possible as a fellow human being. What kind of story is this?[1]

So the root meaning of *incarnation* is "to embody in the flesh." John 1:14 gives us the picture of what this means: The word (Jesus) became flesh and made His dwelling among us. The Incarnation was the trinitarian God's definitive movement toward redemption as Jesus condescended to take on human form. The awesome creator-God drew close enough to His creation to be touched, heard, seen, and remembered.

A Template for the Church

The Incarnation provides a template for the church and its ministry to the world. Just as Jesus drew near, so does the church, for it is now the temple (dwelling place) of the living God. Just as Jesus did not claim right or privilege but set those aside for the sake of the world, so should the church. For thousands of years, followers of Jesus have sought how best to incarnate (put flesh on) the gospel of the kingdom.

We have already made the point that "the earth is the LORD's, and everything in it." In other words, God's work isn't confined to the church. The whole cosmos is being brought back into right relationship with God. So we have emphasized that the church is not the kingdom; it only witnesses to the kingdom. Incarnation is that attitude that allows this witness to take place.

Because God lives in trinitarian relationship, human beings, made as image bearers, are designed for community and truth that is embodied in others. God created us to want to see and touch and taste things for ourselves, so His intention has always been to have human beings reach other human beings with the good news of what He is like. He has always sought to form a community that witnesses to Him as Creator, Sustainer, and Redeemer. This is how Lesslie Newbigin put it:

> How can this strange story of God made man, of a crucified savior, of resurrection and new creation become credible for those whose entire mental training has conditioned them to believe that the real world is the world that can be satisfactorily explained and managed without the hypothesis of God? I know of only one clue to the answering of that question, only one real hermeneutic of the gospel: *congregations that believe it.*[2]

The early Christians understood this reality better than we do. As the church fostered its own identity as *polis, oikos,* and *ekklesia,* thereby resisting the authority Rome claimed for itself, it did not seek to isolate itself from the rest of the world or concern itself solely with caring for its own. The ancient church did not avoid the other inhabitants of the empire, but planted themselves firmly in their midst. A letter found dating from the beginning of the second century reinforces this idea. It shows how Christians lived:

According as each obtained his lot, and following the local cus-
toms, both in clothing and food and in the rest of life, they show
forth the wonderful and confessedly strange character of the constitution of their own commonwealth [*politeias*]. They dwell in their
own fatherlands, but as if sojourners in them; they share all things
as citizens, and suffer all things as strangers. Every foreign country
is their fatherland, and every fatherland is a foreign country. They
marry as all men, they bear children, but they do not expose their
offspring. They offer free hospitality, but guard their purity. Their lot
is cast "in the flesh," but they do not live "after the flesh."[3]

For the church, incarnation is the posture we take toward God's
work in the world. It doesn't mean that it is up to ourselves to embody
God's work and message, though that is a part of it. *Incarnation*, as
I am using the term, means seeking to enflesh what God is already
doing. As we have seen, I am not the creator and sustainer of God's
work, nor is it up to me to accomplish His purposes in the world.
Rather, the community of witnesses enters the world seeking to point
out, draw attention to, and ultimately embody what God is *already*
doing out in the world. We don't do God's work in the world; we
simply participate in God's work in the world that is already underway.
We look for it and seek to join Him in it, allowing Him to use our flesh
and blood to incarnate its reality. He's always at work everywhere, and
if we look long enough or listen long enough, we'll be able to discern
what He is up to.

Many churches have a theology of extraction that creates a Christian
peer pressure to move away from the world in all its forms. Incarnational people and churches, on the other hand, have a habit of living
among people and participating in the natural activities of the culture
around them (1 Corinthians 9:20-23; 10:23-31). The beginning of the
book of Acts shows this to be true. There, Luke references his previous
work (the Gospel of Luke) as a record of "all that Jesus began to do and
teach" (Acts 1:1). The implication, obviously, was that Luke was going
to record what Jesus *continued* to do and teach through His disciples
and His church. The church therefore participates in, and in this sense
continues, the work of Jesus on the earth.

The Community of the Sent

Missional at its essence means "sent." It is the polar opposite of waiting for people to come to us. It's the antithesis of trying to attract them to us, our programs, our buildings, or our gatherings. Mission cannot be separated from incarnation—the taking on of human flesh. The missional part of redemption was Jesus leaving His Father's side in the heavens and coming to us in human form. The incarnational part of redemption was that Jesus took on flesh and lived among us. For us, mission requires leaving, and incarnation determines the ways we go.

Leaving entails intentionally giving up what is comfy, easy, and familiar and going somewhere else, doing something different, and giving up time so we can connect with people. *Missional* means to be sent, so leaving is where living like a missionary really begins. Leaving isn't only just about going overseas. It's about replacing personal or Christian activities with time spent building relationships with people in the surrounding culture. It is creating margin to be with people who don't naturally fall into the category of "those most like me." It's about being intentional as a repeat customer in shops and restaurants, fighting the temptation to withdraw into our holy clubs and subcultures. Leaving means being intentional about finding opportunities that allow us to move beyond what is safe and secure.

For many of us, this represents a dramatic paradigm shift. Instead of focusing the best of our resources on creating an enriching, entertaining, and moving weekend experience, we must readjust our time and efforts to leaving, sending, and incarnating in the world around us. If Jesus is our model for this, we must examine His life and ministry more closely. For Jesus, the Incarnation included at least these four things:[4]

- *Presence.* God came into our midst and "tabernacled" among us in human flesh.
- *Proximity.* Jesus wasn't aloof or unapproachable. He lived among and interacted with the outcasts and the

socially rejected (Luke 19:10). Jesus was not immune from the sufferings, trials, and disappointments of life in this world.

- *Powerlessness.* Jesus emptied Himself of His divine omnipotence and took on the form of a servant (Luke 22:25-27; Philippians 2:6-7). He did this not only to sympathize with us but also to show the power of love and humility to overcome the greatest of evils.

- *Proclamation.* Jesus announced the message of the kingdom in both word and deed and called for a response of repentant faith.

The church's mission is modeled after Jesus' own ministry. He has commissioned us to simply continue the work He initiated. Certainly there is an unbridgeable gap between the ministry, death, and resurrection of Jesus and our witness to those things, but we are to continue Jesus' work. The work that Jesus calls us to is to bear witness to the kingdom of God and call people to life in that kingdom (life in Christ) by our words and actions. As the church, we are called individually and corporately to embody this incarnational way of living like Jesus did:

- *Presence.* Instead of withdrawing or separating ourselves from the world, we engage the world and live within it. At times, incarnation will simply require us to be part of the fabric of the surrounding culture, meeting people on their terms, loving them without an agenda. It is to be in the world but not of it. The worst thing we can do is to isolate people into Christian subcultures.

- *Proximity.* Just like Jesus, we need to be directly active and involved in the lives of the people we are trying to reach. We must be both present and available to them. We must be willing to engage their world and not wait for them to come to us. We learn to speak their language and learn about their lives. As Paul said, "I have become all things to all men so that by all possible means I might save some."

- A theology of *place* is central to incarnation. We need to reclaim houses and neighborhoods and dorm rooms as places where we are available to God and others to participate in God's redemption. We need to understand that where we live is important because all of the law and prophets hang on loving our neighbors.

- *Powerlessness.* Jesus didn't manipulate or coerce people into the kingdom, nor did He use grand displays of power or promise trouble-free living. He used genuine, humble service to break past their skepticism and touch their souls, and then He called His disciples to follow suit (Luke 22:25-26; Philippians 2:5-7).

- *Proclamation.* Just as Jesus initiated the gospel invitation, we are charged with the role of continuing to proclaim it to a lost and dying world (Matthew 28:18-20; 2 Corinthians 5:18-20), and embody its presence through the ministry of the Holy Spirit.

This is difficult and often tedious work. It is much easier to carbon copy a franchise or reproduce another model or method that has worked elsewhere. I am reminded of the story of Simon the sorcerer. Simon evidently was a rather well-known sorcerer who enjoyed his high status. Once he came upon the gospel of Jesus, however, he believed and was baptized.

> When Simon saw that the Spirit was given at the laying on of the apostles' hands, he offered them money and said, "Give me also this ability so that everyone on whom I lay my hands may receive the Holy Spirit."
>
> Peter answered, "May your money perish with you, because you thought you could buy the gift of God with money! You have no part or share in this ministry, because your heart is not right" (Acts 8:18-21).

The message of the kingdom is not a product to be purchased or a template to be copied. Each time and place and circumstance requires that we wrestle with and discover what God is doing *then and there.* More conferences, seminars, church-growth manuals, or ready-made sermons from freesermons.com are not the answers to incarnation. Luke 17:20-21 reminds us that the kingdom of God is not to be pointed at or visited and studied and taken back and replicated. Workshops will not be able to nail it down with bullet points, and training manuals will not be able to ensure success in your area. Instead we must ask these questions: What does it mean to be the church and witness to the reality of the kingdom for these people, in this place, at this time? What does it mean in our context?

This is why so many church plants struggle. What worked for the mother church often doesn't translate into other areas. And this is compounded by our repeated assertions that bigger is better and the answer to the question of what is working is tied directly to where there are numbers. The lie is that if something is big it is worth being copied, but that is taking the easy way out.

Incarnation assaults the most acceptable form of idolatry in the church today: the idea that all this is about my ministry (what I do for God). We rarely pursue God directly (for His own sake) but instead pursue external events and experiences that we call ministry in order to meet our own needs and the needs of others. When we make ministry our pursuit, and an end in itself, we lose the very thing we're after—God's presence and blessing. Ministry is always a by-product of something much bigger and deeper—the pursuit of God himself.[5]

Would You Like Jesus with That?

One way that we may think of this is to contrast two separate but interrelated understandings of the church. For lack of better terms, I'll call them the incarnational understanding of church and the functional/instrumental understanding of church.[6]

Many of us understand the church to be the community of God that He uses to fulfill His purposes (functions) and to do His work. In other words, we see the church as God's instrument on the earth to do certain things. He uses the church like an instrument to do work He wants done. On this understanding the church is where the functions take place: You learn the Bible, get married, have a funeral, learn to worship, find community, and so on. The church is an instrument used by God to perform certain functions in the world.

The natural focus for this understanding of the church is on programs. God uses the church to do things, so we create programs and ministries to do those things: marriage ministries, children's ministries, youth ministries, counseling ministries, and the like. If programs are the focus of the church, we need to spend a lot of time evaluating them. Are the things we are doing the best things we could do? Is this doing what we thought it would? Is it successful? Is there enough "bang for the buck"? If not, we add, change, or remove our programs by bringing in new people or curriculum or whatever.

This instrumental/functional understanding of the church leads inevitably to the church being thought of as the building—you go to church. We go to church because church is the place where we do certain religious things.

To some degree, this is a correct (if unbalanced) view of things. Certainly, the church is to do the work that God has called it to do. But my question is this: Is the functional/instrumental view of church the *primary* understanding we are to have? I don't think so. Robert Webber's comments here are instructive:

> The church, like a tribe, is a cultural community defined by the story of God. This story and shared vision is taught and communicated primarily as a lived experience...Therefore it is important during [discipleship] to experience the biblical nature of the church. The church is not a mere voluntary society of like-minded believers, but a continuation of the presence of Jesus in and to the world. It is the "body of Christ," the real extension and continuation of the incarnation, death, resurrection, and anticipated return of Christ. Therefore the church belongs to the narrative of God's activity in the world. To come into the church is to come into the locus of God's presence. The church not only has a story of God's saving presence

and grace, it *is* the present actualization of the story. To participate in the church is to be disciplined by its self-understanding, ethic, and vision.[7]

The incarnational understanding of the church begins with the understanding that in some strange way, the Incarnation of Jesus continues in and through His people. If we are the body of Christ, then through His church, Jesus still walks the earth in human form. By suggesting this, I am in no way minimizing the continued ministry of Jesus at the right hand of the Father. Rather, I am attempting to get us to think differently about what church might be. In the incarnational understanding, programs are not the focus; *presence* is—the manifest presence of God in our midst. Is God present in the stuff we are doing? Do we need more religious committee meetings? Do we need more people singing nice religious songs? If God doesn't take up residence in our singing, then it is just noise. The problem in many churches is that you can explain what happens there solely by reference to human gifting and resource. I want to be a part of a community where you can't—all I know is that God is present there in some unique way, and none of us can explain it. We are to be this place where God literally takes up residence.

If this is the focus, then the questions we ask are different. Instead of evaluating programs, we ask questions about whom we are pursuing or what are we becoming. Are we becoming more and more the kind of people where God is free to unleash beauty and joy and peace and healing and forgiveness? Are you more free than you were six months ago? Or are you more bound? Are you praising God more than you were six months ago—are you finding yourself bursting out with spontaneous awe more now? Are we becoming like Jesus? More compassionate? Weeping more? More apathetic? Are we becoming the kind of people whose hearts are like God's? The more we become like Jesus and care about the things He cares about, the more He is free to do "God things" in our midst.

Obviously, we have to do something. We can't just sit around; we have to perform certain functions and do certain things. We have to have programs and ministries and budgets and leaders (though even this statement is debatable). But are they the focus, or is the presence of Jesus the focus? Under the incarnational understanding of the church, one doesn't go to church, one is the church. Is the building special? Not at all. Rock Harbor meets in a bar, in a warehouse, and in dorms, shops, and homes all across southern California. The building is just the place where the church gathers, but it isn't the church.

The church focused on the kingdom of God is incarnational. It sees itself as participating and enfleshing the work of God in Christ out in the world. More than just programs and ministries, the church constitutes, in some strange way, the hands and feet of Jesus. As Jesus took the path of descent to become one of us, the church likewise must see itself as drawing near to the world around us.

Chapter 15

Postures of Incarnation

> The community of those who submit to Christ's lordship are in a real sense to *be* Jesus to the world, for through the church Christ himself continues to expand the reign of God in the world. We collectively are his "second" body, as it were, through which he continues to do what he did in his "first" body. Through us, Jesus continues to embody the kingdom of God in the world. Christ dwells in us and among us individually and corporately, and he longs to live *through* us individually and corporately.
>
> GREG BOYD

When we usually use the word *posture,* we refer to the physical bearing of a person, the way he or she carries himself or herself physically. But *posture* can be used another way—to refer to a person's attitude or orientation toward something. What does incarnation require once we are in relationship with people and the world around us? In this, we are fighting human nature at every point: All of us will relapse toward selfishness, apathy, and narcissism if left to ourselves. These postures are the work of the Spirit, not attitudes to be conjured by an act of the will. God emptied Himself, so we need to reverse the values we currently see in the church. The church should not be about popularity or prosperity, but about serving the poor and reconciling racial tension. Christians know God hates poverty and disease. And if that's true, we should fight to change that, to bring about justice and mercy to the world.

A Posture of Expectant Waiting

Doing the hard work of incarnation involves waiting on God. Before anything else can change, I must wait.[1] The work of incarnation can happen only if God speaks into us, peacefully shapes us, and graciously guides us. This wars against our "I need it yesterday!" culture. We prefer immediate change, visible results, or a miracle solution. We are tempted to look for a new meeting, structure, building, or plan. We like to be there now, with no mess, no fuss, no hassle or journey or responsibility or pain. Our ability to wait is inversely proportional to the speed at which we live. We are driven and rushed, often speeding past God-shaped avenues and possibilities and settling for the obvious paths that maintain the status quo.

A Posture of Interruptibility

I believe it was Henri Nouwen who said, "I used to hate interruptions to my ministry until I understood that interruptions were my ministry." Jesus was perfectly interruptible. This is not to say He was without purpose or intention. A great example of this is found in Mark 5. The daughter of one of the leaders of the local synagogue is dying, and Jesus is on His way to the man's house when a woman who had a bleeding problem touches the hem of His cloak. Jesus stops and asks who touched Him. The woman humbly identifies herself, and then Jesus proceeds to listen to her entire story. Can you imagine what you would be thinking if you were one of Jarius' household? Jesus clearly is on His way, yet He takes time to listen to and heal a woman who had been crushed by the religious structures of her day.

One way my family and I try to practice this is through the way we play with our kids. We want our house to be a place that people want to visit, so we have stuffed our driveway and front yard full of balls, basketball hoops, a trampoline, waterslides and pools, fun sprinklers, bikes, scooters, sidewalk chalk, and action figures. We made a conscious decision to put all this stuff in the front of our house rather than in the backyard so that we become interruptible and our neighbors feel free to drop by. We have developed some great neighborhood relationships from this, and we very much enjoy "being present" in our community, watching for the signs that God is at work.

A Posture of Prayerful Discernment

We believe that God is always at work, so every conversation, task, e-mail, meeting, or class carries the opportunity for us to participate in the work of God's redemption. We simply ask the Holy Spirit to wake us up to whatever God is doing in the people around us. Perhaps burning bushes are all around us, if only we'd pay attention. The work of incarnation requires discerning what is of God and what is just a good idea. It takes patience and a great deal of hard work. We listen to the news or read the newspaper differently. We pay attention to the world around us to pick up the currents of the Spirit. We ask God to show us where the kingdom is invading our world and then look for it. Again, all this requires the hard work of paying attention and learning to recognize the sure signs of Jesus. This helps us avoid the real danger of being assimilated by the culture instead of helping to transform it.

The big question is, how do we avoid the twin missteps of separatism (withdrawing from the world) and assimilation (adopting the world's values and priorities)? This is a narrow road to be walked. Selective engagement with culture requires patience, prayer, and discernment. N.T. Wright offers a helpful analogy. Suppose we possessed only the first four acts of a Shakespearean five-act play. Would we archive the play? Or would we call together the Shakespearean scholars and invite them to immerse themselves in the first four acts so they could try to finish it? This situation is similar to where we find ourselves. We have the first four acts of the biblical story: creation, fall, Israel, and Jesus. We are also given the beginning of act five: the church and its mission. The end of act five is the new creation. We must immerse ourselves in the first four acts to know the text well enough to continue the story.

A Posture of Courageous Faith

We present ourselves to the Lord Jesus to be used by Him if He chooses, in whatever way He chooses. This, at times, may require us to look and feel a bit ridiculous. Andrew Purves offers the following suggestions:

- Announce the love and presence of God to people.

- Care for people by listening, affirming, encouraging, or praying.

- Bear witness to Jesus and to His present, living, and reigning ministry of grace to people.

- Help discern and interpret people's life situations by pointing out possible manifestations of grace and blessing.

- Engage in symbolic action. Incarnate the reality that you have been speaking of. Prayer, touch, Communion, confession, pronouncing forgiveness...any of these may be appropriate, depending on the Lord's leading.

As a parent, I find myself constantly talking to our kids about the difference between their outside voices (loud and rowdy) and their inside voices (softer and kinder, with less screaming!). I have found that, in my experience anyway, God has an outside voice (which is direct and grabs attention) and an inside voice (the "still small voice" the Scriptures talk about). For whatever reason, God likes using His outside voice with me.[2]

My family and I were traveling back from Ohio to California via the Houston airport. Our arrival into Houston was late and gave us only ten minutes to traverse the *one mile* between gates before the flight to Ohio departed. My wife literally hijacked one of those beeping carts and coerced the driver into helping us to our gate. We arrived just as the doors were closing. We made it, but not by much. That was when I heard God clearly say, in His outside voice, *There is a reason you are on this plane.*

Yes, I thought, *to get home!* And I began to read a book.

About two-thirds of the way through our flight, a significant commotion behind me was followed by a piercing shriek and an otherworldly series of moans. I turned around and saw a small boy (I later found out he was ten) punching, slapping, and kicking a woman three rows behind me. He appeared to be trying to climb over the seat in front of him, and the woman was attempting to hold him down.

Needless to say, the whole atmosphere of the plane changed instantly and dramatically. I, on the other hand, returned to my book.

Go and offer to help that woman, said the Lord, again using His outside voice. I reluctantly put my book down (I think it was the last Harry Potter book) and thought about how in the world to approach this woman. *Go and offer to help that woman,* Jesus said again.

So I, a very reluctant minister, walked back and put my hand on the woman's shoulder. By this time she was literally laying on top of the kid to keep him in his seat.

I asked if I could help her.

She turned toward me, and I will never forget the look in her eyes. It was one of sheer horror and humiliation. This boy was her son. He was severely autistic and terrified of the airplane, and he was trying to make his way to the exit row so he could climb out. The mom said that she was flying alone with her son for the first time, and she was horrified of the scene he was causing.

I smiled. One of our children is mildly autistic. I thought I knew how to handle this. I went back to my wife and grabbed our bag of goodies. Every parent comes to rely on this bag in cases of extreme airline emergency. It had videos, crayons, Matchbox cars, and treats. But none of these things held any interest for the young boy three rows back. He continued to cry and writhe and attempt to climb out of the headlock his mother had him in.

Why don't you pray for him and ask Me to do something, the Lord interjected.

Now, I have to confess at this point that I have prayed a lot for God to do stuff, and very often none of it happens (at least that I can see). So I kind of rolled my eyes at Jesus, put my hand on this woman's shoulder, and began to pray.

I no sooner had gotten the "dear Jesus" part out of my mouth when everything changed. I am not kidding—the whole scene changed in a heartbeat. It was as if Jesus Himself arrived on that plane and the *shalom* (peace) of God settled over this little boy and his mom. The boy relaxed and melted into his mother's arms, and the mom's eyes and her whole body released their tension.

This is the best I can explain it. One minute, the boy was freaking out. The next, the Holy Spirit revealed His presence and peace, and everything changed.

I went back to my seat, weeping, astonished at God's mercy to a special child and his mom.

As I reflect on that event, I am so thankful that God gave me the grace to step out and trust that He was working. I was uncomfortable, I didn't want to take the risk, and I was worried I would look foolish. Yet God used a clown like me to bring a little of the peace of His rule on earth. I would have been diminished otherwise.

I didn't know it then, but I was doing the work of incarnation—enfleshing the love of Jesus to the broken and hurting around me.

Chapter 16

Baptism as Civil Disobedience

> Jesus was not just a moralist whose teachings had some political implications; he was not primarily a teacher of spirituality whose public ministry unfortunately was seen in a political light; he was not just a sacrificial lamb preparing for his immolation, or a God-Man whose divine status calls us to disregard his humanity. Jesus was, in his divinely mandated (i.e., promised, anointed, messianic) prophethood, priesthood, and kingship, the bearer of a new possibility of human, social, and therefore political relationships. His baptism is the inauguration and his cross is the culmination of that new regime in which his disciples are called to share.
>
> JOHN HOWARD YODER

The church is an alternative community that is formed and sustained by and through practices like Communion and baptism. Public worship services and liturgy are not ways of escaping the real world. Rather, they get us back in touch with it. Certainly, God is at work everywhere and at all times. He cannot be contained in the fleeting moments of corporate worship. Yet those moments, if understood and practiced correctly, have the power to reorient our myopic vision far beyond ourselves back onto the kingdom of our God. Baptism and Communion, as central elements to public worship, provide us with the vision we need to be the church in the world. Now more than ever, as the church stands at the margins of culture, the church must make its worship public and embodied.

The church testifies to the work of God both in its midst and beyond its walls, and the practices of Communion and baptism are designed to be the clearest and most vibrant expressions of the gospel. As such, they cannot be understood or faithfully practiced apart from the whole life of the community. God has chosen baptism and the Eucharist as our most public witness to the nature and reality of the kingdom. They are, in Robert Webber's words, performative symbols.[1] Performative symbols are ways in which God's saving presence is made a reality through physical signs or acts. They perform the story that is being spoken. They point beyond themselves and participate in what they point toward. Performative symbols are based on the doctrine of the incarnation: The human and divine are united in the person of Jesus, so we can affirm that God can and does work through the physical stuff of creation.

Baptism is most of all oriented toward our participation in community. This rite inducts the new believer into the shared practices of the believing community, which is defined and ruled by the story of Christ's life, death, and resurrection. Baptism is a sign of new birth and our new identity in Christ.

Baptism

In this chapter we want to examine baptism in its proper kingdom and eschatological context. Baptism is tied to the great exodus narrative of how God saved the nation of Israel from Egypt through the waters of the Red Sea and into the wilderness. Of equal importance was Joshua's crossing of the Jordan River, leading the nation of Israel into the promised land.

So it is not surprising when we come across John the Baptist out in the wilderness calling people to be baptized in the Jordan River. His whole enterprise smacked of new exodus imagery as he exhorted the people to prepare themselves for the one who would fulfill all of God's promises to Israel.

Rabbinical teaching of the day said that if all Israel would repent for just one day, Messiah—the anointed king—would come. Following that tradition, John the Baptist called people to turn from sin and back to God. People trekked from all over Israel to the Jordan River to confess their sins and receive John's baptism as a sign of cleansing. In a symbolic way, he excommunicated unrepentant Jews and then baptized them back into God's covenant, much like what was done to Gentile converts.[2] If we are to follow Jesus, we must join Him on the riverbank. This is where the kingdom is first revealed because this is where the king is first revealed. To join Jesus means that we acknowledge our own sin, repent, and surrender to Him. To repent means to surrender one's agenda for Jesus' agenda. It means to take on His kingdom message and ministry.

Interestingly, Jesus Himself submitted to John's baptism as a form of solidarity with Israel in repentenace and renewal. The Holy Spirit anointed Jesus as He came up out of the water, and a voice from heaven declared that Jesus was God's true Son and the long-awaited Messiah. Jesus referred to His future suffering and crucifixion as a baptism also.

When John baptized Jesus, all Israel's history was summed up in one symbolic act. Just as Israel went through the Red Sea in the first exodus, so Jesus went through the Jordan in the final exodus. Instead of deliverance from Pharaoh, Jesus offered deliverance from Satan himself, transferring all who follow Him into the kingdom of God.[3] The New Testament writers used several pictures from the Old Testament to describe what baptism means: exodus (1 Corinthians 10:1-2), circumcision (Colossians 2:11-12), and the flood (1 Peter 3:19-21).

As the early church reflected on the nature of the act, it came to have many layers of symbolism. It pointed to new birth, new exodus, and new creation. But most importantly, it came to be linked with the crucifixion and resurrection of Jesus in Romans 6:1-8. There, Paul argues that we share in Christ's death and resurrection so that we may share in His new life. Our old lives are crucified with Christ, and we rise out of the water to new life. Baptism declares the mysterious reality that crucifixion and resurrection weren't events that happened only in the life of Jesus; they happened to us also. Baptism became the central picture of what it means to be born again, as a convert was plunged into the water and blessed in the name of the one God: Father, Son and Holy Spirit (Matthew 28:19). Jesus' own baptism was trinitarian, and so is ours. Baptism is the sign of what the triune God does—forgives, cleanses, regenerates, adopts, and sends the Spirit into our hearts whereby we cry, "Abba, Father."

Baptism is the rite of entry into the Christian life. It not only symbolizes cleansing of sin (water) but also the death of our old lives (as we go down into the water) and our resurrection to new lives in Christ (as we rise up). It signifies our spiritual exodus, our deliverance from Satan's kingdom and our entry into God's kingdom. But baptism is not just a symbol; it is also an event.

It is the event and reminder that the kingdom of God is now within reach. God is establishing His justice and sovereign rule in this world to uphold His law and forgive, receive, and transform sinners. He turns our values upside down. For the kingdom of God to fully come, Jesus had to become the suffering servant of Isaiah 53, taking the place of sinners, satisfying divine justice, and dying the death we all deserved for our sins. In the death of Jesus, God's justice was satisfied (upheld), the moral and legal debt of all our sin was paid in full, and God's mercy was extended to each of us. He didn't quit being a God of wrath and suddenly become a God of love; He has loved us continually from all eternity. But the ground on which He could accept us was dramatically changed. The penalty for sin was paid, and all who have faith in Jesus are freely and fully justified. At the cross, God lifted His wrath from us and placed it upon Himself through His Son (Romans 3:26).

To be a Christian is to be in Christ, that is, baptized into His body, the church, of which each person is a constituent member (1 Corinthians 12:12). This is the basis of Paul's appeal to the church in regard to ordering their lives and relationships with each other. There must be mutual dependence. (The eye cannot dismiss the hand, and the head cannot dismiss the feet. This calls for recognition of different gifts and support for the weaker ones.) But individuals are not absorbed into a nameless, corporate entity. The Trinity is characterized by the distinct persons in relationship, and this offers a pattern for human relationship.

Baptism as Civil Disobedience

Religious conversion (in the modern sense) was practically unknown in the ancient world. You either added your particular deity to the existing pantheon, or you identified him or her with one of the existing gods. Roman religious policy was remarkably tolerant. But it did insist on a gesture of loyalty from all the subjects of Rome to the divine Augustus. This Christians were unwilling to do. They acknowledged only one divine Lord. This is why conversion and baptism were not just private matters between an individual and God, but were social acts with profound social and religious implications. "Faith in Christ was political, ethical, and communal. Living under the reign of God meant a new political allegiance, a new set of ethical values, and a communal life among the people of God."[4]

Faith in Jesus, far from being a private matter solely between the individual and God, amounts to being assimilated into a new people. People believe the gospel and through it become God's covenant people. Gentiles (non-Jewish people), through baptism, are incorporated into the body and life of God's people. Baptism is initiation into a new culture called *church*. In baptism we die to our individualistic consumer preferences and privatized notions of faith and identity, and we rise anew into the community of Christ.

Followers of Christ have a new identity because they have been baptized into Christ and adopted into God's family. We take on a new family culture. The biological family, let alone the nation-state, is no longer the primary source of identity, support, and growth. Seen in this light, baptism is profoundly subversive. This was the center of the church's conflict with the Roman Empire—in its baptism the church boldly insisted that here was a kind of allegiance to God and to others that was more significant and constitutive than that of biological family or the state.

Baptism pictures a transfer of loyalties, the replacement of former allegiances by a new allegiance to Christ as Lord. This confession places us in a new fellowship—the community of those who confess Jesus.

That is why our union with Christ includes inclusion into His body, the church (1 Corinthians 12:13).

Baptism is civil disobedience. The New Testament understands life in the church as a kind of resocialization, an enculturation according to the standards of the kingdom rather than those of the world. When the church and state merged, baptism was stripped of its political significance and subversive potential because in that setting the church was no longer seen as a distinctive and challenging culture. When the church takes itself seriously as an alternative culture, baptism is a subversive act of worship.

Through practices like baptism, the church maintains itself as a community that bears witness to the kingdom reality that Jesus has defeated the powers of Satan and is now bringing all things under His authority. Baptism testifies to the reordering of the cosmos under Christ's rule. As John Howard Yoder says, "The very existence of the church is its primary task. It is itself a proclamation of the lordship of Christ to the powers from whose dominion the church has begun to be liberated."[5]

Baptism as Eschatological Immersion

Baptism symbolizes our spiritual union with Christ. Like Him we are crucified (putting to death our old sinful life) and resurrected (raised to new life). Through baptism, we are immersed in God's story of love and redemption, and in our public confession we anticipate our full participation in His resurrection at the eschatological renewal at the end of the age. The resurrection of Jesus is both the assurance that the new age has begun and the assurance that it will be brought to completion. The resurrection of Jesus gives us a glimpse into our futures.[6]

In linking to both Jesus' death and resurrection, baptism points beyond our initiation into the Christian life to the goal of God's saving activity.[7] This goal includes glorification, the transformation of all believers at Christ's return (Romans 8:11, 1 Corinthians 15:51-57) and our participation in the eschatological community of God. En route to that goal lies the process of sanctification, as the Spirit continually renews us in our Christian walk (Romans 8:9; 2 Corinthians 3:18).

Baptism is eschatological because it is practiced with a view toward our future in the kingdom of God, the glorious eschatological fellowship of God with His people. The believer's story is not consummated in baptism, it is only inaugurated. This act points to the coming of God's reign and symbolizes our hope of participating in that eternal community. For this reason, Paul described the presence of the Holy Spirit, whose coming upon the believer is symbolized by baptism, as a pledge of the reception of God's full inheritance at Christ's coming (2 Corinthians 1:22; 5:5; Ephesians 1:14). This imagery comes from the exodus story, where the promised land was Israel's inheritance and God's presence among the people was both the foretaste of that inheritance and the means by which it would be gained (1 Corinthians 10:1-2). Similarly, the presence of the Holy Spirit in us points inescapably to the same reality. He is the foretaste of our inheritance in Christ and His new creation, as well as the means by which we attain it. In Romans 8:23, Paul calls the Holy Spirit the firstfruits of the coming renewal.

Baptism points to the baptism of the Holy Spirit—the Spirit given so that the church can share in the life and ongoing ministry of Jesus, who now sits in the position of supreme authority at the right hand of the Father. N.T. Wright puts this well:

> The Spirit is given so that we ordinary mortals can become, in a measure, what Jesus himself was: part of God's future arriving in the present; a place where heaven and earth meet; the means of God's kingdom going ahead...The Spirit is given to begin the work of making God's future real in the present.[8]

This means that we live at the intersection of the present and the future. Jesus' resurrection opened the door to God's new creation (He was the firstfruits of what is to come), and the Spirit now helps us to begin to live in that new creation here and now in the midst of the fallen world we live in. This paradox is what baptism represents:

dying to the old and embracing the new even though they are both still present in us and in the world. Learning to live in the new reality is the most difficult task confronting us as disciples of Jesus. The old rules of this world no longer apply, but they are all we know. The church functions both as a reminder and as the living embodiment of this new age, training those who are new how to operate by a different set of rules and values that come from a kingdom "not of this world." We are literally part of God's new creation (2 Corinthians 5:17) and have become the temple of God because He now resides in us (1 Corinthians 3:16).

Implications

As we consider anew the practice of baptism, we are confronted by the cost at which the early church identified itself with Jesus. For them, baptism was a public and subversive declaration of believers' new identity as followers of Jesus the Christ. Once people were baptized, they were exhorted to "live their baptism," meaning that they should live in the reality of what baptism means.

We need to recapture this aspect of baptism today. In baptism our former identities (as Democrat or Republican, addict or failure, son or daughter, employee or employer, white or black) are washed away. Imagine what would happen if a community actually began to live this out and identified themselves primarily as members of God's new people. How subversive would we be if old political or business allegiances were rethought in light of our baptism, or if the bonds of biological family were loosened in the waters? What would happen if the United States was dethroned from its place of eminence in our pledges of allegiance as we pledged ourselves to a kingdom of an entirely different sort? Might we behave differently were we to take the old admonition of "living our baptism" upon ourselves?

Secondly, baptism reminds us of new life. This is a gospel that moves beyond that of "sin management" and into living out our new birth in Christ.[9] In other words, the resurrection (to which baptism points) is good news not simply because we go to heaven when we die but because we can live differently here and now, as part of God's new creation. Through the person and work of Jesus Christ, God fully accomplishes salvation for us, rescuing us from judgment for sin into fellowship with Him, and then restores His creation, in which we can enjoy our new life together with Him forever. Baptism gives us a tremendous picture of our life now in Christ and our call to live according to what we have already received. We no longer act as if it were up to us to earn God's love, for baptism reminds us that we are already secure. My life now is a matter of living up to what is already true of me (in the same way that I became a husband on my wedding day and now get to spend the rest of my life growing into that new reality). Because our identity has changed, we now engage the world from an entirely different point of view.

Chapter 17

Bread and Wine:
The Meal of the Kingdom

> The *method* of the kingdom will match the *message* of the kingdom.
> The kingdom will come as the church, energized by the Spirit, goes
> out into the world vulnerable, suffering, praising, praying, misunder-
> stood, misjudged, vindicated, celebrating: always—as Paul puts it
> in one of his letters—bearing in the body the dying of Jesus so that
> the life of Jesus may also be displayed.
>
> N.T. WRIGHT

I f baptism is the initiating practice for the church, Communion may be called its sustaining practice. It is the ongoing practice of the community that enables us to participate in God's continual provision of new life for God's people. It incorporates us into the life of the kingdom by that act of remembering Christ as the one who teaches and embodies the kingdom. We cannot participate in the life of the kingdom without knowing what that life looks like. In the celebration of the Lord's Supper, we recall Jesus' own table fellowship with those on the margins and those at center, with the one who would betray Him and the many who would abandon Him. We are at the table by God's invitation and on the basis of the work of Christ. We celebrate this meal as a witness to the kingdom and its work in our world. As we practice, we grow into life in the kingdom.

For the church to witness to the kingdom, it should be Eucharistic. This is not simply a matter of *the practice* of Communion, which is focused on practical and theological questions like these: Is Christ present in the elements? If so, how? How often should Communion be celebrated? Who can participate? Who can officiate?[1]

Certainly these are important questions and worth the attention of our pastors and theologians. But I think the Eucharistic nature of the church is deeper than the practice of Communion; rather, it is an issue of the church embodying what Communion signifies and points to.

For some, the Eucharist is magic. A holy person says the magic words, and *presto!* ordinary bread and wine is turned into the actual body and blood of Jesus. For others, Communion is merely a symbol, a bare reminder that Christ died for our sins. My own view is that the truth lies in neither of these two positions, but that is a discussion for another time.[2] For our purposes, whatever your beliefs, the important point is that the Eucharist reorients us in three directions. As Paul says, "Whenever you eat this bread and drink this cup, you proclaim the Lord's death until he comes" (1 Corinthians 11:26).

The Past

Faith is nourished by remembrance. The story began without us, as a story of the way that God is redeeming the world, a story that invites us to join in and be saved by sharing the work of the new people whom God has created in Israel and Jesus. This participation saves us by placing us within an epic story of God's redemptive purpose for the whole world, and by communally training us to fashion our lives in accordance with what is true about the world rather than what is false. Early Christians began not with esoteric speculation about the nature of the incarnation, but instead with stories about the real Jesus, about those whose lives were caught up in His life.

In the Lord's Supper, we are turned backward and not only are reminded of the sacrifice of Jesus on behalf of us but also are placed again within the story of God's people. The central celebration and festival of the Jewish nation was Passover. Passover, of course, was the festival that God commanded the generations of Israelites to commemorate when He delivered them from the Egyptians in the Exodus. One thing that was unique about Jewish sacred meals was that they were more than simply memorials, more than mere rememberings of the events that happened to their forbears centuries earlier. Rather, the

Jews view their festivals as participatory remembrances in the events they celebrate. That is, they don't suppose they are essentially doing something different from the original event. They don't just remember something that happened to someone else, they place themselves again in the story. Even today when Jews celebrate Passover, they say, "This is the night when God brought us out of Egypt." In other words, they don't see the exodus as happening to other people; the focus on the meal is that it happened to *them*.

The technical word for this kind of remembering is *anamnesis*. It is a word of rich significance and does not simply denote recollection of some remote date of bygone history, but instead refers to a participation in the past event itself. The celebration of Passover during and before Jesus' era was not seen as the mere celebrating of a memorial meal of purely symbolic value.[3] Passover is more than mere remembering; it is the way the Jews place themselves in the ancient story.

Jesus adapted the Passover meal and applied elements of it to Himself, signifying the importance of what He was about to do in a new exodus context. He took the Passover bread and used it to point to His own body, which would be given up on behalf of others. He took Passover wine and said that a new covenant (the one Jeremiah spoke of) would be the result of the shedding of His blood. The command to "do this in remembrance of me" is reminiscent of Yahweh's commands to the Israelites to remember the Passover every year for generations. So we can be reasonably confident that in our remembrance of Communion we do not merely memorialize the sacrifice of Jesus as an isolated date from 2000 years ago. We remember it in such a way that we know by the grace of God that we are the people for whom our Savior died and rose again. We are the people whose sins Jesus confessed on the cross. We are the people with whom God has made a new covenant and who are now citizens of His kingdom. The Eucharist brings the past crashing into the present so that everything that defines us from our past—our failures, mistakes, sin, regrets, and hurts—is swallowed up again by the grace of Jesus.

Here's a cultural stereotype: Americans have little to no collective memory. Some of that is a reflection that our nation is barely more than 200 years old. But some of that amnesia comes from our "I want it now" society, our addiction to immediate gratification. We share in that legacy as evangelicals. Again, I am speaking generally (and including myself), but in our never-ending quest for relevance and innovation, we overlook much in our past. As the center of Christianity has moved away from North America, we seem especially susceptible to one of two errors. The first is a nostalgic, over-idealized yearning for the "good old days" of Christianity, when America was supposedly a Christian nation or when prayer was allowed in public schools. The opposite error also beckons: forging ahead with little or no thought about how previous generations of disciples have dealt with some of the pressing issues of today.

In the Eucharist, we are pulled backward and again centered on the core of our faith. This is not out of false nostalgia. Rather, we look back and are reoriented within the community of faith that allows us a balanced, holistic view of the present and future. We are placed again back into the ancient story, reminded that we stand together with millions and millions of others in declaring Jesus to be Lord. The result is that we can reengage the present and the future from a much deeper perspective.

The Present

Paul calls Communion a participation in the body and blood of Christ. Again, much debate surrounds what he means by this. Regardless, it is significant that Communion is not focused solely on the past event of the sacrifice of Jesus, but includes a present communion with Him. This present element to the Eucharist energizes our expectation in worship, prayer, and reflection. Only a thin line separates an ordinary church or Communion experience from an other-worldly one. In Communion the thin partition separating heaven and earth becomes permeable and, like the Israelites in the wilderness, we get a taste now of what awaits us in the promised land (the new creation).

The Lord's Supper is an essential witness to the crucified, risen, and returning Lord. Paul does not assume that the Lord's Supper is a purely symbolic meal. He believes a spiritual transaction is going on (and that a darker spiritual transaction occurred in the meal at the pagan temple).

Our practices of the Lord's Table should also reflect the practices of Jesus as He welcomed sinners to dine with Him. In the ancient Near East, meals were incredibly significant.[4] Mealtimes in first-century Palestine were thought to be pictures of society as a whole. Meals had become religious and social statements, so one's mealtime companions—and who sat where—were invested with serious social, religious, and political meaning. The Pharisees thought of their dining tables as little temples. They insisted on eating only with companions who were in the state of ritual purity (Mark 7:1-4).

To say that Jesus' behavior was scandalous to many in His day would be an understatement. His practice of sharing meals with sinners was a declaration of acceptance and intimacy. Scot McKnight argues, "Jesus saw in his practice of eating with sinners an acted parable of the final constitution of God's kingdom and its forgiveness. The practice symbolized Jesus' entire vision for the kingdom, which was an inclusive and celebrating community."[5]

For Paul, the celebration of communion reversed the social stratification common to Greco-Roman meals and society. This was behind his heated instructions to the Corinthian church on the subject. Evidently, the "haves" in the community were celebrating apart from the "have nots" and using the Lord's Supper to reinforce social and cultural prejudices.[6] Paul desired that the *ekklesia* share the meal in ways that differed from normal Greco-Roman norms and values. Likewise for the community of Jesus today. Does our celebration of the Eucharist point toward the removal of all barriers of race, class, religiousness, or sin? Does it point to the unity that is supposed to exist in the body of Christ? Marva Dawn's comments are demanding:

> To live "the breaking of bread" with congregational integrity—without any barriers between peoples, without any segmentation based

on economics, race, or musical style—demands great weakness. Many of the church marketing gurus advocate churches of homogeneity, appealing to those who are like us so that our churches will grow, but this violates the sacrament of Christ's presence and destroys our testimony to the world that there are no divisions and distinctions among the people of God.[7]

The Future

Finally, and for our purposes most importantly, Communion is eschatological. Paul says that in the Eucharist we "proclaim the Lord's death until he comes." In Communion, the forward comes rushing back into the present. The Lord's Supper has a forward-looking dimension we don't often talk about. N.T Wright puts it this way:

In the Eucharist, bread and wine come to us as part of God's new creation, the creation in whose reality Jesus already participates through the resurrection...If, then, the church is to be renewed in its mission precisely in and for the world of space, time and matter, we cannot ignore or marginalize that same world...Living between the resurrection of Jesus and the final coming together of all things in heaven and earth means celebrating God's healing of this world, not his abandoning it; God's reclaiming of space as heaven and earth intersect once more; God's redeeming of time as years, weeks, and days speak the language of renewal; and God's redeeming of matter itself, in the sacraments, which point in turn to the renewal of the lives that are washed in baptism and fed with the Eucharist.[8]

In the Eucharist and through the death and resurrection of Jesus, this future dimension is brought sharply into play. We must see this as the arrival of God's future in the present, not just the extension of Jesus' past into our present. We do not simply remember a long-dead Jesus; we celebrate the presence of the living Lord. And He lives, through the resurrection and ascension, precisely as the one who has gone on ahead into the new creation, the transformed new world, as the one who is Himself the prototype. We understand Eucharist most fully as an anticipation of the banquet when heaven and earth are made new, the marriage supper of the Lamb.[9] It is the breaking in of God's future into our present.

Implications

Put simply, to orient ourselves around the Eucharist means the church now exists to reenact the ministry and sacrifice of Jesus to the world. Obviously, this is not a literal reenactment. Jesus has died once and for all, and His sacrifice can never be repeated. But Communion offers us a way to see our participation in God's work. Our ways are to become His ways, and His priorities are to become ours. Our purpose is to be found in offering our flesh and blood to the world to be "poured out" on behalf of Jesus. Sometimes the manner in which we minister to the world in the name of Jesus does violence to the Jesus we are trying to glorify.

Because the church is Christ's body, we are to be a gift to the world as Christ is a gift to us all. We are called to embody the sacrifice of Jesus on behalf of the world—to become a living Eucharist, if you will.[10] Paul speaks of his own ministry as sharing in both the crucifixion and resurrection of Jesus.

> But we have this treasure in earthen vessels, so that the surpassing greatness of the power will be of God and not from ourselves; we are afflicted in every way, but not crushed; perplexed, but not despairing; persecuted, but not forsaken; struck down, but not destroyed; *always carrying about in the body the dying of Jesus, so that the life of Jesus also may be manifested in our body* (2 Corinthians 4:7-10; see also Colossians 1:24 NASB).

We are the living Eucharist to the world, here to be broken and poured out for the sake of others. And this means there is a cost. As we benefit in life when Christ gives His body, His Eucharist to us, others gain when we give them ours. This is where we gain our lives by losing them, as they are opened up and poured out for others (Paul refers to his own experience in 2 Timothy 4:6). Communion, then, isn't only the practice of participating in the Lord's Supper. It also forms the shape and content of the church's ministry. John Howard Yoder puts it this way: "To be a disciple is to share in that style of life of which the cross is the culmination."[11]

What does it look like for members of the church to again be sacrificial in their love for others who are not like them? Doesn't everybody love those who love them? To say the church is to be Eucharistic is to say it must embody the sacrificial love of Jesus—a love without boundary, distinction, limit, or worth. How can the church pour itself out for the world? It begins by simply loving people without an agenda. It means that we embrace the path of weakness and descent instead of glorying in our strength and excellence. It means forsaking our narcissism and selfishness and abandoning ourselves to the message and ministry of Jesus. It means doing the hard work of incarnation—we must dive into what God is doing for these people, in this place, at this time.

One of the major causes of the epidemic of irrelevance and dysfunction in our churches is that we have ceased living for something bigger than ourselves. We spend most of our time building our little kingdoms, focusing on our own success and reputation, and in so doing losing the life Jesus has for us but trying to bring it about through our own efforts. We must repent of the hubris of the modern church and embrace again our limits and finitude. We must engage people with humility and honesty about our shortcomings and failures. Churches that do not witness to the power and presence of the kingdom, existing only for themselves, are based on fundamentally mistaken views of the gospel, the kingdom, and the church.

God's people have always been blessed instrumentally. In other words, they have been blessed to give those blessings away. This began with Abram in Genesis 12: "All people on earth will be blessed through you." God told Abram to leave the land he was familiar with because He had something for him to do—a blessing for him to receive. God's blessing is instrumental—His blessing does not end with Abram and is not a blessing for him alone. Abram receives a blessing to become a blessing and dispense that blessing to others.

This is the consistent call of God upon His people—to give away what He has given them.

As David Parker, a pastor acquaintance of mine, has said, the church exists for the benefit of its *non*members. That is why we rightly object to churches that focus solely on themselves. The church was meant to be a gift to the world. Much of the New Testament is based on this: We love with the love we have received; we comfort with the comfort we have enjoyed; we forgive because of the forgiveness we have known. Always and forever, God's favor toward us should in turn lead us into the lives of others.

When we have something so big and wonderful to live for, something so far beyond us, we turn out not to matter as much. We cease being preoccupied with claiming our rights and instead order our lives around the advancement of God's kingdom and mission and the announcement of Jesus' message through evangelism and worship. We are to mirror the kingdom and demonstrate its power, but not through becoming bigger, better, or stronger. Rather, we want to live our lives in a way that allows individual and collective Jesus to manifest His kingdom among us. Concerns about whether we are successful or important simply decrease in value because we become preoccupied with a bigger story. Paul says it this way in Romans 12:1: "Therefore, I urge you, brothers, in view of God's mercy, to offer your bodies as living sacrifices, holy and pleasing to God—this is your spiritual act of worship."

The church exists to worship Jesus and to serve the world. We are no longer here for us—our comfort, safety, prosperity, or success. We must go against a culture in love with power and prestige, and we must ask how we can serve the world around us. We give ourselves away. We want nothing to do with entitlement, manipulation, control, arrogance, or power games; we are interested in how we can serve each other and the world. When you live this way, you align yourself against the culture, and you witness to the kingdom in our midst.

The Eucharist connects us again to the sacrificial nature of our service. For Jesus, the only way the kingdom would truly come was through weakness and vulnerability, sacrifice and love. The kingdom could conquer only by first being conquered in the supreme and unthinkable sacrifice of Jesus. This was the foolishness and weakness of God (1 Corinthians 1:18-25). The coming of the kingdom required the defeat of Christ on the cross. The moment when God appeared weak and foolish, seemingly outsmarted by human and demonic evil, provided the means by which He exposed and judged the evil of empire and religion, and in them, the evil of every individual human being.

The God of Israel and Jesus Christ makes Himself known by entering into a vulnerable relationship with His creatures. God—pre-eminently in the life of Jesus Christ—does not force people to faith but attempts to persuade them to faith. This means the church must renounce any attempt to force or manipulate others into accepting the Christian way of life. We are required instead to affirm our willingness to suffer the consequences of opposition to the kingdoms and powers of this world.

Chapter 18
The Presence of the Future

The Messiah *has* come. The curtain has risen, the last act has begun; all that remains to be fulfilled is the climax of the redemptive drama. Eschatology is not limited to the "end things" of a distant future, the church of which is to be reserved for the final chapter of a theology textbook. The incarnation marks the insertion of a new world into the flow of history; consequently, the "end things" have been made present and there is no longer any chapter of theology lacking in eschatological dimension.

RENE PADILLA

Jesus and the writers of the New Testament spoke of the end times using phrases like "the renewal of all things," "the restoration of all things," and "reconciliation of all things." These images are much different from much of the popular end-times teaching that has been widely accepted in the church. How one sees the end of our story largely determines the predominant messages and methods of the church. This chapter will examine the harm done by a misplaced and misguided emphasis on end-times theology.[1]

The Jews expected that the arrival of the age to come would result in the ending of this current age.[2] One was thought to lead to the other in a linear fashion. But in Jesus something new and unexpected happened. In some mysterious way, the age to come had broken in to this present age while the present age continued. We are now in an interim period between the coming of the kingdom and its fulfillment. The kingdom is now but not yet at the same time. The age to come and this present age coexist in Jesus (and by extension in us). The future age is present, but the present age has not ended. The kingdom was revealed in Jesus, and though it will be consummated at the end of the age, it is now present in Him. The final victory over evil has been won, yet we are surrounded by continued warfare.

Thus, rather than waiting for the last days, we have been living in them since the coming of Jesus. Rather than waiting for the end to come, we are already living in the end times that will be consummated when Jesus returns. Both the resurrection of Jesus and the pouring out of the Holy Spirit attest to this understanding.

In the resurrection of Jesus, what will happen to all of us at the end of time happened to one individual Man in the present. This was contrary to all Jewish belief and expectation concerning the resurrection at that time.[3] Therefore, His resurrection is the beginning of the universal resurrection (to use Paul's phrase, it is the "firstfruits" of the final harvest) before its time. For those in Christ, the transition from death to life has already occurred. Or, to use John's language, those who believe in Christ have *eternal life*—that is, the life of the ages, or life of the age to come—here and now.

A similar point can be made about the pouring out of the Holy Spirit. The Old Testament prophets expected the outpouring of the Spirit as a sure sign of the last days. On the day of Pentecost, the apostle Peter quotes the prophet Joel to make this point. The quotation itself is well-known, but not everyone realizes that the original context of Joel's prophecy is absolutely eschatological (that is, it concerns the signs that will be present at the end of the age). Peter is showing that the age to come broke through in the coming of the Holy Spirit at Pentecost. Those who receive the Spirit receive the power of the world to come.[4] Paul teaches that the Spirit is the down payment, or first installment, of our future inheritance (Ephesians 1:13-14).

We agree that the Holy Spirit is given to empower believers for service and to bring attention to Jesus throughout the world. But to experience the Spirit is also to experience the future age. To live in the Spirit is to taste the age to come.

The last days began with Jesus and Pentecost. We are still living in them. We can speak of the last of the last days, but the last days began with the coming of Jesus and His Holy Spirit, and they continue to this present day.[5] Jesus was the "presence of the future" (to use Ladd's phrase), so the end is present now in and through the community of Jesus, but it still awaits fulfillment and consummation. Jesus was the beginning of the fulfillment of all the hopes and expectations of the Old Testament, but complete fulfillment is still in the future. Jesus is risen, but His resurrection anticipates the resurrection of the dead that will occur at the end of the age. The judgment of God was poured out on Jesus on the cross, and yet judgment will still occur in the future. To experience the presence and power of the Holy Spirit is to partake of the down payment of our future redemption. We pray, "Your kingdom come, Your will be done on earth as it is in heaven," knowing that one day, every knee will bow to Jesus and confess Him as Lord. Paul puts it this way:

> Then the end will come, when he hands over the kingdom to God the Father after he has destroyed all dominion, authority and power. For he must reign until he has put all his enemies under his feet. The last enemy to be destroyed is death...When he has done this, then the Son himself will be made subject to him who put everything under him, so that God may be all in all (1 Corinthians 15:24-28).

For the church to truly reflect the kingdom, the church must live within this eschatological framework, living within the "now but not yet" tension of the kingdom of God. This is what I mean by saying the church should be *eschatological*. It is defined by what has come and what is coming. This has several important ramifications for the church, as Gibbs and Bolger point out:

> The dialectical tension between the church and the kingdom cannot be resolved. The church exists between the time of the inauguration and the consummation of the reign of God on earth. Therefore, it is always the "pilgrim" or the "becoming" church. Furthermore, it is made up of forgiven sinners, not perfected saints, who are at various stages of a life journey of discipleship. Yet the dialectical tension has value in that it safeguards the church from becoming self-focused, institutionally self-sufficient, and

intellectually complacent. The strains and stresses brought about
by the dialectical tension provide a forcible reminder that Christians
are called to live by faith, love, and hope until they stand transformed by the presence of Christ at his glorious return.[6]

The Paradox of the Kingdom and the Mystery of Life

The Christian life finds meaning in the paradox of the kingdom—we are saved, we are being saved, and we will be saved. We
live between the times—we are "already but not yet" people. The
world around us lives in only one age, but we are becoming what
we already are. We are born out of the powers of the future age;
we have eternal life, the life of the ages. If we overstate the present
reality of the kingdom (realized eschatology), we run the danger of
triumphalism and conceive of the Christian life with no suffering,
pain, or failure. If we overstate the future reality of the kingdom
(consistent eschatology) we run the danger of defeatism, escapism,
and the victim/remnant mentality that characterize most other forms
of withdrawal from society.

The eschatological tension implicit in the kingdom is the key to
understanding the Christian life. It allows us to understand we are
not only new creations in Christ but also struggling sinners at the
same time. It helps explain why we see some evidence of the kingdom
(healings, answered prayer, deliverance) and why we don't see more.
The paradoxes in us also exist in the church. The church is the glorious
bride of Christ, but at the same time, it is a frail and often shortsighted
human institution. But of this we are assured: The old human nature is
gradually being overcome by the new human nature, the frail church
is witnessing to the powers and principalities of their sure defeat, and
the "crumbs" of kingdom life we see around us will result in the feast
of the Messiah at the end of the age. We, individually and together,
are glorious contradictions and living paradoxes within which two
ages coexist and overlap.

At times, the kingdom presents itself with such power in the midst
of our world that I am ashamed of ever doubting my faith. Prayers

are answered, the sick are healed, the lost are found, marriages are restored, prodigals come home, worship turns otherworldly, and the words of the Scriptures jump off the page with transforming power. At other times, God seems silent and far off, as if He is concerning Himself with other matters. Or prayers go unanswered for long periods of time, the Bible seems dry, worship is a duty, and prayer is like dust in our mouths. Diseases rage and disasters terrify. Death and sin and evil get more and more press. Living in the overlap of the ages is difficult because of its incompleteness. Life in the kingdom doesn't mean freedom from pain and disappointment. We are not exempt from this fallen world simply because our citizenship is in the *polis* of heaven. Both sides of the tension of the kingdom must be recognized in order to prevent us from despair and disillusionment ("God isn't here," or "He isn't moving") or hollow triumphalism ("just have more faith, and you'll be rich and healthy").

The New Testament writers use phrases like "the present time" (Romans 8:18 NASB), "this present world" (2 Timothy 4:10 NASB), and "the coming ages" (Ephesians 2:7) to attest to the Jewish view that there are only two periods of human history: this age and the age to come. The coming of Jesus into the world was the invasion of the future (the age to come) into the present (this present age).[7] As a result, we can reflect on the life and ministry of Jesus and see the inauguration of the kingdom even though it came unexpectedly, inconspicuously, and modestly. In the crucifixion and resurrection we can see the defeat of Satan and of the powers and principalities that rule this world. And in the ascension and the coming of the Holy Spirit at Pentecost we see our invitation to enter into the realm where Jesus reigns and rules over His people. "We have the privilege of enjoying God's tomorrow in the world of today."[8]

The Thin Line Between Compromise and Withdrawal

This is to say that the church must represent the "now but not yet" eschatological dimension of the kingdom in its message and in its methods. The church lives between the victory of Jesus' crucifixion and resurrection and the triumph and vindication that will characterize the end of the age. When the disciples ask about the coming of the kingdom in the beginning of the book of Acts, Jesus' reply anticipates a delay between the current presence and future fulfillment of the kingdom: "It is not for you to know the times or dates the Father has set by his own authority. But you will receive power when the Holy Spirit comes on you; and you will be my witnesses in Jerusalem, and in all Judea and Samaria, and to the ends of the earth" (Acts 1:7-8).

In other words, the Holy Spirit would be poured out upon the disciples to anoint and empower them to continue Jesus' ministry. That mission would take them from Jerusalem to the uncomfortable soil of Samaria and the unfamiliar soil of the nations. Jesus warned them against needless speculation about His return. Until then His community of disciples was called to continue to proclaim and demonstrate the reality of the kingdom.

The resurrection of Jesus and His ascension to the position of ultimate authority and power at the right hand of the Father, when combined with the Spirit that has been poured out upon His followers, creates the dynamic out of which the church is to minister. Jesus' resurrection assures us that He has conquered sin and death and holds the keys to eternal life, His ascension means that His rule and reign are being extended throughout the comos, and His Spirit anoints and empowers His people to extend the reality of resurrection and ascension to others. Because of this, we proclaim the kingdom from a position of strength and not fear or insecurity. We need not withdraw because the power of the gospel is sufficient to transform communities, nations, and structures. Nor should we compromise to gain acceptance because the kingdom of Jesus is not of this world.

Instead we witness to and preach about a kingdom that destroys all the barriers that keep human beings alienated and separated from each other and from God. The gospel forms a new community made up of new people and leading to a new city located within a new heaven and new earth. Greg Boyd elaborates:

The kingdom of God is not a Christian version of the kingdom of the world. It is, rather, a holy alternative to all versions of the kingdom of the world, and everything hangs on kingdom people appreciating this uniqueness and preserving this holiness. We must always remember that we are "resident aliens" in this oppressed world, soldiers of the kingdom of God stationed behind enemy lines with a unique, all consuming, holy calling on our life. We are called, individually and corporately, to look like Jesus to a rebellious, self-centered, and violent world.[9]

If we fail to understand or appreciate either side of this tension, we will miss the vision of what God has for us *now* and what waits for us in the *not yet*. If both sides are not held in tension, we will fall either into withdrawal and separation from the world around us, or we will delude ourselves into a false triumphalism. Because the resources and power of the age to come are here already, God has given us a mission to participate in His redemptive intent to bring all things back under His gracious rule. No other movement, cause, self-help philosophy, or article of legislation can do this. Without Christ, all other attempts to change the world will fail.

But this shouldn't lead us to defeatism, separation, or some version of escapism. Instead, because we know that the kingdom is here and that the King is present, we should be the most hopeful and prophetic people on earth. Far too often the church has abdicated its eschatological voice to human intuitions or philosophy.

The Thin Veil

The barrier between this age and the future age is now torn. The Scriptures do not distinguish between the "spiritual" parts of this world, but something is now available to ordinary people in ordinary places that had not been available previously. Derek Morphew offers this explanation of "the thin veil":

People worshipping though outward symbols (Heb. 9:8-9) will find themselves carried by the Holy Spirit into an immediacy of God's presence that will be true of the age to come. Christians who understand the kingdom live hovering between two worlds, never knowing when a very ordinary, "this worldly" church service will be transformed into an ultimate encounter, or when a private devotional moment will be injected by the powers of the future resurrection. The kingdom worldview makes us continually open to signs and wonders and overwhelming interventions of God. This also makes us patient when this fails to happen. It is always here, almost here, delayed and future. Every promise of God, every prophetic word, every calling, every ministry we engage in, has the mysterious sense of being continuously delayed by God and yet just around the corner. We live tasting, yet with our mouth watering; filled yet hungry; satisfied yet longing; having all, yet needing all.[10]

Everything has changed now that the kingdom is here. Even the nooks and crannies of everyday life can be transformed by the reality of the Holy Spirit. The kingdom perspective leads to a life of *expectancy*. Although this is much diminished in many of our churches, we live in the expectancy that God could intervene, break through, or show up. He could heal, deliver, speak or convict. The imminent and transcendent could crash together at any moment. We draw a distinction between the omnipresence of God and His manifest presence. Some of our church meetings progress in a very normal, this-worldly way. But sometimes, without warning, an intangible change takes place, and we become aware of God's presence.

I think the problem we have had comes from the wrong conception of heaven. Once you start to think of heaven not as a place miles up in the sky, but as God's dimension of reality that intersects with ours (but in a strange way that is to us unpredictable and uncontrollable), you realize that for Jesus to go into the heavenly dimension is not for Him to go like a spaceman miles up into space somewhere, and not for Him to be distant or absent now. It is for Him to be present but in the mode in which heaven is present to us. That is, it's just through an invisible screen, but present and real.

This isn't a hyped-up sense of emotion or anticipation; Jesus has never responded well to big crowds hyping Him up as the next big thing. We can't convince Him to reveal Himself simply by working ourselves up into a frenzy. The expectation that we are referring to is the simple anticipation and hope that, at any moment, Jesus could manifest His presence through His Spirit, and the very ordinary-ness of this world can be transcended by a foretaste of the future consummation of the kingdom. This is inaugurated eschatology—the understanding that the end has already begun in Jesus and His resurrection.

Chapter 19

Beyond *Left Behind*

This interval [between the first and second comings of Jesus] is not to be a time in which we passively wait for the end. Rather, it is the time in which the kingdom of God that was planted at Calvary is supposed to grow in us and through us to encompass the entire world. People who are submitted to the King, and whose lives are therefore being transformed into a domain in which God reigns, are called the "first fruits" of God, because they manifest in their lives what humanity and the world will look like when God's kingdom is fully manifested (2 Thess. 2:13; James 1:18; Rev. 14:4). We are to show ahead of time the eschatological harvest that is coming; we are to reveal the future in the present, the "already" amid the "not yet"...Whatever else one thinks about the New Testament's eschatology, it certainly does not encourage...irresponsible escapism. The hope offered to believers is not that we will be a peculiar elite group of people who will escape out of the world, leaving others behind to experience the wrath of God. The hope is rather that by our sacrificial participation in the ever-expanding kingdom, the whole creation will be redeemed.

GREG BOYD

The eschatological tension we live in as God's people has been a helpful way of understanding many of the paradoxes we are confronted with in our experience. To live as "now but not yet" people, we must fully come to terms with the implications of this in our lives and witness.

Most of us are familiar with the Lord's Prayer:

Our Father in heaven,
hallowed be your name,
your kingdom come,
your will be done
on earth as it is in heaven.

> Give us today our daily bread.
> Forgive us our debts,
>   as we also have forgiven our debtors.
> And lead us not into temptation,
> but deliver us from the evil one (Matthew 6:9-13).

I want to highlight two parts of the prayer. The first one, "your kingdom come, your will be done on earth as it is in heaven," we have already looked at. Jesus here is connecting God's coming kingdom with God's will being done. This, as we have already suggested, is most simply what it means to live in God's kingdom. We bring the kingdom to earth when we step into God's will.

Prior to understanding the centrality and nature of God's kingdom, I did not understand what this part of the Lord's Prayer meant. But now I realize it perfectly captures the work of Jesus and the hope of His community—that one day His kingdom will come in all its fullness, and God will bring everything back under His rule and reign. It also tells us what we are to be about as God's people in the meantime. It reframes our obedience as something that participates in the wider work of God in the world. I have the opportunity to bring a tiny piece of His kingdom to earth when I step into worship and obedience.

Tomorrow's Bread Today

The other section of the prayer I want to examine is the petition, "Give us this day our daily bread." Many scholars suggest an alternative translation, one that I think has merit. Instead of the usual translation, they suggest a more eschatological reading: "Give us tomorrow's bread today."[1] As it is usually taught, asking for daily bread means asking to have our daily needs met. Nothing is wrong with that prayer, of course, but I think that Jesus has something different in mind here.

The phrase *daily bread* would lead the Jewish mind back to the exodus event and the provision of manna to God's people in the wilderness. Moreover, people commonly assumed in the time of Jesus that at the time of Messiah's coming, God would again rain manna down from heaven. (This is what makes Jesus' "I am the bread of life" comment in John 6 so significant to the Jews.)

In asking for tomorrow's bread today, we are asking for a taste of the kingdom today. To be sure, many "appetizers" of the kingdom are around us, not the least of which is the Holy Spirit given to us as a down payment toward our full inheritance in the consummated kingdom. Praying it this way helps us live in the eschatological paradox we discussed in the last chapter. As we expectantly long for the fullness of God's kingdom to be revealed when Christ returns, we ask God to give us glimpses of the kingdom to nourish us today. Of course, Jesus is the bread that gives us life, and ultimately our prayer is answered in Him. But as people who live at the intersection of two ages, asking God for the bread of the kingdom implicitly acknowledges that "man does not live on [physical] bread alone, but on word that comes from the mouth of God."

Kingdom Justice

We are not simply waiting for the end to come; we are already living in the end, which began with the death and resurrection of Jesus. The eschatological emphasis in some popular novels leads us to devalue the present world in ways that are unhealthy and unbiblical. If the world is simply destined to burn, the only thing that is important is rescuing souls from the fire. The rescue of human souls is, of course, of supreme importance. Jesus came to seek and save the lost, and to give His life as a ransom for many. This emphasis is certain and true.

What is not so obvious today is how we should relate to the world with a more biblical paradigm. Rather than deeming creation as beyond repair, the inaugurated eschatology of the kingdom puts the world in proper perspective. Jesus expressed this in the parable of the sheep and goats (Matthew 25:31-46), where no good deed is forgotten; where every little act of kindness done for the homeless, the criminals, or the hungry is instilled with eschatological importance. Rather than emptying this world of eternal value, kingdom eschatology infuses our present world (and lives) with meaning and significance.

Such a view helps us navigate a path between two important errors of the church. One error is to focus exclusively on the social gospel, as if the job of the church were merely to facilitate cultural renewal and justice. This understanding of the gospel blurs the distinctions between the kingdom and the world and assumes that we can usher the kingdom into this world through our efforts. The obvious concern here is that there is little to no focus on the sacrifice of Jesus, forgiveness of sins, and entrance into the kingdom through salvation.

The other extreme, however is equally erroneous. In reacting to the social gospel, many of us have gone the other direction and narrowed the gospel of Jesus to His atonement for our sins. This, of course, is a huge piece of the work Jesus came to do, but as we have seen, it isn't the whole of His message. Under a misguided emphasis on last-days eschatology, we are left with the understanding that this world is unimportant because it will all burn anyway. So our focus becomes rescuing souls from this sinking ship. But this ignores the here-and-now message of the kingdom in Jesus. This view of the gospel ignores the radical social and political aspects of the message of Jesus; it often ignores the call to participate in the restoration of all things, so we simply withdraw into Christian cultural enclaves and leave the world to its own devices.

What is the real work of the gospel? Is it a capitulation to pluralism's dictates that we work toward racial reconciliation and the elimination of poverty and illiteracy? Does this take away from the "real work" of the gospel, saving lost souls?

If what we have been discussing is correct and the message of the Jesus is the message of the reign of God invading our present world, and if we are correct in suggesting this reign is not confined merely to the salvation of human beings but is also extended to the whole of creation and that God will restore and renew all things, then shouldn't the church seek to participate in the redemption of God wherever it is found? I like Allen Wakabayashi's question: "If the good news that Jesus proclaimed was that God was beginning to reclaim a lost creation and restore it to his creational intentions, does it not call us to live for and seek the love, truth and justice of God in *whatever way it is being challenged in our world?*"[2]

After all, Paul seems to suggest that the redemption of Jesus extends beyond saving individuals from hell to heaven. This is crucial and central to the work of Jesus but does not exhaust its implications. Rather, Paul seems to suggest that Jesus' redemption was being applied to an entire creation that had been distorted and corrupted by the fall. In Romans 8, as we have said, Paul explains that the whole of creation is now in bondage because of the sin of Adam and Eve (Romans 8:19-22). In other words, Paul seems to be suggesting that the redemption of human beings is somehow tied into the redemption of the whole world. Both are broken, and both need to be fixed.

If this understanding is correct, then the separation between evangelism (the saving of souls) and social justice (making the world a better place) is a false one. Creation groans for liberation. Powers and principalities stand behind the political and economic structures of the world that keep people in bondage. The children of God are bearers of, witnesses to, and participants in the redemption of all things in Jesus Christ. We are called to seek the kingdom "on earth as it is in heaven." If this means feeding the homeless, we do that in the name of Jesus. If this means sharing the good news to our neighbors, we do that also. It could mean adopting orphans, mentoring at-risk youth, raising money for HIV or cancer patients, being informed voters, challenging corporate practice in third-world countries, or cooking a meal for a friend.

When the focus of changing the world becomes fixated on the salvation of lost people, the significance of seeking kingdom change around you in other ways is diminished. You go to work and try to be a good Christian, but in your mind you think that the real world-changing drama is in your witness with your colleagues. No! The real world-changing drama is a day-to-day, minute-by-minute affair of bringing the influence of God's kingdom into all areas of life. It's about loving your neighbor and your enemies. It's about using your influence to bring about kingdom changes around you. It's about incarnating the kingdom in that office and

banishing the darkness of sin, death and injustice *wherever* that
darkness manifests itself![3]

I need to make sure I clarify: Evangelism is absolutely central to
the mission of Jesus. The focus of proclaiming and demonstrating the
good news that God has made a way for us to be transferred from the
kingdom of darkness to the kingdom of light is essential to the life of
the church. I am simply suggesting that our participating in the good
news of Jesus doesn't end there. The gospel demands that we work
against sin and its effects whenever and wherever they are found. The
kingdom is about a creation restored, so the church works to join God
in this work. Rene Padilla says, "The Gospel is Good News concerning
the Kingdom, and the Kingdom is God's rule over the totality of life.
*Every human need therefore can be used by the Spirit of God as a beach-
head for the manifestation of his kingly power.*"[4]

It is exactly because we live in the eschatological tension of the
kingdom that we can work for both the salvation of individuals and
the restoration of creation. The kingdom has come *now,* so we have the
resources to make a real difference in the world. But it is also *not yet,* so
we are not under the illusion that we can usher in the kingdom through
our own efforts. And because the end of the age does not result in the
destruction of the earth but rather in its renewal, we can be confident
that our labor here is not empty of significance. Paul exemplifies this
spirit in 1 Corinthians 3:10-15:

> By the grace God has given me, I laid a foundation as an expert
> builder, and someone else is building on it. But each one should
> be careful how he builds. For no one can lay any foundation other
> than the one already laid, which is Jesus Christ. If any man builds
> on this foundation using gold, silver, costly stones, wood, hay or
> straw, his work will be shown for what it is, because the Day will
> bring it to light. It will be revealed with fire, and the fire will test the
> quality of each man's work. If what he has built survives, he will
> receive his reward. If it is burned up, he will suffer loss; he himself
> will be saved, but only as one escaping through the flames.

This suggests that what we do here isn't empty or meaningless. We are not merely rearranging the deck chairs on the *Titanic* by working to make the world better. Nor are we ushering in the kingdom through our own efforts. N.T. Wright makes this note:

> The point of the resurrection...is that *the present bodily life is not valueless just because it will die.* God will raise it to new life.... What you *do* in the present—by painting, preaching, singing, sewing, praying, teaching, building hospitals, digging wells, campaigning for justice, writing poems, caring for the needy, loving your neighbor as yourself—*will last into God's future.* These activities are not simply ways of making the present life a little less beastly, a little more bearable, until the day when we leave it behind altogether. They are part of what we may call *building for God's kingdom*... That is the logic of the mission of God. God's re-creation of this wonderful world, which began with the resurrection of Jesus and continues mysteriously as God's people live in the risen Christ and in the power of his Spirit, means that what we do in Christ and by the Spirit in the present is not wasted. It will last all the way into God's new world. In fact, it will be enhanced there.[5]

The mission of the church is to point toward and witness to God's act of restoration that broke magnificently into the present age with the resurrection of Jesus and the coming of the Holy Spirit. We now work to participate in God's great restorative work. This means emphasizing salvation (God's intent that all humanity should come to a saving knowledge of Him) *and* justice (God's intention on setting the whole world back the way it should be, subsumed under His authority and rule). These are not two different gospels; they are expressions of *the* gospel of the kingdom. The church bears witness to the past and future comings of Jesus by seeking to bring the whole of human life (which includes creation, culture, business, family, politics, and more) under the gracious reign of God. Anytime this happens, and anywhere this happens, we get a glimpse of what life will be like when God is fully back in charge of the world again. Donald Kraybill summarizes this point well:

We don't have a spiritual and social gospel, a salvation and a social justice gospel. Instead we have a single, integrated gospel of the kingdom. This gospel fuses social and spiritual realities into one. Jesus binds the spiritual and social into an inseparable whole. On the one hand Jesus says that true faith is anchored in the heart—not in tithing, sacrifice, cleansing, and other external rituals. On the other hand, Jesus argues that faith in God is always expressed in tangible acts of love for our neighbor. He was, in short, smashing our categories of social and spiritual.[6]

Part 5

Fruit:
For God So
Loved the World

Chapter 20

Election, Exodus, and Diaspora: The Fine Art of Cultural Engagement

> Ivan Illich was once asked, "What is the most revolutionary way to change society: Is it violent revolution or gradual reform?" He gave a careful answer: "Neither. If you want to change society, then you must tell an alternative story."
>
> ALAN HIRSCH

We have argued that the church finds its true purpose and meaning when it gives witness of the real presence and anticipation of the kingdom of God. God is moving all things toward the fulfillment of the kingdom, when human souls and all creation will be brought back into the ordered arrangement God intended. The church participates in this mission by cultivating a communal life that is sustained through the presence of the Holy Spirit and the practices of baptism and Eucharist, which are both eschatological. Fundamental to this line of thinking is the idea of incarnation: The church exists as a parallel community within the world, embodying a real alternative to it. In this chapter, we want to rethink the so-called culture wars that exist in America between conservatives and progressives over what is culturally good, true, and beautiful.

The church that is called to witness to the kingdom should not be surprised to find itself living in contradiction to the world. The pragmatic and shallow relevance that defines our consumer- and market-driven approaches to church reach people only with "gospel lite." As a result, we relinquish the subversive nature of the gospel and the church and settle for popularity.

My assumption is that Christians are to practice selective discernment and engagement with the world. We can listen to the myriad cultural voices and discern the voice of Jesus somewhere in the midst of all the noise. The aim of the church as a culture and way of life is not simply to separate from or uncritically embrace culture.

We are called to selective and discerning engagement. This is dynamic and ongoing. The church at different times and places may respond differently to worldly occupation or practice.[1] There are no black-and-white, absolute rules to follow that allow us to resolve the tensions involved in cultural discernment and engagement. There is no surefire, guaranteed formula to follow. Instead, we must wait, pray, and discern as the community of faith.

Christians in the early church had to decide where they could conform to their society and where they couldn't. They had different opinions about what was appropriate and what wasn't. But it was clear that anyone who would be identified as a Christian had to draw the line here: Jesus is Lord, and there is no other. Anything that compromises the central confession of the church should be jettisoned in its entirety. But how do we draw that line?

From the Margins

For the last 16 centuries or so, the church has been at the center of Western civilization in its music, art, philosophy, science, government, law, ethics, and politics. This may be an overstatement, but it serves to show how little this is the case today. Formerly, discourse in the public square assumed a significant portion of the truth of the Jewish and Christian Scriptures. In those cases, evangelism was simply a matter of extending and clarifying what culture already (for the most part) accepted to be true. Evangelism meant talking to people who already shared 90 percent of our assumptions with us.

Now we live in a postmodern, post-Christian culture. The world around us no longer shares our Christian assumptions. In fact, those assumptions are viewed with a high degree of suspicion. So the church now exists at the margins of society, and entire segments of life and culture exist that are no longer under the church's influence. We have been reduced to being one subculture among many subcultures, one voice among many voices, one truth among many truths. The church could once presume for itself a privileged voice, but it can no longer make this assumption. The home base from which Christians thought to Christianize the world feels less like home, and a growing number of theological voices are helping us to ask whether Christians should have yielded to the temptation of making ourselves at home in the first place.[2] Many in the church bemoan this state of affairs and yearn wistfully for a return to the position the church held in American culture at the beginning of the twentieth century. I do not share their nostalgia. The marginalization of the church is, by and large, a good thing. I agree with Bryan Stone's assessment:

> It may be that it is precisely from a position of marginality that the church is best able to announce peace and bear witness to God's peaceable reign in such a way as to invite others to take seriously the subversive implications of that reign. It may be that through humility, repentance and a disavowal of its former advantages, so that those things that were once "gains" to the church now come to be regarded as "loss" (Phil. 3:7), a church at the periphery *of* the world may yet be a church *for* the world.[3]

It is simply enough to point out that, though there are glittering exceptions, for the most part, the church has done poorly when it has been wed to the power structures of society. Rodney Clapp makes this comment:

> The culture wars have forcefully reminded us that culture as ethos, as a way of life that forms character, is immensely powerful and not at all removed from any realm of life. The culture wars can be welcomed on the count that they help return us to a place where we can conceive of Christianity as a way of life, as a specific manner of being and doing in the world. They make it possible for Christians, like those who inhabit other ways of life, to move more easily and

> directly into the public, the social, the political and the economic
> realms—and do so *specifically as Christians.* The culture wars free
> the church of the Constantinian shackles that have confined it for
> 17 centuries. They make it possible for the church not merely to
> be relevant to culture but to *be* a culture.[4]

What these scholars and others are showing us is that the marginalization of the church is good precisely because it forces the church to see itself as an alternative community that is defined not just by its beliefs, but by its way of life. The earliest Christians were known as Followers of the Way. Now that the church is no longer at the center of cultural life, we Christians find ourselves in a situation much more closely analogous to that of the New Testament believers.

The earliest Christians took the good news out of its original Jewish dress and put Gentile clothes on it without compromising its content. We have much to learn from their ingenuity, fidelity, and enculturation.[5] They lived in a world far more relativistic and pluralistic than our own. But Christianity presented ideas that demanded a choice, not tolerance. They did most of their evangelism on secular ground. They also had a priority for personal conversations with individuals. The home provided the most natural context for sharing the gospel. Church planting (house churches) proved the most effective of all methods of evangelizing in the ancient church. They did not wait for a long time before allowing other churches their independence. They moved fast, relying on traveling teachers and letters from founding apostles to equip fledgling leadership. The team leadership of the early church was on display everywhere. There are many stories of how Christians would not go to the theater, public banquets, or gladiatorial shows. Employment in the army, teaching, and civil service were all regarded with suspicion because of the measure of idolatry involved.

Consider this:[6] In AD 100, there were only 25,000 Christians. By AD 313 (when Constantine granted legal protection to Christianity), there were upwards of 20,000,000.

How did they do this? How did they grow from a small movement to the most significant religious force in the Roman empire in two centuries? They did it under what we would consider "extreme circumstances":

- Christianity was an illegal religion.
- Christians didn't have any church buildings as we know them.
- They didn't have the Scriptures as we know them (or commentaries).
- They didn't have an institution (a denominational organization) or seminaries.
- They had no seeker-sensitive services, youth groups, or worship bands.
- They actually made joining the church difficult and created a significant initiation period to prove that new members were worthy.

This isn't just a quirk of history. We're seeing the same sort of flourishing under the harshest of conditions in China, where most of the above factors are true to this day. The Christian population has grown from 2 million before the persecution under Mao to upward of 80 million Christians today, even though Christianity is still illegal.

Our point is simply this: The cultural situation in America and the West, instead of being a source for Christian anxiety and departure, is precisely the environment needed for true Christian spirituality to grow and flourish, as Dallas Willard notes:

> The Christian gospel does not require cultural privilege or even social recognition in order to flourish. God's work is not disadvantaged by persecution, even to death, and much less than by mere pluralism. As Christians we stand now in the Kingdom of the Heavens, and it is always true that they who are for us are more than they that be against us (1 Kings 6:16). It is always true that the One who is in us is greater than the one who is in the world (1 John 4:4)...

Christians, in a pluralistic society, where there is no presumption in favor of their beliefs or practices, but perhaps a strong bias against, are in the *very best position* to show the true excellence of the Way of Christ. When Elijah called the prophets of Baal to the contest at Mount Carmel, he gave them every advantage that could be given. And when it came his turn to call for fire from heaven to consume his sacrifice, he had his altar and sacrifice flooded three times over with water before he prayed. The "disadvantage" of the water proved to be no problem for Jehovah, who answered by fire to consume the sacrifice.[7]

Beyond Christ and Culture

The relationship of Christians to culture is a critical discussion in the life of the church. Christians are deeply divided over how to interact with a world that has moved beyond Christianity and is now settled in a nice, tolerant, pluralistic, post-Christian view of things. There seem to be several main positions. One position says to focus only on being the best, most faithful church possible. In its more extreme forms, it resists any move by the church to directly influence the world. Then there is the position that says, "We don't like the world, so we'll try to return the United States to its Christian roots." This position often looks to legislation or political action to navigate the world away from its moral and cultural amnesia. Still others suggest that the way to change the world is to bring one heart at a time to Jesus. If you change the people, this thinking goes, you change the world. Lastly, many attempt to accommodate the changes in society by changing some of the distinct beliefs and practices that are historically fundamental to Christian life and witness.

It seems obvious to me that each of these positions has something to say for itself. Faithful church practice, political activism, and sincere and biblically faithful evangelism are all part of the answer. But that is not to say that adding all of these positions together is the answer either. We have been suggesting that Christians should function as a dynamic counter culture that witnesses to the kingdom of God and is nourished by the reality of the Holy Spirit. It is not enough for Christians to simply live as individuals in society. We must live as a particular *kind* of community. Jesus told His disciples that they were like a city on a hill that showed God's glory to the world (Matthew 5:14-16).

We have also argued that it is not enough for the church to exist simply as a culture that runs counter to the values of the broader culture. Christians should be a community radically committed to the good of their communities as a whole. We live in the world for the sake of it. We must intentionally move beyond our comfort and security to serve the common good, paying particular attention to the poor, the outcast, the alien, the orphan, and the widow. The last two chapters of the book of Revelation make clear the ultimate purpose of our redemption. There we see that our redemption lies not in forever escaping the material world, but in seeing the heavens and earth renewed. God's purpose is not only saving individuals but also inaugurating a new world based on the fulfillment and consummation of His kingdom on the earth.

Where then should we look for instruction and wisdom on how best to relate to a hostile world? Perhaps one overlooked source of guidance comes from Yahweh's letter to the exiled community of Israel in Babylon.[8] Found in Jeremiah 29, this letter contains themes, encouragements, promises, and warnings that are instructive for us today. We, like the nation of Israel of old, find ourselves in exile, living as aliens and strangers within the culture of the world. Therefore, I want to concentrate our attention on the themes of election, exodus, and diaspora.[9]

Election

God's blessings have always been instrumental. That is, they were to be passed along. This is hinted at throughout the letter to the exiles. God will keep His promises to them because they are His chosen people. In Genesis 12:3, God calls Abram and makes it clear that his calling is for the sake of the world: "All the nations of the earth will be blessed through you." God's choice of His people has never been on their own merit, nor has it been for their benefit only. Abraham's election and God's covenant with him represent the first expression of

God's redemptive concern for all nations. The salvation of the nations was God's ultimate motivation in making Abraham's name great. This universal purpose dominates the purposes of God's covenant with him (Genesis 18:17-18; 22:18; 26:4; 28:14; Galatians 3:8).

Later, God brings Israel to the base of Mt. Sinai and gives them the law, defining for them what it meant for Israel to be God's people. The law was given to a people already redeemed and rescued, so nothing in the law was an attempt to earn God's approval. Rather, the law was given so that Yahweh would be put on display through the way Israel lived—they would show the rest of the world what He was like and how He was to be worshipped. They were to be a set-apart people because God was holy, and through Israel, Yahweh would reveal Himself to the world. The instructions about taking care of the poor, for example, demonstrated God's own heart for the poverty stricken.

Moses continually reminds the Israelites that God's choice of them is no basis for pride. "It was not because you were more numerous than any other people that the LORD set his heart on you and chose you—for you were the fewest of all peoples" (Deuteronomy 7:7 NRSV). That same theme is echoed throughout the conquest of the promised land, lest Israel think that she was responsible for her new status (Deuteronomy 9:4). Their election as God's chosen people had nothing to do with their merit, faithfulness, or track record. It was simply an extension of grace. And this grace was given instrumentally. Israel was blessed in order to be a blessing to the world.

The New Testament Scriptures take key images of Old Testament Israel and apply them to the church.[10] This means that what God was attempting to do through Israel, He now is seeking to do through the church. We now are to show what God is like by putting Him on display individually and together. Our election is instrumental, just as Israel's was. Paul puts it this way:

> Brothers, think of what you were when you were called. Not many of you were wise by human standards; not many were influential; not many were of noble birth. But God chose the foolish things of the world to shame the wise; God chose the weak things of

the world to shame the strong. He chose the lowly things of this world and the despised things—and the things that are not—to nullify the things that are, so that no one may boast before him (1 Corinthians 1:26-29).

This dose of humility is urgently needed by today's church. Election reminds us of our weakness, our need, and our dependence. It is not a basis for pride or exclusion. Any attempt by the church to engage culture that does not start from this place is doomed to failure. The church must begin its witness to the world with these two ideas: It is grace that set us free and formed us into community, and the purpose of our redemption is to empower us to participate in God's project to redeem the whole world.

Exodus

In Jeremiah 29, God's promise to restore Israel uses exodus language and imagery ("I will be found by you...and will bring you back from captivity"). As we have seen, the exodus motif is the most foundational picture of redemption in the Bible, encapsulating both Old and New Testaments. The imagery of exodus reminds us that we were also once held captive and powerless, and we lived at the mercy and whims of others. Israel was to welcome the alien and stranger because they were once aliens and strangers in Egypt (Leviticus 19:33-34; Deuteronomy 10:17-19).

This idea was central to the ministry of Jesus. In His meals with sinners, conversations with outcasts, and inclusion of the misfits and marginalized in His community of disciples, Jesus shaped the church to be an exodus community. Our treatment of others is to reflect God's treatment of us. We have no place for elitist posturing or isolated judgmentalism because we were once lost too. We love because God loves us. We forgive as we have been forgiven. We are to comfort with the comfort that God Himself provides us. This is the way of the kingdom—God initiates, and we respond under His grace and empowered by His spirit. Cultural engagement must include the spirit of the exodus if we are to properly be present and participate with those around us.

As Christopher Wright suggests, "Exodus-shaped redemption demands exodus-shaped mission."[11] This means that the church should display the same comprehensive concern for the totality of human need that God displayed for Israel in the exodus. Our mission is God's mission; our view of redemption must be derived from His and include liberation from bondage, a new corporate identity and focus, and instruction of how to now live as redeemed people. The exodus of Israel has spiritual, economic, and political/social dimensions, so the work of the church must as well. We are all exodus people. Having been liberated from Satanic authority and the wrath of God against sin, we now work against all injustice, oppression, and bondage in whatever form they take. To remember that we are exodus people is to consider our past (in bondage), our present (living as free people and working with God in the redemption of human beings and all creation), and our future (the renewal of all creation). Because of this, we cannot exclude anybody from the possibility of salvation.

Diaspora

As citizens of another kingdom in the midst of the kingdoms of this earth, the people of Israel constituted a subversive presence within enemy territory. The same is now true for the church. God advises His people toward neither withdrawal nor assimilation. Instead, He instructs His displaced people, "Seek the peace and prosperity of the city to which I have carried you into exile. Pray to the LORD for it, because if it prospers, you too will prosper" (Jeremiah 29:7). So as we live in exile among much larger and sometimes hostile cultural groups, we can work for the peace, security, justice, and prosperity of our cities and neighbors, loving them in word and in deed, whether they believe what we do or not. In other words, we become exemplary citizens in the earthly kingdoms as an extension of being citizens of heaven. This is significant. Israel's mission was not merely to survive as a marginalized community, but to flourish.

The years of exile focused Israel's efforts on retaining her distinct communal identity apart from Jerusalem, the temple, and the priesthood. It forced Israel to find alternative ways of living its ancient stories and parables and drawing communal nourishment from them. No longer could Israel simply point to God's presence in the temple as the sure sign of the people's election. They changed the way they told stories, celebrated feasts, and entered into the collective memory of their people.[12] They were to continue and prosper as a people while participating fully (but discerningly) in the common life of the society around them.

This serves as a model for the church today. This kind of cultural engagement keeps us free from falling into the habits and patterns of this world. If Christians engage the culture simply to acquire power, they will never achieve societal influence and change that is deep, lasting, and embraced by the broader society. We must live in the city to serve all the people in it, not just our own Christian communities. We must lose our power in order to find our (true) power. Christianity will not be attractive enough to win influence except through sacrificial service to all people, regardless of their beliefs.[13] Rodney Clapp puts it well:

> The church in a post-Constantinian world finds itself in a kind of diaspora. It no longer governs or defines the lands in which it dwells. But the church's diaspora heritage lets it know that it need not govern or define. In diaspora it is in some ways freer to witness to God and God's way of life. In diaspora, it has no reigning home to mistake for God's kingdom and is less likely to confuse the power of the sword with the power of the cross. In diaspora it cannot lean on the surrounding institutions to enculturate its children in the ways of God, but must take responsibility to be its own culture. And in diaspora it cannot ignore the outsider, for it lives inside the outsider's walls.[14]

This means that in all our preaching and teaching about the hope that the gospel makes possible, we must emphasize that what the gospel offers is not just hope for the individual but hope for the world. This means that our churches must be deeply involved in the supposedly non-Christian concerns of the society around us so that we witness to the reality that no one and nothing is outside the range of God's love and redemption. The message of Jesus is centered on the kingdom of God (God's kingly reign and rule over all creation), so the seed of the gospel is spread over every part of human life. The whole world and the whole person are in view in the announcement of the kingdom. In every area of life we have the option to live in a way that testifies to and cooperates with that rule, or we live under some other power.

This means that the message of the church in exile has to be about the rule of God in the presence and anticipation of His kingdom, and not about the church itself. For the church to be true to the nature of the gospel, it must care for the well-being of the community at large, and not just for itself. But this doesn't mean that we are just another organization hoping and working for social change. No, this is all done in Jesus' name and for His glory, and because of this, at times, our efforts will not be welcomed. The church is called to be a sign, foretaste, and instrument of God's kingly rule, and it is essential that we keep all our thinking centered on the fact that the kingdom of God is present in Jesus—incarnate, crucified, risen, and coming in judgment. The life of the church in the midst of the world is to be a sign and foretaste of the kingdom only in so far as its whole life is centered on that reality. Through the community of the church, the world is to see what living under God's reign looks like—grace and truth, love and compassion, and justice and mercy. The church is the beachhead from which the kingdom moves to reclaim the world. This is not a community of individual witnesses but rather a witnessing community, where all participate in the redemption of the world. We are to be a foretaste of what the world will be like when God is finally in charge of everything on the earth (as in the heavens).

As a community that now exists on the margins of culture, we carry forward with a hope that speaks deeply to a hope-starved world. But that hope can be fully expressed only in a community that embodies it and fashions its life in light of the reality of the kingdom. The community thus creates signs, parables, foretastes, and appetizers of the kingdom in the midst of the hopelessness of the world. It makes it possible to act both hopefully and realistically in a world without hope, a world that trades in illusions and denial. Bryan Stone says it this way:

> Our evangelistic refusal of vulnerability, humility and marginality is finally a refusal of the way of the cross; a way that forgoes the privileges and security allied with winning and opts instead for costly obedience, incarnation and gospel nonconformity. What the gospel needs most is not intellectual brokers or cultural diplomats but rather saints who have taken up the way of the cross and in whose lives the gospel is visible, palpable and true. It needs disciples who follow Jesus with or without the support of culture and for whom the power of the gospel is demonstrated not through winning, but obedience…

> Creative reconstructions of evangelism are being attempted today, and they succeed in expanding the church by adapting it to new generations that are put off by boring liturgies, irrelevant preaching and stuffy pipe-organ music. But while these reconstructions have triumphed in making the church more relevant to the tastes, expectations, preferences, and quest for self-fulfillment of the unchurched, they have utterly failed to challenge the racism, individualism, violence and affluence (and narcissism) of Western culture. They in no way subvert an existing unjust order but rather mimic and sustain it. Our greatest challenge is to find ways of practicing evangelism in a post-Christian culture without at the same time playing by the rules of that culture.[15]

Chapter 21

Jesus Wept:
Apologies and Apologetics

Stopping and grieving will be most difficult for those of us who have had most to gain from this crumbling regime. We must stop the programs, stop the meetings, stop the denials, stop the machinations, dismantle the structures, face our fears and disappointments, and weep for the absence, weep for the emptiness, weep for the pretence, weep for the fiction. Weep until we can see our barrenness clearly, for only then will we have made room for newness. Ezekiel 10—God leaves the temple—Bored by our rambling, navel-gazing conversations about internal tinkering, God hung up. He walked out displaying a true, holy freedom that shouts clearly over its shoulder that "no temple, no place, no people, no box, no church, no agenda, no theological position will ever require me to stay where I don't want, be co-opted with something I only half-agree with, and be pressed into the service of some cause you made up"...

God will not be co-opted into our programs. This turns out to be the foundation for a huge hope. For if God could not leave, then we would be bound and trapped forever inside structures that God "might just be blessing." How many times have we squirmed at some toe-curling "ministry" yet been snared to our seats by the mantra that "if God touches just one person one tiny amount through this, then it's worth it"? Enough of this psycho spiritual bull—God's holiness gives hope beyond this otherwise perpetual trap of "what if?" and "perhaps."

KESTER BREWIN

When we say, "I love Jesus, but I hate the church," we end up losing not only the church but Jesus too. The challenge is to forgive the church. This challenge is especially great because the church seldom asks us for forgiveness.

HENRI NOUWEN

There is a branch of Christian thought called *apologetics*. The word means, "to make a rational defense" of Christianity. *Apology* was a courtroom term in the first century, and it refers to the case that one would make in a court of law. Early Christian apologists were instrumental in writing to Roman officials, arguing for tolerance of the burgeoning church.

When I came to faith, the writings of modern apologists like C.S. Lewis, Josh McDowell, and J.P. Moreland were critical. I still find great encouragement in them, as do many others. But as I have suggested elsewhere, traditional approaches to apologetics are growing increasingly irrelevant to our culture.[1] We are no longer answering the real questions culture is asking. So I want to propose a new definition of apologetics: saying "I'm sorry" on behalf of the church. Apologetics should include an apology of grief, confession, and repentance. Kester Brewin agrees:

> Only through grief can newness become a possibility—no denial or hanging on…There is a spectacular lack of grief in our churches today—the text of so many Christian magazines, sermons and songs are all woven into an enormous blanket of denial that we wrap warmly around us, smothering the honest doubts with an ever-optimistic hue of "everything is good, and God is with us." Hands are raised, but never to ask questions, only to surrender to programs of services, outreaches, prayer meetings and worship. Grief and repentance are the proper antidote for the culture of denial and cover-up that has so permeated our church and wider society. Ungrieving politicians, CEOs—it seems that most of us live our lives bathed in the dark light of façade, unable to grieve, told to soldier up with stiff upper lips, denying everything. Where are the Jeremiahs to lead us?[2]

I think these are some of the most prophetic words written to the modern church. Brewin is absolutely correct. Lament has little place in our worship, sorrow has little place in our prayer, doubt has no room in our pulpits, and suffering has no place in our gospels. We have, for the most part, ceased being honest with ourselves and with God. And because our world pays attention to our hypocrisy, they can simply place us in the same category as all the other posers and pretenders in society. I want to suggest that grieving has a place in our witness to the kingdom. We grieve because the kingdom isn't yet fully here; but we don't grieve as those who have no hope because our grief has been inaugurated in the life, death, and resurrection of Jesus of Nazareth. So we live in this eschatological tension. And this tension allows us to admit our hopes and failures.

So with all of this in mind, I would like to write a couple of open letters to groups of men and women who have been hurt by the church. I write as a Christian first and foremost, and also as a pastor. I am as flawed as anyone, but I hunger to see Jesus more clearly. I speak only for myself, but I think there are many who would agree with the sentiment behind these words, if not the particulars. I am not apologizing for our positions on these issues. I do believe the Scriptures clearly teach that marriage is covenant between one man and one woman that is monogamous, binding, and heterosexual. I also believe that abortion is most often wrong. What I am apologizing for is *the way we conduct ourselves* while articulating our views on these issues.

I acknowledge that many in the community of Jesus don't fit the stereotypes and sins listed below. By necessity, though, I must paint with a broad brush.

To the Gay and Lesbian Community

I want to begin by simply confessing the great deal of harm that we have done to you in the name of Jesus. Our anger, hostility, and antagonism toward you have no place in the community that is supposed to represent Him. I am so sorry. Far too frequently we in the Christian community are rightly characterized as homophobic, mean-spirited, and narrow-minded.

I have several friends who are gay, and they have enlightened me to the heavy burden that many of you carry when you are rejected, mocked, and discarded by those in the church. Instead of offering helpful care, wisdom, and encouragement, we have often turned you away in disgust. We have done too much talking and not enough listening. I grieve this. And I know that Jesus does also. He had a very tender place in His ministry and priorities for those who were marginalized by the religious leadership of His day.

234 | DEATH *by* Church

I regret that we have not been more faithful to His example. The church has lied to you in at least two ways. We have highlighted homosexuality over other issues in the Christian community. We have railed against homosexual marriage while turning a blind eye toward concerns like quick and easy divorce, premarital and extramarital heterosexual sex, greed, gossip, and anger. Our double standards have served only to highlight our own hypocrisy.

We have also said to you that salvation or coming to Jesus means being automatically transformed into a heterosexual. We seem woefully naive of all the factors involved in this issue. As far as I can tell, one's sexual orientation is not the determining factor in one's eternal destiny. If my friendships are any indication, many yearn to follow Jesus fully and completely and yet continue to struggle to reconcile their faith with their desire for intimacy (sexual or otherwise) with someone of the same sex. We have failed to live out the good news of Jesus. Please forgive us.

I also believe that, at times, the homosexual community isn't entirely truthful to you either. For one thing, the gospel of Jesus Christ reveals that our desires are not our destinies. They can be overcome and placed in their proper context. Our wants don't have to become our needs. Entrance into the kingdom of God through Jesus makes possible those things that, prior to Him, were thought to be impossible. We don't have to live at the mercy of desire. Salvation isn't found in self-gratification, nor is it found in unhealthy repression or denial. Jesus offers a third way.

One last thing. I disagree with those who think your sexual orientation is the most important thing about you. The most important thing about you is that, as a human being, you are made in the image of God. As an image bearer, you are a person who has intrinsic dignity, honor, and worth. You, like the rest of us, are also broken and bent toward what is worst for us. But the good news is that Jesus has come to make things right. He invites you into that redemption. Please don't hold the sins of the church against Him.

I do sincerely ask your forgiveness. I grieve the harm we have done,

and I recognize that if the church had done a better job listening, grieving, encouraging, telling the truth, and giving grace along the way, we
would not be so polarized and alienated from each other today.

To Abortion Providers and Patients

I want to ask your forgiveness for the ways we have polarized,
alienated, and insulted you. I apologize for our aggressive tactics, our
political manipulation, and the taunting that so often accompanies
our interactions with each other.

In our zeal to represent what we see as the lives of the unborn,
we have used methods, messages, and strategies that are simply not
of Jesus. If you are reading this and you have worked for a clinic, or
have had an abortion, or simply believe the pro-choice position to be
correct, I ask your forgiveness for the way the community of Jesus has
treated you.

Jesus had an amazing ability to hang around all kinds of people.
The "sinners" and "outcasts" of His day loved to be around Him while
the religious people were suspicious of Him. I grieve that 2000 years
later, these perceptions of Jesus have exactly reversed.

Please know that that we care deeply about this issue. Behind our
heated rhetoric and misguided attempts at intimidation, most of us
are concerned about the ways in which human life is increasingly
devalued (though, I am ashamed to say, it seems that most Christians
are big fans of war and capital punishment, which further erodes
our credibly on this right-to-life issue). I, for one, wish we had done
a better job welcoming and supporting those women who, in the
absence of such support, chose an abortion. We have not done enough
to ensure that those who wish to bring their babies into the world
have the resources to do so.[3] We have not been realistic about the
effectiveness of our abstinence programs, which do little to decrease
the rate of teen sexual activity and pregnancy. We have not embodied
a radical alternative that opens up possibilities for pregnant women.
Please forgive us.

To Those Hurt, Abused, or Neglected by the Church

I know this is a broad category, but it seemed important to write to the many of you who are like those I come in contact with who have shared their pain with me. Like you, I am appalled when those who claim to love Jesus hurt and abuse those who are vulnerable and powerless. I am ashamed that we have not been more forthcoming in owning our part in these failures and have not dealt with them quickly to protect other potential victims. I am sorry that often our talk doesn't match our walk and that our witness and testimony about God's love is so radically undercut by our hypocrisy on moral issues.

I am sorry for the many Christian leaders who have lived double lives, who have pursued monetary gain through the manipulation of emotion and Scripture, and who have led churches and ministries out of nothing more than ego and greed.

I must add myself explicitly to this list of failures. I am sorry that I don't always live, talk, think, or act in ways that reflect Jesus faithfully.

Please understand that our sin is *precisely* the reason we need saving to begin with. This doesn't excuse a thing, but I want you to know that failure, screw-ups, and mistakes are exactly what you should expect from a community of sinners who call on Jesus for rescue. He does heal, forgive, and transform us, and we are all in process together. But I want to apologize to you for fostering the illusion that the "Christians aren't perfect, just forgiven" slogan is the summation of all that Jesus has come to do in and through us. As I have tried to show throughout this book, God is up to much more, and the church is expected to be much more. I am sorry that we have not taken our identity as God's people seriously enough to be honest when we fail, to grieve and repent of our sin, to work toward restitution and reconciliation, and then to strive, under the power of God's Spirit, to be more like Jesus.

The most important thing, however, is to not hold *our* mistakes against *Jesus.* He is more than a moral teacher or a founder of a world religion. He is what God is like. He was God with clothes on. His heart is God's heart. His power is God's power. His work is God's work. That is why we are so confident of God's love for us. In Jesus, we got to see it in action. He is all that the world was meant to be—wrapped up in the garments of a first-century Jewish rabbi. He was mesmerizing; crowds would travel for miles and listen for days to His teaching. Those whom the religious establishment deemed unacceptable had a special place in His heart. He could be found with the misfits, outcasts, and big-time sinners of His day. He smiled and laughed a lot. He cried over the suffering He found in the world. He grew angry over religious hypocrisy. He was moved with compassion to heal and bring freedom to people who were hurting and in bondage. He is the culmination of all that God has done to bring all things back into proper alignment with Him and His purposes.

Regardless of whether you agree with the specific content of these open letters, I challenge you to consider what our witness to the world would amount to if we led with humility, sincerity, and confession. We have caused much harm in the name of Jesus. Acknowledging this costs us nothing, and the world around us cries out for such an admission. Of course, Bible verses and sermons and the like are sometimes appropriate, but I don't think they belong at the beginning of our conversations with people. Maybe we should train disciples in the art of conversation: less talking, more listening; fewer answers, more questions; less judging, more loving. Maybe the people of God will be more effective if we remember how to relate to people as people, not always as potential converts.

Postscript for Pastors and Church Leaders: The Kingdom-Focused Church

> Our greatest threat is that in reaching secular people we will fail to offer them anything specifically Christian...the scandalous dimensions of the gospel will have been softened, disguised and forgotten or placed on the back burner. We may reach more people, but will reach them with Christianity-lite, a pale reflection of consumer preferences and a market-driven accommodation to felt needs. The subversive nature of the gospel will then have been itself subverted, and that which is unprecedented and radical about the church will have been compromised in favor of mere ratings.
>
> BRYAN STONE

To conclude, I would like to talk specifically to pastors and church leaders about what some of the thoughts in this book might look like in practice.

Redefining How We See the Church and How Others Should See It

Church (*ekklesia*) from the fifth century BC onward referred to an assembly of citizens called to decide matters affecting common welfare. The Hebrew word *qahal* denotes a solemn, deliberative assembly of Israel's tribes. In the Septuagint, *qahal* was translated *ekklesia*—the town meeting of God. Based on Greek civil practice that allowed every Greek citizen to speak into civil matters and/or to propose an agenda for the *polis* (city), the *ekklesia* became the assembly of citizens gathering together to discuss the political issues of the day. The New Testament first uses the word to describe a local congregation or assembly of Christians in 1 Thessalonians 1:1, where it refers to the assembly (church) of Thessalonica. What characterized an *ekklesia* was the ability of anyone to speak, share, and shape. (This is one of the reasons why Paul had to establish his credentials and argue with the church in Corinth. He does not merely proclaim ecclesiastical authority.)

Given all this, it is unsurprising that early observers of Christianity were not struck by its religious (in our privatized sense) qualities. What struck outsiders was the church's total way of life—its culture. The Romans classified Christians as a political society. The church was not just a religious grouping, but one whose religion made it a subversive presence within the wider Roman society. The thoroughly political language suggests that the church saw itself this way.

We have suggested that the church needs to recapture this political element to effectively witness to the kingdom of God. By *political* I do not mean getting the church involved in American politics. Instead, I wish for the church to be recaptured by its understanding of itself as a social, public, and subversive community. We aren't just to see ourselves as a community of individuals who share nothing in common except private religious preferences. Instead we are something much deeper and more compelling than that: We are a community that seeks to be a foretaste of, a sign pointing toward, and a witness to the reality and goodness of God's rule. In this, we participate in God's redemptive intent to renew and restore all of creation.

The church therefore is a people, not a place. It is an alternate reality based on the person of Jesus Christ, not a specific location where people meet for an hour and a half a week. Gibbs and Bolger suggest, "The modern church has identified itself too closely with the centralized temple worship of the Jerusalem church rather than with the household basis of the Pauline model of church." The household was the central institution of first-century society. It included extended family and friends, slaves and servants, and clients and employers.

In light of this background, a first-century Christian would have been puzzled by the question, "Where do you go to church?" for church was a network of people to which one belonged. It was not a once- or twice-a-week association but rather a community of continuous interaction that included a range of activities related to every aspect of life.[1]

To see the church as a building or as the activities that go on in the building is to return to the sacred/secular split that has done so much damage to modern life. If church is only the meeting that occurs at a particular building at a particular time of the week, then the rest of the week is not church. And if church is a spiritual activity, then the rest of the week is not spiritual. But as we have seen, this is simply mistaken. Our formation as disciples of Christ is more influenced by the rest of the week than by the hour or two a week that we meet as a congregation. We must come to see that people cannot be engaged in kingdom life and work if they have reduced salvation, gospel, church, and ministry to only those programs or activities that are part of the church. This is destructive not only to our people but also to our understanding of what a church is.

Rethinking Church Leadership

The early church evolved in two contexts: Jewish and Greek. The Jewish context brought a rich legacy of worship gatherings, both at temple and in local synagogues where people read the law, sang songs, and presented offerings. The minimum requirement for the existence of a synagogue was a group of 10 men to constitute the board of elders. When a Jewish community converted to Christianity, the community would retain the symbolic elements of leadership and worship established in the Torah. Of course, it would be focused on Jesus, and it lacked animal sacrifice. Self-governing Jewish communities had a ruling council to direct their affairs. The council was made up of respected older men called *presbyteroi* (elders). One elder was usually recognized as a presiding elder or ruling elder. In early Christianity, we see continuity with the leadership traditions of Judaism.

Whether in a Jewish or Greek context, the goal of the community

242 | DEATH *by* Church

was the maturation of believers. How do we best present everyone mature in Christ? The New Testament teaches that the leadership of the church affects the spiritual maturity and health of the church. If leaders weren't mature, the form didn't matter. When you look at New Testament instructions to the church in this context, they make more sense. To those Gentile churches that were based on autonomy, Paul spoke a word of order and headship, all in the context of a loving family (1 Corinthians 11–14). To churches in Jewish contexts that were caught up in authority and position, the apostles would emphasize the church as an egalitarian community (1 Peter 2:9).

The Bible obviously leaves a lot of room for differences of method and form, but it isn't completely silent on the subject of church leadership. The qualifications of church leaders are specifically addressed, as well as the nature and character of their leadership (Matthew 23:10-12; 1 Peter 5:1-5).

What I want to stress here, however, is this. From both prescriptive and descriptive passages in the Scriptures, church leadership was always intended to be done in community with other leaders. The CEO model of church leadership simply has no basis in Scripture. It has been harmful to the church and to pastors who find themselves leading in such a model. The horror stories of the immorality, greed, pride, power, and ego of pastors who lead in individualistic and unaccountable environments are legion.[2]

I once met with a well-known pastor who suggested that nothing of importance had been accomplished in the Scriptures without the leadership of a sole individual. I replied that the Jerusalem council (Acts 15) seems a noteworthy exception to his argument. He granted the point but still insisted that CEO style of leadership is necessary for the effectiveness of today's church. Years later, I have come to more of a conviction about the inaccuracy (and danger) of his position. I think the weight of Scriptural examples is significant. Moses and Aaron. Elijah and Elisha. Jesus and the apostles. Paul and Barnabas. Paul and Silas. Paul and Timothy. Jesus appointed the 12 to lead once He ascended into heaven. The 12, in turn, selected men to serve as deacons in the Jerusalem church (Acts 6:1-6). Moreover, in the Jewish contexts we observe in Scripture, we never see a biblical church with just one elder or leader. This does not mean there is not room for one to provide guidance, vision, and direction, but this is always done in the context of a team (Acts 14:23; 15:2; 16:4; 20:17,28). In Acts 21:18, only James is mentioned by name, but elders (plural) are always mentioned. At times, one of the elders was appointed to serve as presiding elder in a group of elders: James in the church of Jerusalem (Acts 21:18), Timothy in the church of Ephesus (1 Timothy 1:3), and Titus in Crete (Titus 1:5). But again, the point is that church leadership was always team leadership and never the sole province of a lone individual. It seems that within the context of the priesthood of all believers, some were called specifically to lead and shepherd the congregation.

The reason I belabor this point is that I have personally seen the benefits of a team leadership approach. I work with Todd Proctor, our lead pastor, and the elders of Rock Harbor to help lead our church. Todd is the team leader. I live in submission to him, as do the rest of our staff. He, in turn, reports to a group of elders who help shape and refine the vision of our church.

Todd and I live in a crazy, sometimes easy and sometimes difficult dance of leadership that not only protects us from our own unchecked egos, but also helps to keep our church dependent on Jesus and not on one personality. As ministry partners, Todd and I work hard at listening, honoring, and submitting to each other. Believe me, sometimes each of us realizes that the CEO leadership model would be easier and more efficient. But it would rob our church and rob us of the unique ways God has used this to mold and shape us.

This isn't the only way to do it, nor is it easy. But we see enough biblically and personally to convince us of the wisdom of this way of church leadership. We know of far too many churches that are led by strong personalities with little to no accountability. Some have elders who are family and friends, or they are paid staff who report to the senior pastor. This is a far cry from the leadership, mutual accountability, and submission that we see in the early church. In light of the present crisis of the church, I cannot recommend highly enough the humility and accountability built into a team leadership model.

Rethinking Church Ministry

From Ephesians 4:11-12 we learn that the leadership of the church exists to prepare, equip, and train the people of the congregation for ministry. Someone who does the work the work of ministry is called a minister. The leaders of the church are not the only ones who do the work of ministry. They do the teaching, equipping, leading, and preparing of people to do the ministry so that the church might be built up. Every Christian is a minister—there are not special people who are in ministry and others who are not. The church doesn't pay us to do the work of ministry; this is where we train and equip ministers to be the best possible ministers wherever they find themselves. If this is correct, then some ways of doing pastoral ministry facilitate the ongoing training and equipping of people better than others. David Parker distinguishes between three models for being God's people as the church.[3]

The first is the temple model of doing church. The temple was designed to emphasize God's holiness and distance from us. The spiritual experience of the temple was distance, with an emphasis on holiness and need for sacrifice. We can all think of churches whose architecture reflects the emphasis of the temple model. The temple was designed for preparation of sacrifice, and it was served by a special priesthood called with that emphasis: to prepare people for a relationship with God. Catholic liturgies and cathedrals are perfect examples of churches build on the temple model. Distance is emphasized, distinctions are made between priests and laity, and sacrifice and proper worship (liturgy) are highlighted.

The second model is based on the Jewish synagogue. After the temple was destroyed by the Romans in AD 70, synagogues came into even more prominence. Instead of sacrifice, the synagogues emphasized the Sabbath. Whereas preparation was the function of the temple, preservation was the function of the synagogue. The distinct laws, identity, and manner of life were preserved through a rabbi's leadership over a synagogue. Instead of highlighting distance, the synagogue stressed discipline. Many churches operate with this same understanding, seeing themselves as teaching centers where law is administered and spiritual discipline happens, all for the goal of the preservation of the people.

What David called the early church model has some overlap with the other two models but ultimately stands in contrast to them. The church is not the temple, a place where God resides. It is not the synagogue, where the family of faith is preserved. Instead, it is the signpost and witness of the presence of the kingdom. It is not about preparation or preservation, but proclamation—the announcement of the good news of the kingdom of God to both those inside and those outside the faith. The focus is not on sacrifice or Sabbath, but salvation. In the same way, spiritual discovery is highlighted, not spiritual distance or discipline. And finally, and most importantly, there is no special priesthood or rabbi, but a team of ministers that leads the church. The idea that the pastor is an all-consuming spiritual leader comes from the way the synagogue would view the rabbi. The much more biblical model shows the body ministering to each other.

Because this is the case, we, as church leaders, are forced to examine the ways we position ourselves as the only authority, minister, or leader, thereby inhibiting the gifts and ministry of others. Ministry in the kingdom is based on the metaphor of a body: All the parts are needed, and they all contribute to the whole. The body called the church is an organic unity that functions as a whole (see 1 Corinthians 12) and must be led with the whole body in view.

We must abandon our own ministry agendas and practices so that Jesus can fill us with His. How severely would our church methods and messages have to be rethought if we were serious about adopting John the Baptist's posture: "He must increase and I must decrease." How much more dangerous would the church be if we really didn't care who got credit for ideas and programs? But as things stand, our names often displace Jesus' name, and our ministries often serve as a poor substitute for the work that He is actually doing. As the church, we can no longer afford to offer people church. We must cease making converts and disciples of the church and must again focus all our efforts on seeing people connect with Jesus in His kingdom. Andrew Purves seems to have church leaders in mind when he writes this:

> Our new basis for ministry is a sharing in the continuing ministry of Jesus, for the church and her ministry can only be found where Jesus is already. We are bumped aside by God with whatever forcefulness is required, so that Jesus stands in our place. He offers the worship, discipleship, faith and ministry that we thought we could offer but can't. The crucifixion of our ministry is stagger-ing good news. Now ministry is possible for us, probably for the first time, as gospel.[4]

In Philippians 3:12 Paul talks about pressing on in ministry because he has been taken hold of by Christ. This is an aggressive picture that means that the ministry of the kingdom isn't up to me. I have a part to play, but it is only in response to the part that God plays. My part depends in every way upon the continuing ministry of Jesus, who is present to and for us in and by the grace and power of the Holy Spirit. As usual, N.T. Wright says it best. Our ministry is based on the life, death, resurrection, and ascension of Jesus, though the latter is most often ignored in our churches. "What happens when you downplay or ignore the ascension?" he asks.

> The answer is that *the church expands to fill the vacuum.* If Jesus is more or less identical with the church—if, that is, talk about Jesus can be reduced to talk about his presence within his people rather than his standing over against them and addressing them from elsewhere as their Lord, then we have created a high road to the worst kind of triumphalism...by trying to maintain that talk of the ascension is really talk about Jesus being with us everywhere, the church effectively presented itself (with its structures and hier-archy, its customs and quirks) instead of presenting Jesus as its Lord and itself as the world's servant, as Paul puts it...Only when we grasp firmly that the church is *not* Jesus and Jesus is *not* the

church—when we grasp, in other words, the truth of the ascension...only then are we rescued from both hollow triumphalism and shallow despair.[5]

Rethinking Strength and Weakness

David Gibbons, a pastor of another church in our area, once spoke to our staff and said that in his church, three questions are asked of any potential leader or staff member. I have hung on to two of the questions he mentioned as a helpful way to cultivate an environment where weaknesses, brokenness, and failure are openly discussed and dealt with.

The first question is, where is your limp? This question is derived from the story of Jacob wrestling with the angel in Genesis 32. His struggle with God results in a limp that Jacob walks with the rest of his life. What lies behind this question is the assumption that God uses our weakness and struggle (2 Corinthians 12:1-10), and that this becomes our platform for ministry. People who are not in touch with their own brokenness are hindered in ministry because God will not share His glory with another. For me, this rings true. The struggles I have had personally with my family or with our church have been precisely the things God has used to allow me to powerfully reach into and touch the lives of others. My entire ministry is different because I have struggled (or am struggling) with food, pornography, anxiety and depression, and greed. I have learned that our strength is not always the most qualifying thing about us. Often it is the weakness and growth sustained from the struggle that makes us usable in the kingdom of God.

The second question is this: What is in your hand? Referring back to God's question to Moses in Exodus, this question was asked of someone who was convinced he had nothing to offer. By asking the question, God demonstrated His willingness to use whatever Moses had close by (in this case, a staff). In other words, in a church culture that often insists that people receive special training, programs or discipleship before they can be set loose to minister, God seems to delight in using people *just as He finds them.* So often we focus on what we don't have, but the Scriptures teach us that we can do something *now.* The power of God brings the staff to life; all we must do is let Him do it.

⌒⌒

As we said at the beginning, the hard work of applying all that we have considered is really up to you. Many more practical ideas could have been given. But to do so might rob the church of its critical role in the world—to seek and discern, again and again, what God is up to in the people around us, and to adjust our ministry and efforts accordingly. The "paint by numbers" and "one size fits all" approaches to church that are popular these days are never what God had in mind for us. For so many of us, we hunger for something more. Something beyond managing a spiritual business, something beyond entertaining spiritual customers, something more than another program or event that doesn't result in life-transforming discipleship to Jesus or connection with others. My hope is that this book has helped reshape some of the conversation about what it means to be the people of God today.

May God bless and guide you into the "life that is truly life."

May Jesus draw you deeper and deeper into His kingdom.

May the Spirit of God breathe life and fire back into His church.

Bibliography

Barna, George. *Revolution: Finding Vibrant Faith Beyond the Walls of the Sanctuary.* Carol Stream, IL: Tyndale, 2005.

Beasley-Murray, G.R. *Jesus and the Kingdom of God.* Grand Rapids: Eerdmans, 1986.

Borg, Marcus J. *Jesus: Uncovering the Life, Teachings, and Relevance of a Religious Revolutionary.* New York: HarperSanFrancisco, 2006.

Borg, Marcus J., and John Dominic Crossan. *The Last Week: A Day-by-Day Account of Jesus' Final Week in Jerusalem.* New York: HarperSanFrancisco, 2006.

Boyd, Gregory A. *God at War: The Bible and Spiritual Conflict.* Downers Grove, IL: InterVarsity Press, 1997.

Boyd, Gregory A. *The Myth of a Christian Nation: How the Quest for Political Power Is Destroying the Church.* Grand Rapids: Zondervan, 2005.

Boyd, Gregory A. *Satan and the Problem of Evil: Constructing a Trinitarian Warfare Theodicy.* Downers Grove, IL: InterVarsity Press, 2001.

Bright, John. *The Kingdom of God.* Nashville: Abingdon, 1953.

Brewin, Kester. *Signs of Emergence: A Vision for Church That Is Organic, Networked, Decentralized, Bottom-Up, Communal, Flexible, and Always Evolving.* Grand Rapids: Baker Books, 2007.

Carter, Craig A. *Rethinking Christ and Culture: A Post-Christendom Perspective.* Grand Rapids: Brazos Press, 2006.

Chalke, Steve, and Alan Mann. *The Lost Message of Jesus.* Grand Rapids: Zondervan, 2003.

Chan, Simon. *Spiritual Theology: A Systematic Study of The Christian Life.* Downers Grove, IL: InterVarsity Press, 1998.

Clapp, Rodney. *A Peculiar People: The Church as Culture in a Post-Christian Society.* Downers Grove, IL: InterVarsity Press, 1996.

Clowney, Edmund P. *The Church.* Downers Grove, IL: InterVarsity Press, 1995.

Cole, Neil. *Organic Church: Growing Faith Where Life Happens.* San Francisco: Jossey-Bass, 2005.

Colsen, Jake. *So You Don't Want to Go to Church Anymore: An Unexpected Journey into the Reality of the Father's Family.* Moorpark, CA: Windblown Media, 2006.

Crossan, John Dominic. *God and Empire: Jesus Against Rome, Then and Now.* New York: HarperSanFrancisco, 2007.

Crossan, John Dominic. *Jesus: A Revolutionary Biography.* New York: HarperSanFrancisco, 1994.

Drane, John. *The McDonaldization of the Church: Spirituality, Creativity, and the Future of the Church.* London: Darton, Longman and Todd, 2000.

Driscoll, Mark. *The Radical Reformission: Reaching Out Without Selling Out.* Grand Rapids: Zondervan, 2004.

Dulles, Avery Cardinal. *Models of the Church.* New York: Image Books, 2002.

Erre, Mike. *The Jesus of Suburbia: Have We Tamed the Son of God to Fit Our Lifestyle?* Nashville: W Publishing Group, 2006.

Erre, Mike. *Why Guys Need God: The Spiritual Side of Money, Sex, and Relationships.* Eugene, OR: Harvest House, 2008.

Ferguson, Everett. *Backgrounds of Early Christianity.* Grand Rapids: Eerdmans, 1993.

Ford, Kevin G. *Transforming Church: Bringing Out the Good to Get to Great.* Carol Stream, IL: Saltriver, 2007.

Galli, Mark. *Jesus Mean and Wild: The Unexpected Love of an Untamable God.* Grand Rapids: Baker Books, 2006.

Garber, Steven. *The Fabric of Faithfulness: Weaving Together Belief and Behavior.* Downers Grove, IL: InterVarsity Press, 1996.

Gibbs, Eddie, and Ryan K. Bolger. *Emerging Churches: Creating Christian Community in Postmodern Cultures.* Grand Rapids: Baker Books, 2005.

Glasser, Arthur F. *Announcing the Kingdom: The Story of God's Mission in the Bible.* Grand Rapids: Baker Academic, 2003.

Green, Michael. *Evangelism in the Early Church.* Grand Rapids: Eerdmans, 2003.

Grenz, Stanley J. *Theology for the Community of God.* Grand Rapids: Eerdmans, 1994.

Halter, Hugh, and Matt Smay. *The Intangible Kingdom: Creating Incarnational Community.* San Francisco: Jossey-Bass, 2008.

Harvey, Barry A. *Another City: An Ecclesiological Primer for a Post-Christian World.* Harrisburg, PA: Trinity Press International, 1999.

Hauerwas, Stanley. *After Christendom.* Nashville: Abingdon Press, 1991.

Hauerwas, Stanley. *A Better Hope: Resources for a Church Confronting Capitalism, Democracy, and Postmodernity.* Grand Rapids: Brazos Press, 2000.

Hauerwas, Stanley, and William H. Willimon. *Resident Aliens: Life in the Christian Colony.* Nashville: Abingdon Press, 1989.

Hirsch, Alan. *The Forgotten Ways: Reactivating the Missional Church.* Grand Rapids: Brazos Press, 2006.

Horsley, Richard A. *Hearing the Whole Story: The Politics of Plot in Mark's Gospel.* Louisville: Westminster John Knox Press, 2001.

Horsley, Richard A., and Neil Asher Silberman. *The Message and the Kingdom: How Jesus and Paul Ignited a Revolution and Transformed the Ancient World.* Minneapolis: Fortress Press, 2002.

Karkkainen, Veli-Matti. *An Introduction to Ecclesiology: Ecumenical, Historical and Global Perspectives.* Downers Grove, IL: InterVarsity Press, 2002.

Keel, Tim. *Intuitive Leadership: Embracing a Paradigm of Narrative, Metaphor and Chaos.* Grand Rapids: Baker Books, 2007.

Kenneson, Philip D., and James L. Street. *Selling Out the Church: The Dangers of Church Marketing.* Nashville: Abingdon Press, 1997.

Kimball, Dan. *They Like Jesus but Not the Church: Insights from Emerging Generations.* Grand Rapids: Zondervan, 2007.

Kinnaman, David, and Gabe Lyons. *unChristian: What a New Generation Really Thinks about Christianity…And Why it Matters.* Grand Rapids: Baker Books, 2007.

Kraybill, Donald B. *The Upside-Down Kingdom.* Scottsdale, PA: Herald Press, 2003.

Ladd, George Eldon. *Crucial Questions About the Kingdom of God.* Grand Rapids: Eerdmans, 1952.

Ladd, George Eldon. *A Theology of the New Testament.* Grand Rapids: Eerdmans, 1974.

Letham, Robert. *The Lord's Supper: Eternal Word in Broken Bread.* Phillipsburg, NJ: P&R, 2001.

London, H.B., Jr., and Neil B. Wiseman. *Pastors at Greater Risk.* Ventura, CA: Regal Books, 2003.

MacMullen, Ramsay. *Christianizing the Roman Empire: A.D. 100–400.* New Haven: Yale University Press, 1984.

McClaren, Brian D. *The Church on the Other Side: Doing Ministry in the Postmodern Matrix.* Grand Rapids: Zondervan, 2000.

McLaren, Brian D. *The Secret Message of Jesus: Uncovering the Truth That Could Change Everything.* Nashville: W Publishing Group, 2006.

McKibben, Bill. "The Christian Paradox: How a faithful nation gets Jesus wrong." Harper's Magazine, August 2005, 31-37.

Meeks, Wayne A. *The First Urban Christians: The Social World of the Apostle Paul.* New Haven: Yale University Press, 1983.

Meeks, Wayne A. *The Moral World of the First Christians.* Philadelphia: Westminster Press, 1986.

Meeks, Wayne A. *The Origins of Christian Morality: The First Two Centuries.* New Haven: Yale University Press, 1993.

Metzger, Paul Louis. *Consuming Jesus: Beyond Race and Class Divisions in a Consumer Church.* Grand Rapids: Eerdmans, 2007.

Minear, Paul S. *Images of the Church in the New Testament.* Louisville: Westminster John Knox Press, 2004.

Moltmann, Jurgen. *Theology of Hope.* Minneapolis: Fortress Press, 1993.

Morphew, Derek. *Breakthrough: Discovering the Kingdom.* Cape Town, South Africa: Vineyard International Publishing, 1991.

Muller-Fahrenholz, Geiko. *The Kingdom and the Power: The Theology of Jurgen Moltmann.* Minneapolis: Fortress Press, 2001.

Myers, Ched. *Binding the Strong Man: A Political Reading of Mark's Story of Jesus.* Maryknoll, NY: Orbis Books, 1988.

Petersen, Jim. *Church Without Walls: Moving Beyond Traditional Boundaries.* Colorado Springs: Navpress, 1992.

Purves, Andrew. *The Crucifixion of Ministry: Surrendering Our Ambitions to the Service of Christ.* Downers Grove, IL: InterVarsity Press, 2007.

Reno, R.R. *In the Ruins of the Church: Sustaining Faith in an Age of Diminished Christianity.* Grand Rapids: Brazos Press, 2002.

Saucy, Robert L. *The Case for Progressive Dispensationalism: The Interface Between Dispensational and Non-Dispensational Theology.* Grand Rapids: Zondervan, 1993.

Saucy, Robert L. *The Church in God's Program.* Chicago: Moody Press, 1972.

Sider, Ronald J. *The Scandal of the Evangelical Conscience: Why Are Christians Living Just Like the Rest of the World?* Grand Rapids: Baker Books, 2005.

Snyder, Howard A., *The Community of the King.* Downers Grove, IL: InterVarsity Press, 2004.

Snyder, Howard A., and Daniel V. Runyon. *Decoding the Church: Mapping the DNA of Christ's Body.* Grand Rapids: Baker Books, 2002.

Stark, Rodney. *Cities of God: The Real Story of How Christianity Became an Urban Movement and Conquered Rome.* New York: HarperOne, 2006.

Stark, Rodney. *The Rise of Christianity: How the Obscure, Marginal Jesus Movement Became the Dominant Religious Force in the Western World in a Few Centuries.* New York: HarperSanFrancisco, 1997.

Stone, Bryan. *Evangelism after Christendom: The Theology and Practice of Christian Witness.* Grand Rapids: Brazos Press, 2007.

Torrance, James B. *Worship, Community and the Triune God of Grace.* Downers Grove, IL: InterVarsity Press, 1996.

Van Gelder, Craig. *The Ministry of the Missional Church: A Community Led by the Spirit.* Grand Rapids: Baker Books, 2007.

Wakabayashi, Allen Mitsuo. *Kingdom Come: How Jesus Wants to Change the World.* Downers Grove, IL: InterVarsity Press, 2003.

Webber, Robert E. *Journey to Jesus: The Worship, Evangelism, and Nurture Mission of the Church.* Nashville: Abingdon Press, 2001.

Wicker, Christine. *The Fall of the Evangelical Nation: The Surprising Crisis Inside the Church.* New York: HarperOne, 2008.

Willard, Dallas. *The Divine Conspiracy: Rediscovering Our Hidden Life in God.* San Francisco: HarperSanFrancisco, 1998.

Williams, Don. *Signs, Wonders, and the Kingdom of God: A Biblical Guide for the Reluctant Skeptic.* Vine Books, 1989.

Williams, Don. *Start Here: Kingdom Essentials for Christians.* Ventura, CA: Regal Books, 2006.

Wills, Garry. *What Jesus Meant.* New York: Viking, 2006.

Wilson, Jonathan R. *Why Church Matters: Worship, Ministry and Mission in Practice.* Grand Rapids: Brazos Press, 2006.

Witherington, Ben, III. *Making a Meal of It: Rethinking the Theology of the Lord's Supper.* Waco: Baylor University Press, 2007.

Witherington, Ben, III. *Troubled Waters: Rethinking the Theology of Baptism.* Waco: Baylor University Press, 2007.

Witherington, Ben, III, and Laura M. Ice. *The Shadow of the Almighty: Father, Son, and Spirit in Biblical Perspective.* Grand Rapids: Eerdmans, 2002.

Wolfe, Alan. *The Transformation of American Religion: How We Actually Live Our Faith.* Chicago: The University of Chicago Press, 2003.

Wright, Christopher J.H. *The Mission of God: Unlocking the Bible's Grand Narrative.* Downers Grove, IL: InterVarsity Press Academic, 2006.

Wright, N.T. *The Challenge of Jesus: Rediscovering Who Jesus Was and Is.* Downers Grove, IL: InterVarsity Press, 1999.

Wright, N.T. *Jesus and the Victory of God.* Minneapolis: Fortress Press, 1996.

Wright, N.T. *The Lord and His Prayer.* Grand Rapids: Eerdmans, 1996.

Wright, N.T. *The New Testament and the People of God.* Minneapolis: Fortress Press, 1992.

Wright, N.T. *The Resurrection of the Son of God.* Minneapolis: Fortress Press, 2003.

Wright, N.T. *Simply Christian: Why Christianity Makes Sense.* New York: HarperSanFrancisco, 2006.

Wright, N.T. *Surprised by Hope: Rethinking Heaven, the Resurrection, and the Mission of the Church.* New York: HarperOne, 2008.

Yoder, John Howard. *The Politics of Jesus.* Grand Rapids: Eerdmans, 1994.

Notes

Chapter 1—Descent into Irrelevance

First epigraph. William Easum, *Sacred Cows Make Gourmet Burger* (Nashville: Abingdon, 1995), 16-17, 19, 21-22. Quoted in Brian D. McLaren, *The Church on the Other Side: Doing Church in the Postmodern Matrix* (Grand Rapids: Zondervan, 2000), 20-21.

Second epigraph. Bill McKibben, "The Christian Paradox: How a faithful nation gets Jesus wrong," *Harper's Magazine*, August 2005, 32.

1. This designation and the references to Rodney Clapp in this paragraph are from his book *Peculiar People: The Church as a Culture in a Post-Christian Society* (Downers Grove, IL: InterVarsity Press, 1996), 19.

2. Clapp, *Peculiar People,* 20.

3. Clapp, *Peculiar People,* 20.

4. For instance, see Ron Sider, *The Scandal of the Evangelical Conscience: Why Are Christians Living Just Like the Rest of the World?* (Grand Rapids: Baker Books, 2005). The statistics to follow come from this book. See also Greg Boyd, *The Myth of a Christian Nation: How the Quest for Political Power is Destroying the Church* (Grand Rapids: Zondervan, 2005), 13-14.

5. In fact, one Barna survey indicated that the percentage of born-again Christians who had experienced divorce was *higher* than that of non-Christians (26 percent to 22 percent). See Sider, *The Scandal of the Evangelical Conscience,* 18-20; see also Boyd, *The Myth of a Christian Nation,* 136-37.

6. Michael Horton, "Beyond Culture Wars," *Modern Reformation,* May-June 1993, 3. Quoted in Sider, *The Scandal of the Evangelical Conscience,* 13.

7. Sider, *The Scandal of the Evangelical Conscience,* 17.

8. David Kinnaman and Gabe Lyons, *unChristian: What a New Generation Really Thinks about Christianity…and Why It Matters* (Grand Rapids: Baker Books, 2007).

9. Kinnaman and Lyons, *unChristian,* 26.

10. Kinnaman and Lyons, *unChristian,* 27.

11. In fact, many young believers within the church share the same negative perceptions as outsiders. See Kinnaman and Lyons, *unChristian,* 33.

12. LifeWay Research survey of 1023 Protestants, conducted April and May, 2007, cited in Cathy Lynn Grossman, "Young adults aren't sticking with church," *USA Today,* August 6, 2007. Available online at www.usatoday.com/news/religion/2007-08-06-church-dropouts_N.htm.

13. Kinnaman and Lyons, *unChristian,* 47:

    In virtually every study we conduct, representing thousands of interviews every year, born-again Christians fail to display much attitudinal or behavioral evidence of transformed lives. For instance, based on study released in 2007, we found that most of the lifestyle of born-again Christians were statistically equivalent to those of non-born-agains. When asked to identify their activities over the last thirty days, born-again believers were just as likely to bet or gamble, to visit a pornographic website, to take something that did not belong to them, to consult a medium or psychic, to physically fight or abuse someone, to have consumed enough alcohol to be considered legally drunk, to have used an illegal, nonprescription drug, to have said something to someone that was not true, to have gotten back at someone for something he or she did, and to have said mean things behind another person's back.

See also Eddie Gibbs and Ryan K. Bolger, *Emerging Churches: Creating Christian Community in Postmodern Cultures* (Grand Rapids: Baker Books, 2005), 19-22.

14. Alan Hirsch, *The Forgotten Ways: Reactivating the Missional Church* (Grand Rapids: Brazos Press, 2006), 35.

15. See George Barna, *Revolution: Finding Vibrant Faith Beyond the Walls of the Sanctuary* (Carol Stream, IL: Tyndale House, 2005), 49.

16. Statistics from H.B. London Jr. and Neil B Wiseman, *Pastors at Greater Risk: Real Help for Pastors from Pastors Who've Been There* (Ventura: Regal Books, 2003).

17. "Death by Ministry" statistics and presentation by Darrin Patrick and republished by Mark Driscoll. Available online at theresurgence.com/mdblog_2006-05-24_death_by_ministry.

18. Neil Cole, *Organic Church: Growing Faith Where Life Happens* (San Francisco: Jossey-Bass, 2005), xxv.

19. Cole, *Organic Church*, xxv.

20. Gibbs and Bolger, *Emerging Churches,* 72.

21. 1 Peter 4:17.

Chapter 2—Garage-Sale Jesus

First epigraph. Hugh Halter and Matt Smay, *The Tangible Kingdom* (San Francisco: Jossey-Bass, 2008), 115.

Second epigraph. Paul Louis Metzger, *Consuming Jesus* (Grand Rapids: Eerdmans, 2007), 97.

1. Hirsch, *The Forgotten Ways,* 106-7.

2. Hirsch, *The Forgotten Ways,* 107.

3. For a pretty complete list see www.alittleleaven.com.

4. Adelle M. Banks, "Trade Association: Sales of Christian Products Reach $4.6 Billion." Available online at www.beliefnet.com/story/221/story_22154_1.html.

5. See Mike Erre, *The Jesus of Suburbia* (Nashville: W Publishing Group, 2006), 97-113. Barry Harvey, *Another City: An Ecclesiological Primer for a Post-Christian World* (Harrisburg, PA: Trinity Press International, 1999), 3.

> Christians, particularly in North America, constitute for the most part a rather indistinguishable lot in the modern world, assuming along with virtually everyone else that their purpose in life is to pursue their own interests in every sphere allotted to them by the institutions of our commercial republic...They regard religion almost exclusively as a private and inward matter, quite often as a form of therapy designed to make their lives more fulfilling. They see little or nothing wrong in regarding the church as simply another vendor of goods and services.

6. Hirsch, *The Forgotten Ways,* 109-10.

7. Philip D. Kenneson and James L. Street, *Selling Out the Church: The Dangers of Church Marketing* (Nashville: Abingdon Press, 1997), 67.

8. John Drane, *The McDonaldization of the Church: Spirituality, Creativity, and the Future of the Church* (London: Darton, Longman and Todd, 2000), 28-29.

9. Christine Wicker, *The Fall of the Evangelical Nation: The Surprising Crisis Inside the Church* (New York: HarperOne, 2008), 123.

10. Just kidding about that last one (kind of).

11. Drane, *The McDonaldization of the Church,* 42-43.

12. I came across a blog entry a while back that had the following quote. I cannot find the reference for it or its original source, but it captures exactly what many of us are sensing about the church.

   Mark Matlock, president and founder of WisdomWorks Ministries, spoke on the church and culture. He compared the values of culture to the values of the kingdom. Cultural values: identity, controlling the process, critique of others, and achievement of outcomes. Kingdom values: denial of self, submission to God and others, serving others, and trusting God for outcomes. He closed with the following comment: The institutions that house the church have become works of culture, not the kingdom.

13. David Swanson, "The Glory and the Grief." Available online at blog.christianitytoday.com/outofur/archives/2008/02/.

14. Available online at videochurchblog.typepad.com/my_weblog/2008/02/page/2/.

15. Hirsch, *The Forgotten Ways,* 110.

16. Needless to say, even the phrase itself is a capitulation to consumer culture. The concept of church shopping is utterly antithetical to the view of the church in the New Testament.

17. McKibben, "The Christian Paradox," 33-34.

18. Kenneson and Street, *Selling Out the Church,* 23.

19. See Kenneson and Street, *Selling Out the Church,* 49-53 for more on this. See also 1 Corinthians 4:7 and Acts 8:20.

Chapter 3—The King and His Kingdom

Epigraph. Frederick Buechner, quoted in Brian D. McLaren, *The Secret Message of Jesus: Uncovering the Truth That Could Change Everything* (Nashville: W Publishing Group, 2006), 199.

1. And if you don't, my friend Doug Berry will personally refund your money. (He won't really. He has just always wanted to see his name in print.)

2. John Bright, *The Kingdom of God: The Biblical Concept and Its Meaning for the Church* (Nashville: Abingdon, 1953), 7-10, 18; Robert L. Saucy, *The Church in God's Program* (Chicago: Moody Press, 1972), 83. Arthur Glasser, *Announcing the Kingdom: The Story of God's Mission in the Bible* (Grand Rapids: Baker Academic, 2003), 20-21:

   God's right to reign and rule over all creation and over all the peoples of the world must be univocally understood. This brings together the message of the OT and NT narratives because the Kingdom of God is one of the most central themes of the Bible. Although explicitly a New Testament theme, we are deeply persuaded that the Old Testament can also be understood from this perspective...The lordship of Christ can be best understood when it is informed by OT concepts of kingship.

   Derek Morphew, *Breakthrough: Discovering the Kingdom* (Cape Town, South Africa: Vineyard International, 1991), 8:

When we look at the Word of God from the perspective of the centrality of Christ, we realize that the message, ministry and self-understanding of Jesus are inseparably linked to the kingdom. Jesus came announcing the kingdom. His parables explained the kingdom, and his miracles bore witness to its presence. In fact, the theme of the kingdom as preached by Jesus Christ unites the whole flow of biblical truth, from Moses, through the Prophets, the Writings, the Gospels, the Epistles and the Revelation of John.

Robert Saucy, *The Case for Progressive Dispensationalism: The Interface Between Dispensational and Non-dispensational Theology* (Grand Rapids: Zondervan, 1993), 27: "The kingdom…best encompasses the full meaning of God's work in the history of Scripture."

3. I'll retain the traditional usage of *Old Testament* and use *Hebrew Scriptures* as synonymous. *Yahweh* is the proper name of the God of Israel.

4. For more information, see George Eldon Ladd, *Crucial Questions About the Kingdom of God* (Grand Rapids: Eerdmans, 1952), 45-49; or Bright, *The Kingdom of God,* 17-44.

5. Ancient kings used *images* of themselves to extend their rule to the far reaches of their kingdoms.

6. See Genesis 9:9-11; 17:4; Exodus 19:5; 2 Samuel 7:11-16; Jeremiah 31:31-34. Covenants come in two kinds: the unconditional royal grant (like the Abrahamic covenant) and the conditional vassal treaty (like the Mosaic covenant). The New Covenant fulfills the covenant made with Abraham (see Galatians 3:6-14; 4:21-31). It is unconditional and perpetual.

7. Genesis 12:1-3.

8. Morphew, *Breakthrough,* 15 and following; Ladd, *Crucial Questions About the Kingdom of God,* 61 and following. See Isaiah 24:23; 33:22; 52:7; Zephaniah 3:15; Zechariah 14:9 and following. The Jews saw the kingdom to come both in terms of an earthly reign of a descendant of David (Isaiah 9:11) and also a cataclysmic intervening of God at the end of the age, marked by the dramatic appearance of the Son of Man (Daniel 7). In each case, God was to defeat Israel's enemies and establish her as chief among the nations settled in the land once promised to Abraham.

9. Arthur Glasser explains:

> There is both differentiation and intimate correlation between God's universal rule and his kingly rule over his people. As creator and redeemer he will finally and fully triumph in human history. As a God who is faithful to his covenants, God will bring his people to a golden age of salvation. We cannot adequately understand the Old Testament unless we take into account the full measure of the Old Testament's record of failure. We must consider the details of Israel's persistent apostasy and from this perspective review the hopes and expectations so vividly set forth by the prophets: God will ultimately realize his covenantal goal for his people. Through this hope we can begin to appreciate the uniqueness of Jesus Christ: he is the other Israel—by a totally obedient life, a truthful witness to his generation, and a substitutionary atoning surrender of his life in death, Jesus establishes a new and unbreakable covenant of grace and salvation that will embrace all nations (Jer. 31:31-34; Ezek. 39:24-28). He makes possible the ultimate triumph of God in history (*Announcing the Kingdom,* 22-23).

10. Regarding God's universal reign over creation, see 2 Kings 19:15; Psalm 29:10; 99:1-4; Isaiah 6:5; Jeremiah 46:18. For God's particular reign over Israel, see Numbers 23:21; Deuteronomy 33:5; Isaiah 43:15.

11. See Morphew, *Breakthrough*, 21-22. The river Nile was the domain of the god Ha'pi. The first plague (turning the Nile to blood) was the effective demonstration of Ha'pi's death. Heqit, the goddess of fertility, was the subject of the second plague. She was symbolized by frogs, and when they began to multiply beyond control, it was a clear sign to the Egyptian people that Heqit was herself subject to the God of Israel. The killing of livestock targeted three deities who were represented by the bull (Apis), the cow (Isis) and the ram (Ammon). The powerful sun god, Ra, was blotted out during the ninth plague when darkness settled over the land at daytime.

12. Morphew, *Breakthrough*, 23.

13. Exodus 19:6.

14. See Harvey, *Another City*, 44-47.

15. N.T. Wright, *The New Testament and the People of God* (Minneapolis: Fortress Press, 1992), 307; see also Harvey, *Another City*, 46.

16. A suzerainty treaty was a treaty between unequals (as opposed to an ancient parity treaty, made between two equal parties for mutual benefit). The covenant between Yahweh and His people at Sinai is an example of a suzerainty treaty—it follows the conventions of the day. Egypt had been defeated in battle, so Yahweh could now enter into a new agreement with Israel as a conquering king. But this treaty was different from those of the day: Yahweh, the conquering King and Suzerain, would live among his people (Deuteronomy 4:32-34). This was unheard of. Usually, kings ruled lands and peoples from a distance or through representatives.

17. How can God be King and David be king at the same time? This apparent contradiction is answered in the Incarnation: Jesus is fully divine (God) and fully human (man). As God, He is the eternal Son of God. As human, He is the son of David. He reigns on God's throne and David's throne simultaneously. What appears to be a contradiction in the Old Testament is resolved in the New.

18. See Nehemiah 9:36-37. For more on this, see N.T. Wright, *Simply Christian* (New York: HarperSanFrancisco, 2006), 79.

19. The word *eschatology* refers to the study of last things or the end of history. It includes more than heaven and hell—it also refers to the strongly held belief of most first-century Jews and virtually all early Christians that under the guidance of God, history was headed toward God's new world of justice, healing, and hope. Regarding the end of the present age and the beginning of the new, see Harvey, *Another City*, 52, and N.T. Wright, *The New Testament and the People of God*, 298-99.

20. Clapp, *Peculiar People*, 86; see also N.T. Wright, *The New Testament and the People of God*, 466; Harvey, *Another City*, 55.

21. In the fourth Gospel, John substitutes the phrase *eternal life* for *the kingdom of God*. See McLaren, *The Secret Message of Jesus*, 36-37; Ladd, *Crucial Questions About the Kingdom of God*, 57. The phrase *kingdom of God* is equivalent to *kingdom of heaven*. See Ladd, *Crucial Questions About the Kingdom of God*, 63-64. Elsewhere, Ladd writes, "It is the coming of God's Kingdom (Mt. 6:10) or its appearing (Lk. 19:11) that will bring this age to its end and inaugurate the Age to Come. It is important to note, however, that *basileia* (*Kingdom*) can designate both the manifestation or coming of God's kingly rule and the eschatological realm in which God's rule is enjoyed. In this sense, inheriting eternal life and entrance into the Kingdom of God are synonymous with entering into the Age to Come" (*Theology of the New Testament*, 64). Likewise, Wright notes, "God's kingdom and the Kingdom of Heaven mean the same thing—the sovereign rule of God (that is, the rule of heaven, of the one who lives in heaven), which according to

Jesus was and is breaking into the present world, to earth" (*Surprised by Hope,* 201). See also Ladd, *Crucial Questions About the Kingdom of God,* 121-27.

22. In the New Testament, *basileia* (a noun) is usually translated as "kingdom," but the term refers to the act of God reigning.

23. George Eldon Ladd, *The Gospel of the Kingdom* (Grand Rapids: Eerdmans, 1994), 19.

24. Ladd, *A Theology of the New Testament,* 78-81.

25. Allen Mitsuo Wakabayashi, *Kingdom Come: How Jesus Wants to Change the World* (Downers Grove, IL: InterVarsity Press, 2003), 30.

26. See Donald Kraybill, *The Upside-Down Kingdom* (Scottsdate, PA: Herald Press, 2003), 18.

27. I don't mean to imply that Jesus meant exactly the same thing His contemporaries did by the phrase, but rather I am trying to give the flavor of the dynamic nature of the kingdom and how one enters into it. As Wright so aptly demonstrated, Jewish hope about the coming kingdom centered on several ideas: (1) God would fulfill all his promises to Israel, (2) Israel would be delivered from the oppression of foreign nations, (3) God would bring judgment upon the nations (particularly Israel's enemies), and (4) God would usher in a new era of justice and peace. Obviously, Jesus conceived of the kingdom in different terms (N.T. Wright, *Simply Christian,* 100).

28. See Mishnah, Berachot 2:2. The remainder of this section is adapted from Robert Lindsey, "The Kingdom of God: God's Power Among Believers," Jerusalem Perspective Online.

29. For example, in Mark 1–8, Jesus is the Warrior King, advancing God's reign against the powers of darkness. In Mark 8–16, Jesus is the Suffering Servant of the Lord who comes to bear away our sorrows, take our sins, and then be vindicated. He triumphs through suffering. See John Howard Yoder, *The Politics of Jesus* (Grand Rapids: Eerdmans, 1994), 24-25.

30. For Jesus, the ministry of John was the transition to the ministry of the kingdom (Luke 7:24-28; Matthew 11:14). The turning point from the old (the Law and he Prophets) to the new came in the ministry of John. John was the last and greatest of the prophets; since his ministry, the kingdom is working in the world and is the focus of God's work in the world. Jesus saw His own ministry as the fulfillment of the Old Testament promises, short of the final, eschatological consummation (Luke 4:21).

31. See Erre, *Jesus of Suburbia,* 79-83.

32. See Wright, *The New Testament and the People of God,* 280-338 for more on the varied expectations of first-century Jews regarding the kingdom and the Messiah.

33. George Eldon Ladd, *A Theology of the New Testament* (Grand Rapids: Eerdmans, 1993), chapter 6. See also Oscar Cullmann, *Christ and Time: The Primitive Christian Conception of Time* (Louisville: Westminster John Knox Press, 1964).

34. This eschatological tension has puzzled modern scholars. Some, like Albert Schweitzer in the *Quest for the Historical Jesus,* think that Jesus was mistaken about the nature and coming of the kingdom. They argue that Jesus expected the final consummation of the kingdom to come in His lifetime or soon thereafter (Matthew 10:23; Luke 9:27).

Others, like C.H. Dodd in *The Parables of the Kingdom,* argued the opposite extreme and held that the kingdom was fully and completely present in Jesus' ministry (Luke 10:9; 11:20). This view is called *realized eschatology* because the kingdom was fully realized in Jesus.

A third position is the view of traditional dispensational theologians. In this view, the kingdom is relegated to the future and literal reign of Christ on earth during the millennium. Dispensationalists argue that Jesus offered the fullness of the kingdom to Israel during His ministry. Their subsequent rejection of Him as Messiah forced God to delay the arrival of the kingdom until Jesus' return.

35. See Kraybill, *The Upside-Down Kingdom*, 26.

36. See Ladd, *A Theology of the New Testament*, 45-49. See also N.T. Wright, *The New Testament and the People of God*, chapter 6; *Jesus and the Victory of God*, 202-10; *The Resurrection of the Son of God*, 578-583.

37. The same can be said for Pentecost. The coming of the Holy Spirit was another sign of the age to come. Peter references this in Acts 2.

38. See Ladd, *A Theology of the New Testament*, 48:

> In brief, this age, which extends from creation to the Day of the Lord, which in the Gospels is designated in terms of the parousia of Christ, resurrection and judgment, is the age of human existence in weakness and mortality, of evil, sin and death. The Age to Come will see the realization of all that the reign of God means, and will be the age of resurrection into eternal life in the Kingdom of God.

39. Jesus compares the kingdom to a mustard seed (Matthew 13:31-32), yeast mixed into flour (Matthew 13:33), treasure buried in a field (Matthew 13:44), a pearl of immense value (Matthew 13:45-46), a net gathering fish (Matthew 13:47-50), workers in a vineyard (Matthew 20:1-16), a banquet (Matthew 22:1-14), and money entrusted to servants (Matthew 25:14-30).

40. Morphew, *Breakthrough*, 71.

41. Jesus saw the future consummation of the kingdom in Daniel's terms: the dramatic coming of the Son of Man at the end of this age (Matthew 24:29–25:46). The Son of Man will judge the nations (Matthew 25:31-32), and His disciples will share in the judgment of Israel (Luke 22:29-30). Many of His parables contain these elements. Wheat and weeds grow together until harvest (Matthew 13:30), when good and bad are separated at the end (Matthew 13:47-52). Everything will be disclosed in the coming judgment (Luke 8:16-18), and a great banquet will signify that the kingdom has fully come (Matthew 22:1-14).

42. Morphew, *Breakthrough*, 92-93.

Chapter 4—The Kingdom of the Church or the Church of the Kingdom?

Epigraph. Metzger, *Consuming Jesus*, 36-37.

1. For more on how the view espoused here relates to traditional eschatological concepts like the millennium, see Ladd, *A Theology of the New Testament*.

2. Colossians 1:20; Acts 3:21; Matthew 19:28, respectively.

3. Ephesians 1:22.

4. Matthew 28:20; Acts 1:8.

5. 1 Corinthians 10:11. See Harvey, *Another City*, 64.

6. See Yoder, *The Politics of Jesus*, 33-34.

7. We should remember that for Paul, the Jews never replace the Gentiles and vice versa; God simply uses the one to reach the other and forms a new humanity out of those Jews and Gentiles who come to faith in Christ. In some ways, this new identity replaces the old distinctions that kept people far from God (Galatians 3:28).

8. Harvey, *Another City*, 170 and footnote 31.

9. This section follows Ladd, *A Theology of the New Testament*, 107-19, quite closely.
10. Ladd, *A Theology of the New Testament*, 108 (see Matthew 19:28; Luke 22:30).
11. Glasser, *Announcing the Kingdom*. 224:

> The word *ekklesia* is used twice by Matthew. Inasmuch as the context of 18:17 concerns the disciplinary process that is to be followed within the community (18:15-35), it substantiates what we have said earlier about Jesus' provision of the interim community. Jesus granted Peter the keys of the kingdom (16:19)—this does not means that Peter gained the exclusive right to admit persons into the church or excommunicate them from fellowship. The metaphor of keys was used elsewhere by Jesus to represent the sort of knowledge that makes entrance into the kingdom possible (Luke 11:52). Binding and losing was related more to his preaching than to disciplinary authority he may have exercised during the course of this ministry. These were given to carry the divine revelation of Jesus to humanity.

12. Of course, we see obvious differences between the ministry of the divine Son of God in human skin and the ministry of very broken and sinful human beings. But that is why Pentecost (the coming of the Holy Spirit) is so important. We were baptized and anointed with the same Spirit as Jesus. That is the basis for our authority and power—our union with Him through His Spirit.
13. Matthew 28:16-20; Luke 24:45-49; John 20:19-23; Acts 1:7-8.
14. In this context, the phrase *the baptism of the Holy Spirit* gains special significance.
15. Some dispensationalists believe that *kingdom* refers exclusively to the Davidic monarchy and the nation of Israel, and *church* refers to the body of Christ, which has a completely separate destiny than does the nation of Israel. In this view, Jesus offered Israel the real, millennial, Davidic kingdom, but when they rejected it, He began to form something new: the church.
16. Glasser, *Announcing the Kingdom*, 221.
17. Ladd, *A Theology of the New Testament*, 117-18.
18. Ladd, *A Theology of the New Testament*, 119.

Chapter 5—Interlude: Why This Matters

Epigraph. Richard Rohr, "Holy Fools: Ushers of the Next Generation of the Church," *Sojourners Magazine*, July 1994. Quoted in Tim Keel, *Intuitive Leadership: Embracing a Paradigm of Narrative, Metaphor, and Chaos* (Grand Rapids: Baker Books, 2007), 67.

1. Gibbs and Bolger, *Emerging Churches*, 90.
2. I know this is one of those "No, duh!" kind of statements, but for a long time I have felt and acted as if it were up to me to do God's work, so I would cheerlead, cast or articulate vision, rally people behind campaigns and programs, and try to be an entertaining teacher.
3. My own community, Rock Harbor church, is a large, attractional community that is trying (and sometimes succeeding and sometimes failing) to put this into practice. How can we be a church that is kingdom minded? How can we bless other churches instead of stealing people from them? How can we avoid the mentality that bigger is better because bigger means that God is moving? The lead pastor of our church, Todd Proctor, has led the way in asking questions like these. This is what his heart is for the church. We'll get into the particulars in a couple of chapters, but I wanted to affirm him here even though he'll never read this. He skims the books I write and does not look up the endnotes. But just in case—Todd, can I have a raise?

4. N.T. Wright, *Simply Christian*, 200.
5. Here are the exceptions: Matthew 15:21-28; Mark 8:1-10; Luke 7:1-10.
6. Clapp, *Peculiar People*, 32, 75, 95; Robert E. Webber, *Journey to Jesus: The Worship, Evangelism, and Nurture Mission of the Church* (Nashville: Abingdon Press, 2001), 13.

Chapter 6—More than a Ticket: Why the Four Spiritual Laws Need to Add a Few

Epigraph. Boyd, *The Myth of a Christian Nation*, 29.

1. Mark 1:21-28,32-34; 5:1-20.
2. This section summarizes work done by Don Williams in an unpublished paper.
3. This worldview is articulated and defended beautifully by Greg Boyd in *God at War: The Bible and Spiritual Conflict* (Downers Grove, IL: InterVarsity Press, 1997).
4. When Jesus spoke of the kingdom of God as having drawn near or come, He was also announcing that it lies on a collision course with all human rule or authority. Satan is determined to thwart the progress of the kingdom. Jesus taught that the Father gave Him authority to rule (Matthew 11:27; 28:18; Luke 10:22). He will exercise this rule until the dominion of Satan, sin, and death is brought to a complete end (Mark 9:1; 13:26; 14:62; Luke 11:20-22). Paul later added that Jesus will eventually return this authority and rule to the Father (1 Corinthians 15:24-28).
5. See Glasser, *Announcing the Kingdom*, 188. "The finger of God" (Luke 11:20) was the phrase the Egyptian magicians used when they could not account for the disasters that fell on Egypt through Moses' confrontation with Pharaoh (Exodus 8:19). The signs achieved by the finger of God were demonstrations of the power of God that led to the exodus of the Jews from Egypt. Here Jesus saw His works of exorcism as the kingdom's preliminary assault on the power of evil in the earth.
6. See Christopher J.H. Wright, *The Mission of God: Unlocking the Bible's Grand Narrative* (Downers Grove, IL: InterVarsity Press Academic, 2006), 268-72 for an account of all the dimensions of the salvation of Israel in the Exodus.
7. N.T. Wright, *Simply Christian*, 75; N.T. Wright, *The Challenge of Jesus: Rediscovering Who Jesus Was and Is* (Downers Grove, IL: InterVarsity Press, 1999), 159. Glasser, *Announcing the Kingdom*, 94:
   > God redeemed his elect people from Egypt so they could be his agents in liberating the nations. When the apostle Paul later sought to understand the meaning of the cross of Christ, he would fall back on this early major triumph of Yahweh. In fact, Paul made almost 40 references to the Exodus in his epistles.
8. See Ezekiel 5:5-9.
9. See Isaiah 1:11-15; 29:13; Jeremiah 7:9-10; Ezekiel 10:18.
10. See Isaiah 24:4-6; Jeremiah 2:7.
11. Glasser, *Announcing the Kingdom*, 150:
    > The prophets had spoken of a new exodus (Jer. 31:2-6, 15-22; Ez. 20:33-38; Hos. 2:14-20). But Isaiah poured into this concept something that went before beyond any restoration of the old monarchy...Isaiah oscillated in his description of the servant of the Lord, ranging from Israel, blind and deaf (42:19) to a righteous remnant (44:1; 51:6-7); finally he is the new Moses about to lead God's people into a new exodus from the captivity of sin. He is the great servant—in his sinlessness—who takes people out in mission to the nations. The wealth of messianic predictions

are found in three distinct though interrelated figures—whether a Davidic king, a divine son of man, or a suffering servant—all are the embodiment of wisdom and righteousness; all act in judgment, and all possess the spirit of God.

12. Glasser, *Announcing the Kingdom,* 75.

13. Some people ask why Paul doesn't use kingdom language more often. The first answer is that he uses it more than they may realize. Paul mentions the kingdom in connection with the gospel (1 Corinthians 4:15,20; Colossians 1:13,23; 1 Thessalonians 2:9,12; 2 Thessalonians 1:5,8). But because of the political overtones involved in preaching a kingdom, Paul wisely preferred for the most part to translate what he had to say into other categories, such as eternal life, salvation, or justification. Repentance and faith are essential human conditions, though Paul prefers to use synonyms for repentance such as dying to sin and putting off the old man.

The second answer is that Paul was incredibly subversive in his choice of language. He continually takes the empty language and slogans used in paganism and emperor worship and fills them with new meaning because of Jesus. To say that "Jesus is Lord" was to declare politically, religiously, and economically that no other lord (such as Caesar) could be acknowledged. This is kingdom reality. Paul was, first and foremost, a missionary. His mission, as reflected in his writings, was to take the Semitic gospel and to translate it into Hellenistic language and concepts. The Greeks had none of the Old Testament background that would have been necessary to make sense of the phrase "the kingdom of God." So instead, Paul uses phrases like "in Christ" or "being saved" to proclaim the same reality. The shift from kingdom language in the Gospels to church language in the epistles reflects a shift from Jewish to Greek culture.

Chapter 7—Hammer and Tongs

Title. This title has nothing to do with the material in this chapter (which is about the implications of the last one). I just thought it would make a cool chapter title.

Epigraph. N.T. Wright, *Surprised by Hope: Rethinking Heaven, the Resurrection, and the Mission of the Church* (New York, HarperOne, 2008), 227.

1. Don Williams, *Start Here: Kingdom Essentials for Christians* (Ventura, CA: Regal Books, 2006), 36.

2. N.T. Wright, *Surprised by Hope,* 200.

3. Ephesians 1:10. Glasser, *Announcing the Kingdom,* 155-56:

When Messiah comes he will be the means whereby Israel is converted and transformed by the Holy Spirit in accordance with the new covenant. This will be far more efficacious than the old covenant because the people will be given a heart of flesh—he will place his spirit within his people—thereby making possible their walking in his statutes and observing his ordinances (Jer. 31:31-33; Ez. 36:24-27). Further, when Messiah comes he will "restore David's fallen tent...repair its broken places, restore its ruins and build it as it used to be" (Amos 9:11)...Thus the New Israel becomes the gathering point around which the nations assemble in order to participate in God's salvation. The key passage is Isa. 2:2-4—in one sense this gathering will be in response to God's imperative eschatological summons, through the preaching of the good news of the kingdom by the church. In another sense it will take place on the last day...then, at long last, it will be said, "Israel will be...a blessing on the earth" (Isa. 19:24)—the promise made to Abraham will have been finally fulfilled. When Messiah comes he will judge the nations for their sins and for their treatment of Israel (Mal. 3:2)—in the Old Testament, the final salvation that the Messiah brings will be all-inclusive. It will embrace the reconciliation of sinners to God, the forgiveness of their sins, the renewal of nature, the removal of the curse of death, and the wiping away of all tears (Isa. 25:6-8; 11:6-9). It will embrace the totality of human existence and will be cosmic in its significance.

4. N.T. Wright, *Surprised by Hope,* 103.
5. Williams, *Start Here,* 15.
6. Romans 12:1.
7. Erre, *Jesus of Suburbia,* 77-96.
8. Ladd, *A Theology of the New Testament,* 73.
9. Ladd, *A Theology of the New Testament,* 72.
10. For more on this, see Clinton Arnold, *Three Crucial Questions about Spiritual Warfare* (Grand Rapids: Baker Academic, 1997).

Chapter 8—The Big Story of God's People

Epigraph. Keel, *Intuitive Leadership,* 144-45.

1. N.T. Wright, *The Challenge of Jesus,* 36; The Resurrection of the Son of God, 200-6.
2. Ben Meyer, *The Early Christians: Their World Mission and Self-Discovery* (Wilmington, DE: Michael Glazier, 1986), 96:

    This scheme is recurrent in Acts. First, the word is offered to Jews, who split into camps of believers and unbelievers. The believers by their faith constitute restored Israel, heir of the covenant and promises. Now and only now may Gentiles find salvation, precisely by assimilation into restored Israel.

    See also N.T. Wright, *The New Testament and the People of God,* 93, 96; see also N.T. Wright, *Climax of the Covenant* (Minneapolis: Augsburg Fortress, 1994), 150-51. The church as new Israel does not nullify God's election of old Israel and those within it who do not now believe in Jesus.
3. N.T. Wright, *Jesus and the Victory of God,* 473; see also N.T. Wright, *The Challenge of Jesus,* 44.
4. N.T. Wright, *The Challenge of Jesus,* 53.
5. Stanley Hauerwas and William H. Willimon, *Resident Aliens: Life in the Christian Colony* (Nashville: Abingdon Press, 1989), 32-33.
6. Clapp, *Peculiar People,* 36.
7. Matthew 16:24. Neo, a character in Brian McLaren's *A New Kind of Christian,* puts it perfectly when he asks for "a postmodern consideration of what salvation means, something beyond an individualized and consumeristic version. I may have a personal home, personal car, personal computer, personal identification number, personal digital assistant, personal hot-tub—all I need now is personal salvation from my own personal savior…this all strikes me as Christianity diced through the modern Veg-o-matic." Brian D. McLaren, *A New Kind of Christian: A Tale of Two Friends on a Spiritual Journey* (San Francisco: Jossey-Bass, 2001), 130.
8. See Steven Garber, *The Fabric of Faithfulness: Weaving Together Belief and Behavior* (Downers Grove, IL: InterVarsity Press, 1996), 160-61.
9. Georges Florovsky, "Empire and Desert: Antinomies of Christian History," *The Greek Orthodox Theological Review,* winter, 1957, 133-34; quoted in Harvey, *Another City,* 21-22.

10. See Stanley Hauerwas, *A Better Hope: Resources for a Church Confronting Capitalism, Democracy, and Postmodernity* (Grand Rapids: Brazos Press, 2000), 211-212.

11. Paul explains that this mystery is the summing up of all things in Christ (Ephesians 1:9-10). It shows itself clearly in the reconciliation of Jew and Gentile into one new humanity through the cross (Ephesians 2:14-16 and 3:2-6, where the word *mystery* occurs three times).

12. Obviously, this was the intent. As Paul's instructions to the church at Corinth show, the early church was still very much a work in progress.

13. See Kraybill, *The Upside-Down Kingdom*.

14. Harvey, *Another City,* 59.

15. Michael Green, *Evangelism in the Early Church* (Grand Rapids: Eerdmans, 2003), 253-72.

16. For more on this point, see Ramsay MacMullen, *Christianizing the Roman Empire* A.D. *100–400* (New Haven, CT: Yale University Press, 1984).

Chapter 9—One Is the Loneliest Number

Epigraph. Lesslie Newbigin, *The Gospel in a Pluralist Society* (Grand Rapids: Eerdmans, 1996), 22. Quoted in McLaren, *The Church on the Other Side,* 183-84.

1. See Hauerwas and Willimon, *Resident Aliens,* 77-78.

Chapter 10—The Church at the End of the World

First epigraph. C.S. Lewis, quoted in W. Vaus, *Mere Theology: A Guide to the Thought of C.S. Lewis* (Downers Grove, IL: InterVarsity Press, 2004), 167.

Second epigraph. Webber, *Journey to Jesus,* 68.

1. Bryan Stone, *Evangelism after Christendom: The Theology and Practice of Christian Witness* (Grand Rapids: Brazos Press, 2007), 15; Glasser, *Announcing the Kingdom,* 17; Hauerwas and Willimon, *Resident Aliens,* 43.

2. Jonathan R.Wilson, *Why Church Matters: Worship, Ministry and Mission in Practice* (Grand Rapids: Brazos Press, 2006), 80 and following.

3. N.T. Wright, *The Challenge of Jesus,* 53.

4. Glasser, *Announcing the Kingdom,* 17.

5. Christopher Wright, *The Mission of God,* 23.

6. See 2 Corinthians 5:19.

7. N.T. Wright, *Surprised by Hope,* 104-5.

8. Erre, *The Jesus of Suburbia,* 97-113.

9. Craig Van Gelder, *The Ministry of the Missional Church: A Community Led by the Spirit* (Grand Rapids: Baker Books, 2007), 72-89. I will use his terminology and adapt his material; any mistakes or misunderstanding in this section are due to me.

10. Ephesians 2:21-22; 1 Peter 2:4-5.

11. I use this term here because Van Gelder does. I myself am not a huge fan of the term because it is too elastic. Much like the words *emergent* or *postmodern, missional* comes loaded with meaning but lacks clarity and precision.

12. Van Gelder, *The Ministry of the Missional Church,* 93.

Chapter 11—Missional Church 101

Epigraph. Halter and Smay, *The Tangible Kingdom, 38.*

1. Gibbs and Bolger, *Emerging Churches,* 91.
2. McLaren, *The Church on the Other Side,* 36.
3. Andrew Purves calls this "the crucifixion of our ministry."
4. Howard Snyder, *The Community of the King,* quoted in Glasser, *Announcing the Kingdom,* 200-201.

Chapter 12—The Confessional Church and the Subversive Jesus

Epigraph. Andrew Purves, *The Crucifixion of Ministry: Surrendering Our Ambitions to the Service of Christ* (Downers Grove, IL: InterVarsity Press, 2007), 30.

1. For example, see Romans 10:8-9; Philippians 2:9-11.
2. Williams, *Start Here,* 16-17.
3. One of the early Christian apologists, Theophilus, in his letter to a man named Autolycus, asserted that with Christians, "temperance dwells, self-restraint is practiced, monogamy is observed, chastity is guarded, iniquity exterminated, sin extirpated, righteousness exercised, law administered, worship performed, God acknowledged." From "Letter to Autolycus," 3.15, in *The Ante-Nicene Fathers: Translation of the Writings of the Fathers Down to A.D. 325,* vol. 2 (Grand Rapids: Eerdmans, 1971), 115. The philosopher Aristides wrote, "They do not commit adultery nor fornication, nor bear false witness, nor covet the things of others…They are eager to do good to their enemies; they are gentle and easy to be entreated…[They] live holy and just lives, as the Lord enjoined upon them." Both quoted in Webber, *Journey to Jesus,* 31.
4. See Erre, *Jesus of Suburbia,* 1-20.
5. Tertullian's comments are indicative of the attitude of the early church: "One soul cannot be true to two masters—God and Caesar." Tertullian, *On Idolatry;* quoted in Webber, *Journey to Jesus,* 34.
6. N.T. Wright, *The New Testament and the People of God,* 350.
7. McLaren, *The Secret Message of Jesus,* 96.
8. Clapp, *Peculiar People,* 81.
9. Harvey, *Another City,* 18.
10. Hauerwas and Willimon, *Resident Aliens,* 12.
11. Hauerwas and Willimon, *Resident Aliens,* 45.
12. Wilson, *Why Church Matters,* 24.
13. Romans 12:1-2.
14. Wilson, *Why Church Matters,* 32.
15. McLaren, *The Secret Message of Jesus,* 69-70.
16. See Isaiah 1:10-17; Amos 5:21-27 for more on this point.
17. Hauerwas and Willimon, *Resident Aliens,* 46-47.

Chapter 13—Worship in the Upside-Down Church

Epigraph. Boyd, *The Myth of a Christian Nation,* 29-30.

1. Karl Barth, *Church Dogmatics,* 4.3.2; quoted in Hauerwas and Willimon, *Resident Aliens,* 83.

2. See Erre, *Jesus of Suburbia.*
3. My many other talents include diaper changing, snotty-nose wiping, Xbox 360 playing, football watching, Pearl Jam listening, wife snuggling, office organizing by making piles on the floor, and crafting long sentences.
4. Okay, only one more time, I promise: This is only one way to think about this stuff. We don't claim to have it all figured out. But I do think this way embodies confessional worship in ways that aren't the norm in church.
5. Gibbs and Bolger, *Emerging Churches,* 67.

Chapter 14—Flesh and Blood: The Incarnational Nature of the Church

First epigraph. Hauerwas and Willimon, *Resident Aliens,* 51.

Second epigraph. Madeleine L'Engle, *Walking on Water;* quoted in Gibbs and Bolger, *Emerging Churches,* 65.

1. Of course, this is not the end of the story. The Spirit comes to live among us and even inside us (which is the only way to make sense of Jesus' statement that it was for our good that He went back to the Father). And the whole story ends (or begins, depending on your perspective) with God coming down from heaven to dwell with a renewed humanity on a renewed earth (Revelation 21–22).
2. Quoted in Keel, *Intuitive Leadership,* 155.
3. *The Epistle to Diognetus,* 5.4-8; quoted in Harvey, *Another City,* 24.
4. Hirsch, *The Forgotten Ways,* 132.
5. Purves, *The Crucifixion of Ministry.*
6. This material isn't original to me, but I haven't the slightest clue where I first heard this.
7. Webber, *Journey to Jesus,* 106.

Chapter 15—Postures of Incarnation

Epigraph. Boyd, *The Myth of a Christian Nation,* 30.

1. Kester Brewin has a great section on waiting in his book *Signs of Emergence: A Vision for the Church That Is Always Organic, Networked, Decentralized, Bottom-Up, Communal, Flexible, and Always Evolving* (Grand Rapids: Baker Books, 2007), 41-57.
2. This could be because He thinks I'm quite special. It could also be because a two by four to my soul is usually required to get me to do anything.

Chapter 16—Baptism as Civil Disobedience

Epigraph. Yoder, *The Politics of Jesus,* 52.

1. Webber, *Journey to Jesus,* 41.
2. Williams, *Start Here,* 39.
3. N.T. Wright, *Jesus and the Victory of God,* 453; Williams, *Start Here,* 40.
4. Webber, *Journey to Jesus,* 65.
5. Yoder, *The Politics of Jesus,* 150.
6. Wakabayashi, *Kingdom Come,* 62-63.

7. Stanley J. Grenz, *Theology for the Community of God* (Grand Rapids: Eerdmans, 1994), 522.
8. N.T. Wright, *Simply Christian*, 124.
9. Dallas Willard, *The Divine Conspiracy: Rediscovering Our Hidden Life in God,* (San Francisco: HarperSanFrancisco, 1998). 41-42.

Chapter 17—Bread and Wine: The Meal of the Kingdom

Epigraph. N.T. Wright, *Surprised by Hope,* 112.

1. Ben Witherington, *Making a Meal of It: Rethinking the Theology of the Lord's Supper* (Waco: Baylor University Press, 2007), 27:

     Our views of communion range from the magical to the trivial; communion is a form of symbolic proclamation—the word made visible, of the community's most sacred beliefs and values…meals, perhaps more than any other social event in antiquity, encoded the values of a society…also in the Passover—there is nothing here about the transformation of the elements into something they were not before.

2. See Witherington, *Making a Meal of It,* for an excellent treatment of the subject.
3. Witherington, *Making a Meal of It,* 10.
4. Witherington, *Making a Meal of It,* 10-11.
5. Quoted in McLaren, *The Secret Message of Jesus,* 161.
6. Metzger, *Consuming Jesus,* 60-61.
7. Marva J. Dawn, *Powers, Weakness, and the Tabernacling of God* (Grand Rapids: Eerdmans, 2001).
8. N.T. Wright, *Surprised by Hope,* 263-64.
9. See Paul S. Minear, *Images of the Church in the New Testament* (Louisville: Westminster John Knox Press, 2004), 56-57 for more on this point.
10. I first heard this from Rob Bell.
11. Yoder, *The Politics of Jesus,* 38.

Chapter 18—The Presence of the Future

Epigraph. Rene Padilla, quoted in Glasser, *Announcing the Kingdom,* 215.

1. This chapter relies heavily on Morphew, *Breakthrough,* 96 and following.
2. N.T. Wright, *The Challenge of Jesus,* 178.
3. N.T. Wright, *The Challenge of Jesus,* 137. Wright also weaves this theme throughout *Surprised by Hope.*
4. The Old Testament promised that in the new age of salvation to come, the Holy Spirit would be poured out from heaven and given not just temporarily to a privileged few, but as the permanent possession of God's people (Psalm 139:7-10; Isaiah 11:1-3; Ezekiel 37; Joel 2:28-29). Jesus' anointing by the Holy Spirit was the conclusive sign that the new age—the age of salvation promised in the Old Testament—had begun.
5. While very much beyond the scope of this work, if this view is correct, then this suggests that both dispensationalism (at least in most of its traditional forms) and cessationism are dramatically mistaken.
6. Gibbs and Bolger, *Emerging Churches,* 90.
7. Cullmann, *Christ and Time,* 44-45:

The decisive battle has already been won. But the war continues until a certain, though not as yet definite, Victory Day when the weapons will at last be still. The decisive battle would be Christ's death and resurrection, and Victory Day his Parousia. Between the two lies a short but important span of time already indicating a fulfillment and an anticipation of peace, in which, however, the greatest watchfulness is demanded. Yet it is from the decisive battle now won and the Victory Day yet to be achieved that this span of time gets its meaning and its demands. If this interval of time is given greater and greater extension there will, of course, be consequences that must be described in detail. But the constant factor is from the outset the presence of this tension. This means that I see the general foundation for the whole New Testament in a salvation-historical orientation. This is all the more true as the victory achieved in that decisive battle is understood in retrospect as the obvious consequences and crowning of the preceding events.

8. Glasser, *Announcing the Kingdom,* 192.
9. Boyd, *The Myth of a Christian Nation,* 85.
10. Morphew, *Breakthrough,* 100-102.

Chapter 19—Beyond *Left Behind*

Epigraph. Boyd, *The Myth of a Christian Nation,* 68, 72. If you wonder how the eschatology of the kingdom relates to traditional dispensational eschatology (the rapture, tribulation, millennium, and so on), see Ladd, *Crucial Questions About the Kingdom of God.*

1. Don Williams, *Start Here,* 84-85; Glasser, *Announcing the Kingdom,* 192-93; Wakabayashi, *Kingdom* Come, 71-74; N.T. Wright, *The Lord and His Prayer,* 40-41.
2. Wakabayashi, *Kingdom Come,* 45.
3. Wakabayashi, *Kingdom Come,* 85.
4. Quoted in Wakabayashi, *Kingdom Come,* 86. We have suggested that the powers and principalities that Paul discusses in Ephesians 6 lie behind the social, economic, and political structures of the world. So the work of renewing those structures in the name of Jesus is a core part of our warfare against the god of this world. See Boyd, *God at War,* 51-61, for more on this. Boyd argues that "when we 'take up arms' against corporate greed, and when we follow the call of the Lord in feeding the hungry, clothing the naked, sheltering the homeless, befriending the guilty, embracing the socially repulsive, and siding with victims, we are participating in God's cosmic struggle against cosmic chaotic forces of destruction" (*God at War,* 90).
5. N.T. Wright, *Surprised by Hope,* 193, 208-9.
6. Kraybill, *The Upside-Down Kingdom,* 28-29. He points to the story of Zaccheus as a perfect illustration of this point.

Chapter 20—Election, Exodus, and Diaspora: The Fine Art of Cultural Engagement

Epigraph. Quoted in Hirsch, *The Forgotten Ways,* 53.

1. From Clapp, *A Peculiar People,* 154-55.
2. Stone, *Evangelism after Christendom,* 11.
3. Stone, *Evangelism after Christendom,* 11.
4. Clapp, *A Peculiar People,* 75.

5. The following thoughts are taken from Michael Green, *Evangelism in the Early Church*, 161-202.
6. Taken from Hirsch, *The Forgotten Ways*, 18-19.
7. Dallas Willard, "Being a Christian in a Pluralistic Society." Available online at dwillard.org/articles/artview.asp?artID=17. Accessed 12/20/02.
8. See Harvey, *Another City*, 145.
9. Inspired by Clapp, *A Peculiar People*, 147-49; and Harvey, *Another City*, 135-65.
10. See Kenneson and Street, *Selling Out the Church*, 136-37.
11. Christopher Wright, *The Mission of God*, 275.
12. Harvey, *Another City*, 143-50.
13. "Live such good lives among the pagans that, though they accuse you of doing wrong, they may see your good deeds and glorify God" (1 Peter 2:12; see also Matthew 5:16).
14. Clapp, *A Peculiar People*, 149.
15. Stone, *Evangelism after Christendom*, 12-13.

Chapter 21—Jesus Wept: Apologies and Apologetics

First epigraph. Brewin, *Signs of Emergence*, 54-55.

Second epigraph. Henri Nouwen, *Bread for the Journey: A Daybook of Wisdom and Faith* (New York: HarperCollins, 2006), from the reading for October 27.

1. Erre, *Jesus of Suburbia*, 175-80.
2. Brewin, *Signs of Emergence*, 52.
3. See Boyd, *The Myth of a Christian Nation*, 144-46 for an example of how we might do better.

Postscript for Pastors and Church Leaders: The Kingdom-Focused Church

Epigraph. Stone, *Evangelism after Christendom*, 14-15.

1. Gibbs and Bolger, *Emerging Churches*, 100.
2. This model opens the door to some of the sobering statistics we looked at in chapter 1. I personally know of five church or parachurch leaders who have committed adultery and have been removed from ministry. (One has since been restored—an amazing story for another time.) In each case, the CEO leadership model had been embraced. I am not suggesting that this was the cause of moral failure, but I believe that if the team leadership that we see in Scripture were more in evidence today, we would see fewer examples of ministry failure and burnout.
3. These thoughts come from personal conversations.
4. Purves, *Crucifixion of Ministry*, 24.
5. N.T. Wright, *Surprised by Hope*, 264.

It's a Harsh,

Crazy,

Beautiful,

Messed Up,

Breathtaking

World...

And People Are Talking About It...